QUESTIONING:
A NEW HISTORY OF
WESTERN PHILOSOPHY

> We have to *learn to think differently* – in order, perhaps very late, to achieve even more: *to feel differently.*
>
> (Friedrich Nietzsche, *Daybreak*, 103)

QUESTIONING:
A NEW HISTORY OF
WESTERN PHILOSOPHY

Gideon Baker

EDINBURGH
University Press

Edinburgh University Press is one of the leading university presses in the UK. We publish academic books and journals in our selected subject areas across the humanities and social sciences, combining cutting-edge scholarship with high editorial and production values to produce academic works of lasting importance. For more information visit our website: edinburghuniversitypress.com

© Gideon Baker, 2022, 2024

Edinburgh University Press Ltd
The Tun – Holyrood Road
12(2f) Jackson's Entry
Edinburgh EH8 8PJ

First published in hardback by Edinburgh University Press 2022

Typeset in 10/13 Warnock Pro by
IDSUK (DataConnection) Ltd,
Croydon, CR0 4YY

A CIP record for this book is available from the British Library

ISBN 978 1 4744 9806 7 (hardback)
ISBN 978 1 4744 9807 4 (paperback)
ISBN 978 1 4744 9808 1 (webready PDF)
ISBN 978 1 4744 9809 8 (epub)

The right of Gideon Baker to be identified as the author of this work has been asserted in accordance with the Copyright, Designs and Patents Act 1988, and the Copyright and Related Rights Regulations 2003 (SI No. 2498).

Contents

	Acknowledgements	vii
	INTRODUCTION	1
1.	SOCRATES	13
2.	DIOGENES	21
3.	PLATO	31
4.	ARISTOTLE	41
5.	EPICURUS	53
6.	PLOTINUS	63
7.	AUGUSTINE	73
8.	DUNS SCOTUS	83
9.	ECKHART	93
10.	SPINOZA	103
11.	KANT	113
12.	KIERKEGAARD	125
13.	NIETZSCHE	135
14.	HEIDEGGER	147

15.	WEIL	157
16.	ARENDT	169
17.	BADIOU	179
18.	BUTLER	189

Glosses	201
References	207
Index	213

Acknowledgements

Questioning requires that the order of things seems questionable in the first place. My greatest thanks must therefore go to my parents, Bruce and Sylvia, who put the world in question for me. How grateful I am today for your otherworldliness!

My thanks also to those who read and commented on earlier drafts of various chapters: Bruce Baker, Naomi Baker, Nathaniel Baker, Edwin Bikundo, Venessa Ercole, Dan Halvorson, Ashley Lavelle, Vassilios Paipais, Julia Rudolph and Anne Stuart. As I was unable to take on board everything they said, each one is naturally blameless for the mistakes and omissions in what follows. I am also grateful for the feedback of three anonymous reviewers and for the guidance provided by Carol Macdonald at Edinburgh University Press. The book is dedicated to Ashley Lavelle, who has helped me to see the possibilities of a questioning founded on friendship.

Where possible, I have used established book, chapter and section numbers (rather than the publisher's page numbers) in order that readers can look up my references in whatever edition they have to hand. For the Nietzsche references, *PTAG* is *Philosophy in the Tragic Age of the Greeks*; *HH* is *Human, All Too Human*; *D* is *Daybreak*; *GS* is *The Gay Science*; *Z* is *Thus Spoke Zarathustra*; *BGE* is *Beyond Good and Evil*; *GM* is *On the Genealogy of Morality*; *A* is *The Antichrist*; *EH* is *Ecce Homo*; *TI* is *Twilight of the Idols*; and *WP* is *The Will to Power*.

Introduction

THIS BOOK PROVIDES A narrative arc of the Western philosophical tradition as a history of questioning – in particular, questioning of what it is to be, or maybe to become, human. As the twentieth-century philosopher Martin Heidegger observed, human beings are the only beings for whom being is a question (Heidegger 1996: 6).

Of course, Heidegger's claim, too, is questionable: for one thing, why should being human be experienced as having to question what it is to be human? Is this not the same prejudice that led Socrates to ask, at the dawn of Western philosophy, whether the unexamined life is worth living? This is a question posed to the living by philosophy, but why not put the shoe on the other foot and pose the question to philosophy: from what standpoint outside of life do you presume to question it? Socrates's question presupposes a lack that the living need to account for, a lack that itself can be put in question.

Seeking to overcome this sense of lack, Nietzsche (*TI*, 'Errors', 7) insisted on 'the innocence of becoming' (*die Unschuld des Werdens*). Apart from refusing to be questionable, do innocents question everything? Is it possible to *be* innocent while asking everybody and everything for its justification? Nietzsche's innocents know that, finally, there *are* no reasons, so what would all this questioning be about? Do we question out of a religious impulse to find the reason behind all things, also known as God? Do we question because we no longer have the strength to say: thus it is and there is no reason why? Did even Socrates, full of such brave questions (he accepted the punishment of death for it, after all), question because he couldn't see the point of life and secretly wanted to die?

Questioning, being itself questionable, is a veritable black hole. How, then, can we steer clear of the event-horizon of the question which, once we have crossed it, will allow us no return? The methodology informing this book assumes that there is a way: to approach the question as a *history* of questioning. Everything has a history, *is* its history, and questioning is no different in this regard:

> You want to know what the philosophers' idiosyncrasies are? ... Their lack of historical sense for one thing [...]. They think that they are showing *respect* for something when they dehistoricize it, [...] when they turn it into a mummy. (Nietzsche, *TI*, 'Reason', 1)

The book is therefore structured as a series of studies of the place of questioning in the work of individual philosophers throughout the Western tradition. Each chapter considers the place of questioning in the particular philosopher's work while also linking this contribution to my own reflections on questioning, a reflection which unfolds chapter by chapter.

The near balance of ancient and modern philosophers – plus two from the Middle Ages – is deliberate. There is a tendency to see questioning as a post-critical (i.e. post-Kantian) aspect of modern philosophy, which makes pre-critical metaphysics seem essentially un-questioning. But this view obscures the way in which Immanuel Kant's Copernican revolution in philosophy is in some ways only an intensification of the history of questioning that is Western philosophy.

My choice of the Ancients is wide-ranging: for the classical period it covers Socrates, Plato and Aristotle but also makes room for the less well-known Cynic philosopher, Diogenes of Sinope. There is a chapter on Epicurus. I have included a chapter on Plotinus, a relatively neglected philosopher from late Antiquity and the source of the enduring Neoplatonist strain of thinking in the Western tradition. Plotinus represents the autumn of Greek philosophy before the rise of Christianity. He is perhaps the last Western thinker before Baruch Spinoza, 1,400 years later, for whom questioning aims at understanding the oneness of the world before its fracture into the two worlds of Christianity.

Between ancient and modern Western philosophy, Christianity and Greek philosophy came together in fascinating and diverse ways in innumerable great thinkers, starting with the Church Fathers. Of these I have included Augustine of Hippo – the most influential theologian of the Western Church and a man himself much influenced by the Neoplatonism of Plotinus. Between Augustine and the subject of the next chapter, Duns Scotus, opens a chasm of 800 years. This reflects that, in the Western Church, unlike in the Eastern Church and in Islam, Greek philosophy went into abeyance since almost all the writings of Antiquity were lost. The rediscovery in the twelfth century (by way of Islamic scholars), first, of Aristotle and, later, of Plato, inspired theologians such as Thomas Aquinas, Duns Scotus and Meister Eckhart (a contemporary of Duns Scotus and the subject of Chapter 9) to bring Christian doctrine and Greek philosophy back into conversation just as they had been in late Antiquity.

The modern philosophers are chosen to reflect the sweep of Western philosophy from the seventeenth century (when modern philosophy, so the conventional story goes, was sparked by Descartes's *Meditations*) up until the present. I start with Spinoza (a near contemporary of Descartes) and finish with two contemporary philosophers: Alain Badiou and Judith Butler. In between I select Kant (eighteenth century); Søren Kierkegaard (early nineteenth century); Frederic Nietzsche (late nineteenth century); and three twentieth-century philosophers – Martin Heidegger, Simone Weil and Hannah Arendt. Not all would have called themselves philosophers. Kierkegaard and Nietzsche were even self-styled anti-philosophers. But anti-philosophy is still philosophy, determined by what it rejects even if, for the same reason, it often presents a clearer vision of that which it seeks to overcome.

I recognise that to give an account of Western philosophy in book-length form, with the many omissions this requires, is perhaps the most questionable thing of all here. Like political careers, it is destined to end in failure. Yet no matter how many pages one devotes to it, the history of Western philosophy can only ever be glimpsed from a certain perspective. And perspectivism should not be confused with relativism. Since one's perspective is a gift rather than a possession, my perspective is not mine alone.

I also recognise that many will question the need for more reflection on Western philosophy. Today, other voices rise up to question how a European tradition could ever have been mistaken for the wisdom of the world. As a work that seeks to question Western philosophy, this book shares this impulse. Never doubting that it is not universal,

I try to show what is distinctive, not to mention questionable, about a history of questioning. But I do not claim some privileged perspective from outside of Western philosophy. I want not to denounce but to illuminate. Indeed, my own experience, and I suspect the experience of most people in the anglophone world, is that I was taught little European philosophy (this was true even at university, where I studied political philosophy). For those, like me, who want to know more about what they do when they question, I hope to provide some answers.

Another questionable aspect of my choice of philosophers is that they are mostly men. To be sure, out of the five philosophers selected from the last century, three are women. This indicates that while the history of Western philosophy has been patriarchal, its future need not be. But when it comes to ancient, medieval and early modern European philosophy, I do not want to give the false impression that Western philosophy has been inclusive. Since a central aspect of my discussion is the *questioning* of Western philosophy, I consider it important to take the history of this tradition as it is rather than as we want it to be. The lack of diversity of Western philosophy reflects (but has also shaped) the masculinity of metaphysics, with its ideal of autonomous reason. Yet the emphasis on inclusion also presupposes that exclusion is questionable, and the critique of exclusion is something that Western philosophy has contributed much to.

Questions of Time

Western philosophy is parochial as well as patriarchal. Western philosophy is by no means philosophy *per se*. Yet even such a critique of the Western tradition, precisely *as* critique, is squarely a part of the tradition it criticises, as I will show. This doesn't mean that nothing can shift where this tradition is concerned, but it does mean that breaking with it (if that is what we want to do) is harder than it appears. Given the extraordinary reach of Greek thought into every corner of our lives and every corner of our world, to understand it better is to better understand our world – its limits but also its possibilities.

Take, for example, the modern technologies which shape our world and which seem, on the surface, so unrelated to the past. What does a computer have in common with a Greek temple? And yet, as Heidegger (1978: 217) argued, 'the essence of technology is by no means anything technological'. Rather, it is the *techne*, the making or the producing, by which the Greeks saw beings (for example the stones that are used to fashion a temple) as things to be put to work, that is decisive. When we put rare metals to use in our computers, and also when we put *ourselves* to work at the computer, we echo an ancient ontology of 'putting to work'.

> Thus questioning, we bear witness to the crisis that in our sheer preoccupation with technology we do not yet experience the essential unfolding of technology. [Yet] the closer we come to the danger, the more brightly do the ways into the saving power begin to shine and the more questioning we become. For questioning is the piety of thought. (Heidegger 1978: 238)

Questioning the present leads us to the past, and in understanding the past we can hope for new ways of being in the world in the present. But who is this 'we'? It is those who, questioning more fundamentally, go beyond mere critique, which can never surpass that which it questions.

There is little fundamental questioning of the present in Western culture because of the dominant understanding of time in European modernity. Inheriting the linear time of Christianity (where time is a *history* stretching from creation via the incarnation to the final judgement), denizens of the West assume that what is chronologically distant must be far from being relevant, too. But if we think of Western time as more of a whirlpool, where the frenetic movement is not a movement *away* from Greek metaphysics but rather a movement *around* it, things start to look different. Like the symptom in psychoanalysis, which is always an expression of the same infancy no matter how old we get, moderns can never get past metaphysics. Such is the power of what Heidegger called 'the commencement' (*der Anfang*) that it is 'essentially longer' than every '"history" proceeding from it as a sequence of occurrences'. History, in other words, is only ever 'the history "of" the commencement' (2015: 116–17). Given that the commencement determines its own end, then even the future is only that which arrives from out of the commencement (Heidegger 2012: 36).

Western modernity is still circling *around* its commencement in Greek metaphysics, as can be seen by the enduring centrality of questions of identity in the West. Although the mode of identity that concerns us changes – according to Foucault (1980), today it is sexuality – the metaphysical quest for essences, for that which endures, is as significant today as it was 2,500 years ago. To posit identity in a world of change is exactly what Plato did. And don't think for a moment that opting for difference over identity is a way out of this fixation with identity. As Heidegger observed, the reversal of a metaphysical statement remains metaphysical. To suggest that there *is* only difference is to make difference the principle of identify which metaphysics ever seeks after.

We can see this whirlpool of metaphysical history playing out in questioning, too. Questioning can seem like a modern and progressive thing to do. But, as Nietzsche insisted, questioning does not begin with the 'death of God' in the nineteenth century, which was really only a symptom rather than a cause. Having questioned everything else, European culture was always going to get around to doubting God in the end. But the *impulse* to question everything, which Nietzsche calls the will to truth, is ancient. By haranguing people to question after the truth of existence, was it Socrates who made questioning seem a perfectly normal and healthy activity (when in fact we are always pulling the rug from beneath our feet)?

Questions of Eternity

It is not only the process of questioning that threatens meaninglessness. According to Nietzsche, what is *questioned after* is also at stake in the collapse of the highest values. For Nietzsche, Greek philosophy and its legacy is a history of metaphysics – that is to say, of questions about what is timeless (*meta* means after, so metaphysics is that which is beyond the physical world). Plato's account of the creation of the world in *Timaeus* is a good example of metaphysics. Timaeus tells the story, which meets with Socrates's approval, that the maker and father of the universe must have worked from a pattern based on some unchanging principle. The alternative, that the world is accidental, 'is a blasphemy even to mention' (*Timaeus* 29a). Since the world is the fairest of all things created, the Demiurge must have 'had his eye on the eternal' when giving form to it (*Timaeus* 29a).

This is a good example of how Greek philosophy questions after a changeless world when, in our world, there appears to be only change. This search for a 'true world' outside of time makes our time-bound world seem to lack something; according to Nietzsche it disenchants it and thereby leads to despair. Or, to put it in Heidegger's terms: in looking only to what is eternal rather than to what is given in time, we crowd out the call of Being, missing that even ideas of eternity are only given to finite mortals *in* time. Human finitude comes 'before' infinity.

Building on Michel Foucault's late lectures delivered at the Collège de France shortly before his death in 1984, I challenge this long-standing equation of philosophical questioning with nihilism. I don't doubt that metaphysical-type questions can introduce nihilism (the devaluation of our brief worldly existence), but Greek philosophy did not only ask these sorts of questions. Indeed, Foucault, following Pierre Hadot (2002), showed that ancient Greek philosophy was much more a way of life than the search for a set of timeless principles. The sorts of questions that most of the ancient schools asked were questions about how to live rather than questions about eternity.

The Stoics, for example, although they had a cosmology, were much more interested in the ethical question of how to comport themselves resolutely in a world where time sweeps everything away. The ancient Cynics, meanwhile, explicitly excluded questions about the cosmos from their concerns, often by ridiculing the whole enterprise: 'To someone who was talking about astronomical matters, [Diogenes] said, "And how many days did it take you to get down from the sky?"' (Diogenes Laertius, *Lives of Eminent Philosophers* 6.39). Cynic philosophy was earthy because it was earthly; it did not seek the timeless truth of the heavens but to point people to the true life:

> An astronomer was pointing [...] to a diagram representing the stars, and was saying that 'these here are the wandering stars'; on hearing this, Diogenes said, 'Don't lie, my friend, it's not these that are wandering astray, but those over there' – pointing to the people standing around. (Stobaeus 2.1.23; in Hard 2012: 29)

Nobody more than the Cynic philosopher challenged the idea that philosophy asks loftily about eternal things. Reacting against the metaphysical abstractions – as he saw them – of Plato, Diogenes of Sinope did not think that it was necessary to answer the question 'what is a human being' in order to live the true life. His plucked chicken presented to Plato (here's a biped without feathers for you!) was supposed to demonstrate this as much by the method employed (a chicken has a body, unlike Plato's forms) as by the point it made (that the search for a general definition of a human being is a pointless exercise when the only question that matters is: how should I live?).

This resistance to questions posed about intangible things was present in Epicurus, too, who, lounging in his garden, wondered how it was that the Platonists over the wall in the Academy were more interested in disembodied souls than in their bodies. The question of whether the soul has an afterlife seemed to Epicurus to be motivated less by the need to answer the question and more by the fear of death. Isn't it obvious, he asked his friends, that nothing of a person can survive her physical extinction? In which case, the Platonists fear nothing.

But although they were unsure that the Platonists, in particular, were asking the right questions, it was not the case that the Cynics and the Epicureans ceased to question. Philosophy as a way of life in Antiquity was inseparable from questioning, since no philosophical school doubted for a moment that the true life of philosophy was different from conventional living. Questioning of received wisdom was something that all the schools had in common, though the Cynics undoubtedly pushed this the furthest.

Who Gets to Question?

This raises a concern about the elitism of questioning in the Western tradition. Given that all the ancient schools disdained everyday life in some way, calling followers of philosophy to a different path, is questioning only for the few? Nietzsche was honest enough to admit that the time and space needed for questioning is not something one can enjoy unless other people do the hard work. Nietzsche retired early on a small pension, which enabled him to question in ways he had never been able to when tied down to a day job as a professor in Basel. Working and questioning seem to exclude one another, but how many people can afford not to work?

On closer inspection, however, things are not so simple. Yes, even Epicurus living simply in his garden had slaves (we know because he gave them manumission in his will). But Diogenes was abandoned by his slave, Manes, and came to see this as stroke of good fortune – to have a slave is to be dependent on him. Slavery cuts both ways. Living a precarious existence of poverty and wandering, the Cynics demonstrated that the life that puts conventional living in question need not be elitist in the usual sense. Yes, such a life is not for the many, but not because they are excluded from it, rather because they are not capable of it.

Nietzsche noticed that, in fact, Socratic questioning itself was the beginning of the end for elites. The heroes of the Greek Homeric age gave no reasons for what they did, since to have to give an account of oneself is to be a bit like a slave. Nobody asked King Agamemnon (one of the central characters of Homer's *Iliad*) whether taking Achilles's slave girl off him was a good idea; and not only because they didn't dare to but also because a king doesn't have to have reasons. The rise of reason with Socrates sounded the death knell for heroic impunity. Even Alexander the Great had to seek out Diogenes, since Alexander couldn't ignore that giving an account of himself was necessary if he didn't want to be bettered by a beggar.

Foucault (2011) shows in his last lectures that the questions posed by the Cynics in particular, questions about citizenship and the state, are the point of emergence of the sorts of radical questioning that has led, in Western modernity, to revolutionary politics and the avant-garde. If this is right then, far from Western philosophy being the problem that contemporary questioning needs to overcome, it is only thanks to Western philosophy that radical questioning is given at all. Locating his own critical perspective not outside of but firmly within the Western philosophical tradition, Foucault shows that it is possible to question power while remaining in an affirmative relationship to this tradition.

If the relevance of questioning is a constant throughout Western philosophy, then some of the answers Western philosophers gave, such as Epicurus's atomism or Nietzsche's doctrine of the eternal return, may look like they have been left behind by modern scientific theories. But we will see that Epicurus was actually quite indifferent to exactly how we explain lightning, for example, just as long as we don't attribute it to an angry Zeus. Curing people of their fear of the gods was his true aim. Similarly, Nietzsche's eternal return is not really a cosmological theory, but rather (perhaps) a test – can you love the world even to the extent of wishing everything that happens in it to recur eternally? And *this* question will be as relevant to future generations as it was to his own. Think of all the things you find most horrifying in history and then try to will them to recur for ever. That is just as difficult a test for you as it was for Nietzsche in the nineteenth century. Indeed, after Auschwitz, is it even possible?

Solipsism

We shall see that other aspects of questioning in the Western tradition are not so easily projected into the future. Some questions seem to have become obstacles to thinking. For example, the eighteenth-century

German philosopher Immanuel Kant's critical prohibition on thinking the world as anything other than a world that is given for *us* was, as he understood himself, revolutionary (not suffering from false modesty, Kant called it a Copernican revolution in philosophy, referring to Copernicus's realisation that the sun and not the earth was the fixed point of our solar system). But it has been hard to escape from the thought wrought by this revolution, which for many philosophers in the Western tradition has started to feel like a prison. If the world is only that which is given to us, then we seem to be trapped in what Quentin Meillassoux (2008: 5) has recently called correlationism. Correlationism is the double bind whereby 'we only ever have access to the correlation between thinking and being, and never to either term considered apart from the other'. As we shall see later, correlationism remains central to philosophical questioning, especially in the form of deconstruction.

If all our questions about the world are those in which *our thinking them* is always already in question, then how do we ever get back to the 'great outdoors', the world as such, that philosophers before Kant took for granted. Of course, Kant would say that those philosophers were just naive, not noticing that they were implicated in their own questions. But there seems something a little gloomy about realising that all our questions about the world are really questions about us.

This problem, if such it is, might perhaps be sidestepped with the recognition that Western philosophy did not start out with questions about the world but really with questions about us. While the pre-Socratic natural philosophers did want to know what was in the great outdoors, Socrates had ceased to find any interest, as he said himself at his trial, in what lay above his head or beneath his feet. His questions, as we shall see in the next chapter, concerned the nature of virtues such as courage and justice; in other words, questions about the living of a life and how to do it well.

Disenchantment

I will finish these opening reflections on the question by returning to the theme of nihilism, which is essentially related to questioning. There is no doubt that the will to truth – the drive to ask questions – of Western philosophy has opened the door to nihilism. Indeed, philosophy itself has been killed off by this seeking after truth! The lust for truth ends up finding that nothing is true: not even God, not even philosophy.

Questioning disenchants the world because it puts everything in doubt, like a love affair which begins to end precisely when the questions start – where were you last night? The very act of questioning existence makes existence seem to lack something. This is perhaps the weakness of Heidegger's claim that questioning is the essentially human way of being. The human being might only be the questioning being when she has lost her way of being in the world. In fact, Heidegger (1996: 132, 1978b: 50–1) admits that the question of Being only suggests itself in anxiety – in other words, when we lose our foothold in the world. Questioning is related to the loss of enchantment.

Disenchantment was the twentieth-century French philosopher Weil's theme. Not even re-enchantment with the world will help us. There is still separation here, and in the rapprochement between the individual and the world (as, for example, in Nietzsche's *amor fati* – love of fate), there is still the individual. Weil's passion for *de*individuation, for the extinction of all traces of self, was sourced in a Platonic tradition that has emphasised that the One-all is everything. The individual is only an illusion.

Yet the disenchantment with the world that questioning produces does have individuating effects. Putting something in question is to gain a perspective on it that we previously lacked. Returning to the example of a love affair: it is only when I first doubt my lover that I awake from the spell in which my lover's life was entirely absorbed in mine. Doubting, I emerge from the *in*difference of love as a distinct individual who knows himself poorly and wishes to know more.

And just as the individual emerges in the process of disenchantment, so does the world. Putting the world in question is already a sign of disenchantment. We can never be fully *in* the world again. Having once asked what the world is *for*, we have put ourselves outside it as if looking on. We will retain this separateness from the world we question even if we are no longer estranged from it. Again, the example of a love affair is apposite. Once the questions start, estrangement follows. And even if this estrangement is overcome and we go on together, our love is never innocent in the way it used to be. We *notice* our lover now, sometimes in hope, sometimes with suspicion. But we will never take our lover for granted again.

This is how a world soured by questioning can be. It has been lost, but for the same reason it is now findable in a way that would never have been possible before. The disenchantment wrought by questioning is an opportunity for love of the world.

But this is not all. Strange as it sounds, the world can only love itself by way of our questions. Nowhere is this made clearer than in the seventeenth-century Dutch philosopher Spinoza, where contemplation of the world, or 'the mind's intellectual love of God', is *at the same time* the very love 'by which God loves himself' (Spinoza, *Ethics* Part V, Proposition 36). For Spinoza, God and Nature say the same thing, which means that our questions about the world are the means by which the world first catches sight of itself.

1 Socrates

SOCRATES (WHO DIED IN 399 BCE) posed a lot of questions. Not that he had many answers. But then people with answers don't need to ask questions. Indeed, Socrates believed that questioning is so important that the unexamined life is simply not worth living, a statement that Plato (Plato, *Apology* 38a), his student, attributes to Socrates at the trial at which he was sentenced to death. Does the fact that this sentence was handed down because Socrates was believed to be undermining authority with his questioning make Socrates a martyr for the question? Socrates was prescient enough to see that his death was likely to ensure his reputation as a 'wise man' for posterity: 'because they will say I am wise even if I am not' (*Apology* 38c). Even at the last, a question.

Our sense of Socrates's questions is not beyond questioning, either. We are dependent largely on Plato's Socrates, and no serious student is ever entirely true to his or her teacher. Yet it is clear enough that Socrates's questions were of a different order from the questions that were usually posed in the political arena, or *demos*, that dominated the life of Athenian citizens such as him. Ancient Athenian democracy, participatory as it was, put a premium on rhetoric. Indeed, a great deal of shame was attached to speaking badly in the Assembly. A good rhetor, naturally, would use questions to help him win the argument, perhaps putting off his opponent with what we would still call a rhetorical question today: a 'how would you know?', for example. Rhetorical questions give only the *appearance* of dialogue, for example when the speaker poses a question which he then goes on to answer himself. Rhetorical questioning, political as it is, concerns itself above all with the surface of things.

For Socrates, this type of questioning, while undoubtedly requiring ability, has no relation to truth. For his own part, he claimed to have 'not the slightest skill as a speaker – unless, of course, by a skilful speaker [you] mean one who speaks the truth' (*Apology* 17b). There was something somewhat rhetorical in Socrates affecting not to be able to speak well. Indeed, Socrates knew that he, too, had been accused of making 'the weaker argument stronger', as rhetoricians prized themselves on being able to do (*Apology* 18c). But Socrates was keen to distinguish himself from the teachers of rhetoric, the sophists who charged for their services: 'if you have heard anyone say that I try to educate people and charge a fee, there is no truth in that either' (*Apology* 19d). His care for truth made Socrates's questions, unlike those of rhetoric, confrontational: there is a 'reason for my being unpopular' (*Apology* 23c). The rhetor seduces his audience; the one who tells them the truth will doubtless offend them. Questioning, then, requires the courage of truth: 'I am fairly certain that this plain speaking of mine is the cause of my unpopularity' (*Apology* 24a).

As well as being different in content from his contemporaries' questions, Socrates's questions were also new in kind. There had been questions before: was the universe composed of fire? Of water? Of tiny atoms, perhaps? There had been profound questions about whether everything is constant change, or an unchanging One. There had been questions, in short, about the world; but these were not Socrates's questions. Socrates reminded his jurors of this – have any of you ever heard me even mention what is beneath the ground or above in the heavens? he asked, referring to the dwelling places of the Greek gods (*Apology* 19b–d). Socrates knew that his accusers could not justly convict him of asking questions about anything beyond everyday existence. Socrates's questions had not been questions about the world of nature or the gods but questions about what it means to live, in the sense of living well.

To live well, for Socrates, is to take care of ourselves. This care we must take is care not for the body so much as the soul. Socrates's thoughts on care can be found in Plato's dialogue, *Crito*, where Socrates insists that we must care not for opinion but only for truth. Just as a gymnast must care for his body, so we also should look after that part of ourselves that distinguishes between good and bad and that can be corrupted through neglect.

At his trial Socrates gave the example of how once, when Athens was temporarily under the rule of tyrants, he had been commanded to go and summon innocent men for execution. Fearing doing this injustice more than his own death, Socrates refused the order. Socrates's question is why this sort of behaviour is rare. It might seem obvious that people don't want to expose themselves to physical danger, but the question remains of why they seem to care so little about having an ugly soul: 'Are you not ashamed that you give your attention to acquiring as much money as possible, and similarly with reputation and honour, and give no attention or thought to truth and understanding and the perfection of your soul?' (*Apology* 29e).

For Socrates, the victims of his questioning should not be annoyed 'with me' but with themselves (*Apology* 23d). Rather than turning their wrath on the one who exposed the injustice in their soul, there is 'only one thing to consider when performing any action; that is, whether [one] is acting rightly or wrongly' (*Apology* 28b–c). This one thing to consider is really the *only* question for Socrates: I should not even ask whether an action will threaten my life, only whether it will make me a good or a bad person.

However, enquiring into the state of souls involves different sorts of questions to those that ask after nature. Soul-health concerns intangibles. Things like justice, courage and love are not present in the way that material things are. They are not present to the senses, but they *are*. We know when they are present and when they are absent, don't we?

> My mind and my lips are literally numb, and I have nothing to reply to you [Socrates]. Yet I have spoken about virtue hundreds of times, held forth often on the subject in front of large audiences, and very well too, or so I thought. Now I can't even say what it is. (Plato, *Meno* 80b)

What *is* virtue, for example? To know its difference from vice we must be familiar with it in some way, mustn't we? When asked, however, we prove able to say nothing that can stand up to even rudimentary questioning. We feel familiar with things that we nevertheless cannot claim to know. Indeed, Socrates made out that this was all he knew. His reply to poor Meno (whose mind and lips were numb) was to reassure him that, if he felt perplexed, then this was only because 'I infect [people] with the perplexity I feel myself' (*Meno* 80c). Socrates's wisdom was only his realisation that he wasn't wise: 'it seems that I am wiser [. . .] to this small extent, that I do not think that I know what I do not know' (*Apology* 21d).

But if we really know nothing, what purpose can questioning have? Socrates encounters a problem here, as Meno pointed out (*Meno* 80d). How to question after something we don't know at all? It's a bit like having a map but no destination. How will we know it even if we find it? An answer to a question can only *be* a convincing answer if we in some way already know what we're looking for.

Socrates's response to this challenge was one that would be taken up by his student Plato and then have a very long afterlife in Platonism, Neoplatonism and Christianity. The response was this: When I question after things like virtue or courage, I have a vague notion of what I'm looking for because I have some recollection of them. Where does this recollection come from? It comes from the world of ideas, where the essences of things like virtue and justice reside. And how did I come to have been to this other dimension? The soul,

> since it is immortal and has been born many times, and has seen all things both here and in the other world, has learned everything there is. So we need not be surprised if we can recall the knowledge of virtue or anything else which, as we see, it once possessed [. . .] [F]or seeking and learning are in fact nothing but recollection. (*Meno* 81c–d)

Why did Socrates start to ask questions in the first place? The answer that he gave at his trial recounts a story that began 100 miles to the west of Athens, at Delphi. In Antiquity, Delphi was the home of the Delphic oracle, who spoke in riddles to those who sought the advice of Apollo, god of prophecy. Socrates tells us that a friend of his, Chaerephon, asked the oracle who the wisest man in Athens was. He was told, in strangely certain terms (where is the riddle here?): Socrates. But Socrates, having only questions, *did* take the oracle's pronouncement as a riddle. Refusing the easy road of being flattered (and thereby deceived) by Apollo's seeming praise, Socrates asked what it could mean to say that he was the wisest (*Apology* 21b):

When I heard the oracle's answer, I said to myself 'What does the god mean? Why does he not use plain language? I am only too conscious that I have no claim to wisdom, great or small; so what can he mean by asserting that I am the wisest man?'

Asking his audience to see his adventures in questioning as 'a sort of pilgrimage undertaken to establish the truth of the oracle' (*Apology* 22a), Socrates effectively sets out to disprove Apollo, who he implicitly groups with the sophists ('Why does he not use plain language?'). Socrates is sceptical, almost impious towards the god who refuses the *parrhesia* (plain speaking) that Socrates holds so dear. Not that Socrates was convinced he knew what piety was. At the end of Plato's dialogue *Euthyphro* (15c), Socrates ends the discussion of the meaning of piety by pronouncing his dissatisfaction: 'Then we shall have to start our enquiry about piety all over again from the beginning; because I shall not give up of my own accord until I have learnt the answer.' Having questions gives us the motivation to seek answers.

Another example of Socrates's stubborn commitment to questioning comes at the end of a dialogue with the sophist Protagoras. Socrates reflects on how the outcome of the discussion is like an adversary, pointing the finger and saying:

> 'What an absurd pair you are, Socrates and Protagoras. One of you [Socrates], having said at the beginning that virtue is not teachable, now is bent on contradicting himself by trying to demonstrate that everything is knowledge [...] which is the best way to prove that virtue *is* teachable [...] Protagoras, on the other hand, who at the beginning supposed it to be teachable, now on the contrary seems to be bent on showing that it is almost anything rather than knowledge; and this would make it least likely to be teachable.' (Plato *Protagoras* 361a–c)

That Socrates and Protagoras have switched arguments must be, for Protagoras, a problem. He is a sophist after all and if he is seen to adopt his adversary's position then he has lost the debate – who will pay for his services again? Socrates, however, seems relaxed, amused even, about changing his mind. If the point *is* questioning, then arriving at a different position is a success, not a failure. The only people who never change their opinions are people with no questions: 'Whenever

I succeed in disproving another person's claim to wisdom in a given subject, the bystanders assume that I know everything about the subject myself' (*Apology* 23a).

They assume wrong. Perhaps, as Heidegger (1998) argued much later, to be a human being *is* to be a being that questions. For mortal men and women, who do not have forever to work it out, the question of what it is to be human must remain a question rather than an answer. To err is human, we say, as if it were a bad thing (which is why we follow up with: to forgive divine). But maybe the very possibility of error is what is divine in us? After all, beings who do not err would also be without the possibility of being other than they are. It certainly seems as if Socrates saw becoming other than we are as necessary to living the true life. As Plato makes him say at the end of *Laches* (201a):

> I maintain, my friends, that every one of us should seek out the best teacher whom he can find, first for ourselves, who are greatly in need of one, and then for the youth, regardless of expense or anything. But I cannot advise that we remain as we are.

Not wanting to stand still didn't mean that Socrates sought to flee death. If soul-health is the only health that matters, then death, something that befalls bodies, not souls, isn't something to fear. Indeed, it is precisely the having of questions rather than answers that leads Socrates to think that the fear of death is illogical. After all, not knowing what death *is*, he has no reason to dread it. To be afraid of what comes after death, 'is only another form of thinking that one is wise when one is not; it is to think that one knows what one does not know' (*Apology* 29a). Indeed, since truth is more important than life (since souls have priority over bodies), it is not Socrates who will suffer from his death, but the Athenians who will lack the care he takes of them with his questions: 'you will harm yourselves more than me' (*Apology* 30c).

Having received his sentence, Socrates refused to take the chance of escape from Athens because to do so would mean breaking the law. Socrates (Plato, *Crito* 50e) mused about how Athens was like his mother and father – the city had given him the laws that had made his life possible, and he couldn't forsake her now that those same laws were turned against him. To obey the law when its suits and break it as soon as it goes against our individual interest would, Socrates saw, make all law impossible (imagine only stopping your car at red lights when you feel like it). To escape from under the law – this time the sentence of death on his own head – would have been to contradict himself – to say one thing and do another. And this, for Socrates, since it would sever his relation to truth, was a fate worse than death. As Plato's *Gorgias* (526d–e) has Socrates say:

> Renouncing the honours at which the world aims, I desire only to know the truth, and to live as well as I can, and, when I die, to die as well as I can. And, to the utmost of my power, I exhort all other men to do the same.

Socrates's exhortation that others, too, should seek after truth highlights the universalism of questioning: 'I shall question [. . .] everyone I meet, young or old, foreigner or fellow-citizen' (*Apology* 30a). Socratic questioning knows no distinctions of age or nationality; questioning is for all.

Another legacy of Socratic questioning is the dialectical method by which Socrates questioned. Unlike ancient wisdom (or modern wisdom, for that matter), which posited timeless truths and so had no real need of questions, Socrates only ever had more questions. As the twentieth-century critical theorists Horkheimer and Adorno argued (2002), this means that Socrates's dialectical (questioning) method is defined by its negativity – truth claims are not made, rather there is the attempt to undermine existing truth claims and to seek for better claims that themselves will then be subject to scrutiny (negation). This dialectical process has no end – the point is not to settle on the 'right' answer that will put a stop to discussion. The *process* of questioning is everything.

Negative dialectics, then, is precisely negative. It wants to pull the rug from under our feet, not to point to firm ground on which we might stand. And in opening up the prospect of life as one long debate, it makes us wonder if anybody but free men like Socrates, who could call upon the labour of women and slaves, would have the time or energy for it. Is the dialectical method really the best way to think or is it merely an expression of having too much free time? The devil makes work for idle hands.

There is also the question of whether negation can construct or only deconstruct. The tradition of Western philosophy suggests that building on Socrates's negative dialectics makes for thinkers who are much better at deconstructing truth claims than constructing truths. Indeed, since Nietzsche, modern Western philosophy has found it increasingly difficult to claim to be anything other than deconstructive – a form of philosophical self-reference that thinkers from Heidegger to Jacques Derrida have not sought to deny. As Derrida (1978: 280–1) admitted with admirable honesty, 'we can pronounce not a single deconstructive proposition which has not already had to slip into the form, the logic ... of precisely what it seeks to contest'. Negation is dependent on what it negates. Like a rebellious teenager who needs parents or teachers in order to define herself by her rejection of them, without affirmation negative dialectics would have nothing to work with.

But as outlined in the Introduction, our chief question to Socrates is to wonder how it is possible for one of the living to put the rest on notice that they must justify their existence? The old cliché that when you point your finger, the three other fingers point back at you, will be seen to apply to the history of Western philosophy. The questioning of existence that, after Socrates, came to characterise this tradition has come back to haunt it. Now the questions are asked of Western philosophy itself.

Is it fair to link Socrates to the nihilism of a questioning that can only say no: no, perhaps even to life itself? This is Nietzsche's charge against Socrates. In *Twilight of the Idols* Nietzsche ('Socrates', 1) thinks that Socrates let slip the truth on his deathbed: he really did hate life after all. For Socrates's last request was that a cock be sacrificed to Asclepius, the god of healing. According to Nietzsche, Socrates proved thereby to be tired of life and grateful for death's approach. *This* is where questioning gets you.

But in the last series of lectures that he ever gave, Michel Foucault (2010) contests this reading of Socrates's last request. Rather than finding the dying Socrates not able to care-less about life, Foucault argues that Socrates wants to honour Asclepius for the *healing* that a life of care-full questioning has accomplished. The sacrifice is an *affirmation* of life lived questioningly, that is care-fully, not a negation. 'What is it that Socrates always says, which is nothing new, and which is his last wish that he will convey to his children, his circle, and his friends? "Take care of yourselves" This is Socrates' testament, his final wish' (Foucault 2011: 110–12). And this care of the self is the same as a lifelong questioning of self and others.

2 Diogenes

THE CYNICS (FROM WHOM we get our word cynicism) saw themselves as Socrates's children but, like many ambitious offspring, also sought to outdo their philosophical parent. The most legendary of the Cynics was Diogenes, who was born around fifty years after Socrates in either 412 or 404 BCE. If we were being strictly chronological, this chapter would deal with Plato before Diogenes (although contemporaries, Plato was the older of the two), but it is important to consider Plato and Aristotle side by side, so we will put Diogenes first. Mythological as aspects of the life of Diogenes as recorded by the tradition undoubtedly are, stories of him from generations of Cynics tell us much about the radical questioning of received wisdom that stood at the heart of the Cynic way of life in Greek antiquity.

Diogenes was indeed cynical. Yet he was not only critical. To the contrary, he demonstrated that questioning can also be affirmative: giving to the one who questions a freedom that those who live more conventional lives lack. After all, to question norms is also to raise the possibility of living without them. Crates, Diogenes's 'student' (not that Cynics, having no school, really had students), is said to have rescued one Metrocles from despondency after Metrocles farted loudly while giving an important speech. Visiting this young man, who had locked himself away in shame, Crates, consuming a great pile of pulses, 'farted in his turn' and said: 'it would have been quite a wonder if he had not released the trapped air as nature demanded' (Diogenes Laertius, *Lives* 6.94).

Another often-used example of the link between questioning and freedom in the Cynic tradition is the false freedom of sovereigns, who are sovereign only in name. While kings can only exercise their sovereignty by way of their dependence on a whole host of servants, courtiers and soldiers, the Cynic, renouncing all property and attachments, is dependent on nothing and no one. The Cynic, not the sovereign, is the true king. As Diogenes put it (referring to Philip II of Macedon, whose son, Alexander the Great, was tutored by Aristotle): 'Aristotle breakfasts when Philip pleases and Diogenes when Diogenes pleases' (Plutarch, *On Exile* 12.604d, in Hard 2012: 53). Indeed, such was Diogenes's conviction that the life free of power and possessions was the true life, he was 'fully prepared to compete in happiness with the King of the Persians' (*Gnomologium Vaticanum* 201, in Hard 2012: 12). And this from first an exile, second a beggar and finally a slave.

Perhaps most enduringly of all, what Diogenes exposed by way of his questioning was a common ground beneath differences of identity, a ground that all people share regardless of which gender they are or which country they come from. Diogenes called this egalitarian ground *phusis* (or *physis*), which we will translate as 'coming-into-being' ('nature' is how most translations of the ancient Greek would have it, but we shall shortly see why this is not quite right). Of *phusis*, Diogenes said that we should live according to *it* rather than the laws or customs of any particular state (Diogenes Laertius, *Lives* 6.71). We will explore the cosmopolitan implications of living according to *phusis* later. For now, it is important to mention that Cynicism, almost uniquely in Greek philosophy (Plato's *Republic* is the only other exception here), was capable of conceiving of women's parity with men. In apocryphal letters from Diogenes and Crates to the female Cynic, Hipparchia, women are portrayed as men's equals in philosophy (letters in Hard 2012: 172–3). Cynicism was also the least elitist philosophy in Antiquity. Lucian (1968: 99) tells us that it was 'composed for the most part of serfs and menials'.

The Cynics used to say that great as Socrates was at putting things in question, nonetheless at the end of the day he went home to his wife and slippers (Aelian, *Historical Miscellany* 4.11, in Hard 2012: 36). What they meant by this was that Socratic questioning failed to question everything. What Socrates didn't question, or at least not directly, was *nomos*, the customary or conventional ways of life that include marrying and having children, for example. Indeed, far from questioning *nomos*, Socrates, as we saw, thought that the laws of the land should be taken with the upmost seriousness, which is why he accepted Athens's sentence of death when he could have fled into exile. Inasmuch as he did not question *nomos*, then, Socrates's commitment to living the true life of philosophy did not go far enough for the Cynics.

Nobody could ever accuse Diogenes of failing to question customs. This was a man who lived naked in a barrel in the marketplace in Athens, who masturbated in public and who begged – aggressively. 'He was once begging from a skinflint, and the man was slow to respond. "Come on, man", said Diogenes, "I'm asking you for money to feed myself, not to pay for my funeral".' (*Lives* 6.56)

This begging was, for a Greek, especially shocking. After 2,000 years of Christianity people in the West have become accustomed to the idea of charity – to the notion that some people being dependent on the kindness of others is, if not ideal, then certainly not the worst thing that can happen to a person. But the ancient Greeks felt differently. To them, dependency was truly and unbearably ugly. To be dependent was ultimately to be a slave, and the Greeks had slaves who, above all, they did not want to be identified with. Free-born men were defined precisely by their not being slaves – which is why citizenship was so highly prized in Diogenes's day. Indeed, in one sense all of ancient Greco-Roman thought is a meditation on what is appropriate for a free man.

The people of Diogenes's time therefore saw any display of dependency not only as pitiful (which is probably closer to our reaction today) but as utterly unsightly. In some ways, begging was even worse than slavery, for at least a slave provides his labour in exchange for a living. Nothing could exhibit a slave-like dependency more than a life of begging – the very life that the Cynics embraced wholeheartedly. Indeed, we are told that Diogenes was once sold into slavery and that, in order to emphasise better that he was nothing but a commodity to be exchanged for money, he lay on his belly like a fish (Plutarch, *On Tranquillity of Mind*, in Hard 2012: 59). This was a man who literally did not know the meaning of shame.

What was Diogenes doing flat on his belly in the slave market other than demonstrating a stark truth: most free men are slaves to custom, but Diogenes, although now a slave, is free. This courage to tell the truth of the situation the Cynics called *parrhesia* (straight- or plain-speaking), which for them was the answer to Socrates's question: how should we take care of ourselves? 'When asked what is the finest thing in life, [Diogenes] said: *parrhesia*' (*Lives* 6.69).

Another noteworthy difference of the Cynic from the Socratic life is that where Socrates saw care as a matter of seeking the truth (after all, his wisdom was only knowing that he did not know), Diogenes seems to have felt that he had found it. What can explain this extraordinary confidence by which Socratic questioning is transformed, with Diogenes, into answers? A doing that seems to ask all the questions of others (you fool! why do you follow the customary ways?! As Diogenes shouted at every passer-by) and none of itself?

The answer that Diogenes gives to Socratic questions about love, courage, justice and so on is in a sense to say: don't worry about it! Living conventional lives, we concern ourselves with these things because they matter to questions of who to marry, how to conduct ourselves in battle, how to gain the recognition of our peers, and so on. But for Diogenes there could be no truth in any of this. In other words, Diogenes's certainty was not so much a positive as a negative thing – he defined the true life as *not* marrying, as *not* being a citizen, as *not* caring for reputation, and so on: 'When someone asked him how one can best gain a reputation, he replied, "By holding reputation in contempt"' (Lucian, *Defence of the Portrait* Study 17, in Hard 2012: 23).

But something very positive emerged from all this 'negativity', and this seems to be how the Cynics were able to move beyond Socrates's questioning in order to actually get on with living the true life rather than just talking about it. What was this positive force? It was that, in rejecting customs and citizenship, the Cynics found that nothing at all separated them from people with different customs and from people from other states. It is therefore no accident that, as far as we know, Diogenes was the first to call himself a *kosmopolites* or cosmopolitan (*Lives* 6.63):

> Buyer: Then first, my good fellow, where do you come from?
> Diogenes: Everywhere.
> Buyer: How do you mean?
> Diogenes: You're looking at a citizen of the world (*kosmopolites*).
>
> (Lucian, *Philosophies for Sale* 7, in Hard 2012: 3–4)

Diogenes's questioning of the Greek conception of citizenship as belonging to a particular state (in Diogenes's day a city-state) is much more radical than it appears to us today, inheritors as we are of his cosmopolitanism. After all, Aristotle had spoken the Greek mind on the subject when, in Book I of his *Politics*, he argued that humans are by nature political animals, which means that they belong to some polity. Not to belong to a political community, to be *apolis*, is, for Aristotle, to be either a beast or a god. Human beings belong *somewhere*, not anywhere like roaming beasts or everywhere like the gods. To be without a state is not to be fully human for Aristotle, something which is expressed in the ancient Greek fear of exile as a fate worse than death.

But for Diogenes, to be an exile not only made it possible to be a brother to all (rather than to only a few fellow citizens), it also meant an end to dreary home-staying: 'To someone who said to him, "The Sinopeans have condemned you to exile", he replied, "Yes, and I've condemned them to stay where they are"' (*Lives* 6.49). Exile, indeed, was for Diogenes a *condition* of philosophy, because only those who are cast out of their homeland are really free to question conventions (*Lives* 6.49). Like fish who cannot see the water they swim in, we find it very difficult to separate nature from nurture in our own culture. Sent abroad, however, we will find ourselves with more questions about what is 'natural'. As Diogenes said: there 'was the time when I was such as you are now; but such as I am now, you will never be' (*Lives* 6.56).

As well as preparing the way for future cosmopolitans, the potency of Cynic questioning was that the mission of care that Socrates had still described (in a typically Greek gesture) as care for oneself, became, for the first time, a mission of care for all people, everywhere: 'I'm a liberator of humanity, a healer of human ills' (Lucian, *Philosophies for Sale* 8, in Hard 2012: 4). And the Cynics took this mission of universal care very seriously. It explains their wandering and also why they clearly understood all their rudeness and abruptness at people living more conventional lives as doing those people a great favour: 'When he was in need of money, he would say to his friends that he was asking for what he was owed, and not for charity' (*Lives* 6.46). This upbraiding of everyone was indeed what Diogenes saw as the distinction of his practical, lived philosophy from the empty abstractions of Plato: 'a man who has practiced philosophy all this time and never caused pain to anyone' (Plutarch, *On Moral Virtue* 12, in Hard 2012: 33).

This mission of universal care (expressed by way of an indiscriminate rudeness!) is why, as I claimed earlier, we should understand the

Greek word *phusis* (recalling that Diogenes said that we should live according to *phusis* rather than *nomos*) as 'being' or 'existence' rather than (in the usual translation) 'nature'. Living according to nature can very well justify hierarchy, as indeed it has done many times. Take, for example, the aristocratic senatorial class of Rome, who justified their elevated existence to the plebeians (from which our word plebs derives) by saying that some part of the body politic has to play the servant of the others if the body is not to starve:

> [Rome's] only hope lay in finding a solution for the conflicting interests of the two classes in the state: by fair means or foul the country must recover its internal harmony. The senatorial party accordingly decided to employ Menenius Agrippa as their spokesman to the commons... [He] is said to have told [the commoners] the following story: 'Long ago, when the members of the human body did not, as now they do, agree together, but each had its own thoughts and the words to express them in, the other parts resented the fact that they should have the worry and trouble of providing everything for the belly, which remained idle, surrounded by its ministers, with nothing to do but enjoy the pleasant things they gave it. So the discontented members plotted together that the hand should carry no food to the mouth, that the mouth should take nothing that was offered, and that the teeth should accept nothing to chew. But alas! while they sought in their resentment to subdue the belly by starvation, they themselves and the whole body wasted away to nothing.' (Livy, *The Early History of Rome* 2.32.7–11)

Diogenes's 'living according to nature' is a very different beast from this deeply conservative defence of rank, which appeals to nature in the narrow sense of the hierarchical arrangement of organic life. The *phusis* that Diogenes wants us to live by seems to be something more than just nature in this sense. It looks to be more a term for being, or existence as such. Diogenes seems to be saying that, in living by the light of common *being*, we will see that everyone *is* equally. Both free man and slave are equal in existence. It is only by the light of *nomos* (convention) that inequality appears. To take a famous example of this from the life of Diogenes: when Alexander the Great conquered Corinth (where Diogenes happened to be at the time), he went to find Diogenes and found him sunbathing in a square. Alexander said: tell me one thing I can do for you and it will be yours. Diogenes, who had failed even to acknowledge the great king's presence and who was still lying on the ground replied: stand out of my light! (*Lives* 6.38).

What are the Cynics telling us with this story? Surely an illustration of the fundamental equality between people that customs cover over with their fine robes and fancy titles. Diogenes pretends not to see a king, only another man who happens to be blocking his light (he is sunbathing after all). Diogenes is demonstrating that the differences between the two men only *appear* to be – that if one were to strip away their clothes and their pretensions, they would stand, naked, as equals. Diogenes is like the little boy in Hans Christian Andersen's tale who is the only one to have the courage to say that the king's new clothes are imaginary and that he is really as bare as a newborn baby. Likewise, Alexander was only god-like because people had come to view him as such. In truth, he was a mortal man like any other.

Diogenes's confidence that his questioning had given him answers seems to be located right here. For when we question conventional lives, we do not find a truer form of them but rather that they have *nothing* of truth about them. We should therefore stop living them. And by stop, the Cynics do not mean in order to start with a new, somehow better, set of conventions, but really just that – to *stop*, with nothing in addition. Ceasing to indulge the half-truths that make up so much of everyday living, we find, not nothing, but rather a form of living that, in its very bareness, is true.

Diogenes sees questioning as a form of life that unfolds as follows: if you will have the courage of truth, then you will not be able to live as others do. Indeed, without this difference in living, philosophical questioning is nothing. 'I am thinking of the first night of Diogenes [...] as long as philosophers do not muster the courage to seek an entirely different lifestyle and demonstrate it by their own example, they will come to nothing' (Nietzsche, unpublished fragment from notebook of 1874).[1] Yet although the true life will be different from conventional lives, this difference is not (like the difference of Alexander from his subjects) a difference that cannot be bridged. Rather, it is one that is open to all who would have the courage to make the difficult and dangerous crossing.

Before we move on from Diogenes, we should perhaps pose a question to him (knowing now that he would ask plenty of questions of us).

---

[1] www.nietzschesource.org/eKGWB/NF-1873,31[10]

Diogenes: why is truth the most valuable thing? For despite the appearance that earthy Cynicism was fundamentally different to the creeping otherworldliness of Platonism, the shared Socratic inheritance of Cynicism and Platonism is evident in the unquestioning regard for truth as the highest value. For Plato, unchanging truth is that in which all beings have their being, while for Diogenes the true life is the only one worth living. Truth is the common measure here, even if the Cynics asked more about the true life than the truth of being (they thought it worthless to pursue the study of logic and physics, for example).

In this sense, as Foucault's study (2011) of the Cynics shows, Cynicism in many ways was only an intensification of Socratic questioning rather than something other than it (according to Diogenes Laertius [*Lives* 6.54], Plato had already described Diogenes as 'Socrates gone mad'). Diogenes, like Socrates, did not doubt that the true life is lived in the open, that it doesn't dissemble or lie. Only he pursued this principle to the extent of hiding nothing at all of his life, not even his body and his bodily needs. Similarly, Diogenes shared with Socrates the belief that it is better to die than to live a lie, except that he forced this principle to the point of seeking confrontation with political power, something that Socrates (as he admitted during his trial) always sought to avoid. No more than Diogenes did Socrates believe that power could have any relation to truth, but he interpreted this as meaning that his truth-telling mission was apolitical. For Diogenes, on the other hand, the Cynic really tests his capacity for truth only *in* an open confrontation with political power.

Finally, Diogenes, in questioning custom to the point of rejecting customary lives, again only follows the lead of Socrates. For although Socrates did not reject the life of citizenship, his endless questioning was bound, eventually, to involve questions about citizenship itself. Indeed, in dialogue with Aristippus, Socrates shows how even though the non-citizen is least free, nonetheless free men (citizens) remain slaves of their states (Xenophon, *Memorabilia* 2.1.14). In other words, Diogenes's rejection of the state and his proud description of himself as *apolis* (someone without a state) is a logical extension of Socratic negation. What does nature know of citizenship? How necessary, then, can it be for life?

In Diogenes we see the full force of questioning once it is untethered from any anchor in convention. Once I question everything, I must also question my allotted place in the world. And if questioning shows nationality to be nothing, then neither does anything divide the sons and daughters of Zeus. Unlike Aristotle (*Nicomachean Ethics* 4.6.1126b), for whom 'it is not proper to have the same care for intimates and for strangers', I can now consider myself *kosmopolites*, a citizen of the world. The negativity of questioning is productive of positive new possibilities, in this case of what the Stoics called, borrowing from the Cynics, the 'brotherhood of man'.

3   Plato

PLATO'S APPROACH TO QUESTIONING was built on what he took to be a fundamental distinction between truth and opinion. As he argued in the *Republic* (534a), while opinion (*doxa*) is concerned with the world of change and includes all forms of belief (*pistis*) about things, philosophy asks only after the true world which does not change. Knowledge of these eternal themes (*epistêmê*) is the aim of the philosopher.

As a student of Socrates who died because of it, Plato (427–347 BCE) was well aware of the unsettling consequences of philosophical questioning. As well as undermining social order, questioning also threatens cynicism in the one who questions. This is why, in the section of *Republic* (538d–e) that he devoted to the education of the philosopher, Plato specified that philosophical questioning must not begin too young (not that the old, set in their ways, are capable of it either):

> [B]ut what happens when [the young philosopher] is confronted with the question, 'What do you mean by "honourable"?' When he gives the answer tradition has taught him, he is refuted in argument, and when that has happened many times and on many different grounds, he is driven to think that there's no difference between honourable and disgraceful, and so on with all the other values, like right and good, that he used to revere. What sort of respect for their authority do you think he'll feel at the end of it all?

The problem, Plato elaborated, is that, disabused of conventional notions but not yet arrived at the truth, philosophical questioning tempts the young to seek only pleasure. Finding nothing to be true and not yet fully embarked on the true life, the young questioner will be seduced by 'a life which flatters his desires' (*Republic* 539a). Indeed, even the way he questions will be marked by pleasure-seeking: 'You must have noticed how young men, after their first taste of argument, are always contradicting people just for the fun of it [...] like puppies who love to pull and tear at everything in reach' (*Republic* 539b). For Plato, the worst thing in all of this is not that the young questioner discredits himself, but that, in making questioning all about him, he risks the reputation of philosophy. Unlike opinion, which is worthless precisely because everyone will have their own, truth is a collective endeavour, the way of life of philosophy.

What, then, does philosophical questioning aim at if it must avoid the sophist temptation of questioning for individual gain (such as showing that you're the smartest person in the room or trying to win an argument in the law courts)? True knowledge, for Plato, seeks to know 'what is *as* it is' (*Republic* 478a). Philosophers, as lovers of truth, seek after 'the eternal and the immutable' (*Republic* 484b). Those who question starting from opinion, meanwhile, are 'lost in multiplicity', subject to the 'vicissitudes of change and decay' (*Republic* 485b). Philosophical questions ask after *being*. Questioning in order to form mere opinions grasps, effectively, after nothing. For what *is*, in the sense of being timeless, is knowable, while opinion, concerned only with what pertains in the here and now, is 'knowledge' of that which, changing all the time, is effectively unknowable (*Republic* 477a). For example, if I have an opinion about love based on a love affair I happen to be having right now, then I really know nothing. To know love is to know what love *is* even in those times and places when it does not involve me. True questioning avoids the solipsism of always starting from me.

Genuine knowledge, then, is a collective enterprise whereby I question not from myself but rather question the other, just as she questions me. This feature of Socratic questioning infuriates Thrasymachus in Plato's *Republic* (336b–c):

> What nonsense have you two been talking, Socrates? Why do you act like idiots by giving way to one another? If you truly want to know what justice is, don't just ask questions and then refute the answers simply to satisfy your competitiveness or love of honour. You know very well that it is easier to ask questions than answer them. Give an answer yourself and tell us what you say the just is.

But as Plato writes in his Seventh Letter (341c–d):[1]

> [Philosophy] does not admit of exposition like other branches of knowledge; but after much conversation about the matter itself and a life lived together, suddenly a light, as it were, is kindled in one soul by a flame that leaps to it from another, and thereafter sustains itself.

Philosophy seeks out truth in a dialectical manner as we proceed together 'by question and answer' (*Letter VII* 344b). As (Plato's) Socrates says to Meno: having demonstrated that neither you nor I really know what virtue is, 'I am ready to carry out, together with you, a joint investigation and inquiry into what it is' (*Meno* 100b). To be sure, in principle truth can be obtained. As Socrates says to Thrasymachus: don't think that just because we give way to one another's questions that we are 'less than completely serious about finding it' (*Republic* 336e). Truth, even more than gold, is something that begs to be discovered. But we cannot search for truth alone. And when we do arrive at truth, we must not claim it for ourselves, for it has only come to light in this context of a questioning with others (*Letter VII* 344e).

So important is the link between questioning and philosophy that, in Plato's dialogue *Phaedrus*, the difference between philosophy and opinion is essentially that, unlike opinion, philosophy has questions. Philosophy alone does not pretend that it has the truth in advance. In *Republic* (337e), Socrates responds to Thrasymachus's challenge to stop asking questions of others and start providing definitions of his own: 'How can someone give an answer [...] when he doesn't know it and doesn't claim to know it?' If philosophy displayed its knowledge in advance of questioning then, far from being the search for truth, it would be nothing other than the dissimulation of what is already known, which would make it identical to opinion (*doxa*).

In the great struggle against opinion, Plato targets the sophists in particular, those teachers of the arts of rhetoric. Given that it can speak for or against the same thing, rhetoric is indifferent to truth. Indeed, for questioning to be other than rhetorical dissimulation, it is insufficient to say that questioners *seek* the truth. In representing truth as something external our questions seek after, we would be echoing the claim of sophistry that the truth can be possessed. Philosophical

---

[1] There is some dispute as to whether Plato's Seventh Letter is genuine.

questioning rather stands in an ongoing *relation* to truth. True questioning is not having of knowledge but a capacity of the soul (Foucault 2010: 330–1, 352). Only the soul can be changed by truth; indeed, the soul *is* this capacity for truth. Truth is nothing more or less than the soul which it modifies (Foucault 2010: 335).

The true philosopher, transformed by questioning, *changes*. The sophist, meanwhile, remains stuck with his opinion. Worse, although he fights tooth and nail for this opinion, this is only in order to win the argument, as rhetoric demands. The sophist *has* the measure of truth, which is why he can sell his services as a teacher of wisdom (*sophia*). The philosopher, meanwhile, must yield to the rigours of questioning, which is a pact of mutual submission to the truth: I only get to question the other inasmuch as she questions me. For the questioner-philosopher, truth is a process, not a possession.

While the sophist, by definition, is bad at his art if his rhetoric does not win the argument, the philosopher does not need to win at all. Recall our earlier discussion of Plato's *Protagoras* – Socrates's admission at the end of this dialogue that he and Protagoras (a sophist) have switched arguments points to the essential difference between philosophy and sophistry. Socrates is not embarrassed to be seen to have changed his mind. Protagoras, meanwhile, must not *appear* to change his mind, although whether he really does so is of no concern. Philosophy, Plato is telling us, is the *movement* occasioned by questioning, a capacity for change that sophistry can only disavow. Unlike the sophist who must (seem to) stand his ground, the true questioner must err.

If Socrates questioned what virtues such as courage are in order to live well, then Plato asked, more abstractly, what it is for something like courage *to be* as such. For one thing, Plato notes that the being of something like beauty ('beauty-in-itself') is not accessible to the senses, in this case to vision (*Republic* 507b, see also 597). When I see a beautiful face, I do not see beauty 'itself', but an *appearance* of beauty, one of many such appearances in the world. But beauty *itself* cannot be regarded as many but as one; and this one is something that is only intelligible, not visible. In other words, for all particular things there is first the *idea* of that thing in the intelligible realm and only second the appearance in the material world of copies of this form. For something to be intelligible does not mean that it is thinkable or conceivable, as if the existence of that thing was somehow separate from its idea. Much more than this, a thing such as beauty *is* only by way of its intelligibility. The beautiful face is not already beautiful, only then for the idea of beauty to help me to think it; no, the beautiful face *is* only beautiful by way of its participation in the idea of beauty.

Where does the idea of beauty, along with all the other ideas, reside? Plato (*Republic* 509d) calls it 'the intelligible order or region' and it is to this world, which does not change, that we must direct our questions. Asking after our world, where nothing stands still for a moment, is tilting at windmills, an exercise in futility: 'fixed on the twilight world of change and decay, [the mind] can only form opinions, its vision is confused and its opinions shifting, and it seems to lack intelligence' (*Republic* 508d). The one who questions must therefore turn away from this 'world of change until [his] eye can bear to look at reality, and at the brightest of all realities which is what we call the good' (*Republic* 518c–d). By looking away from what is mutable towards the immutable, the philosopher will find the light of pure knowledge. The one who stays with shadowy opinion, meanwhile, lives 'in a dream from which he will not awake on this side of the other world' (*Republic* 534c–d).

Although it is not at all clear that Plato believed that the ideas reside in another world, it is easy to see why, many centuries later, the nineteenth-century German philosopher Nietzsche said that otherworldliness begins with Plato. The notion that what appears in the world is not all there is can, and did, lead to more *idea*listic readings than perhaps Plato intended, culminating in the conception that this world is but a pale shadow of the true world beyond. Indeed, four centuries or so after Plato, people influenced by the new Platonism of that time came to feel that the material world was a prison and that their souls longed for escape back to the world beyond from which they came (these people were called Gnostics). This Neoplatonism was also influential on the Christianity which emerged around the same time as it. The borrowing of the otherworldliness of Platonism by Christianity is why Nietzsche (*BGE*, Preface) called Christianity 'Platonism for the "people"'.

But long before Nietzsche, plenty of philosophers thought that Plato had got off on the wrong foot with his 'world' of ideas. Plato's student, Aristotle, was one of them (as we shall see in the next chapter). Diogenes was not much impressed, either. We have already heard about how, on hearing Plato's definition of human beings as bipeds without feathers, Diogenes plucked a chicken which he then presented to Plato with the words 'here's your man!' Plato, the Cynics said, was thereby forced to refine his definition of human being with the extra predicate of 'having broad nails' (in order to distinguish human finger and toenails from a chicken's claws). What Diogenes was poking fun at was Plato's notion that one can arrive at an understanding of what it is to be human by way of an 'idea' of what is common to human being. Plato's ideas might give us definitions of things, but these are ultimately empty and certainly cannot help us to answer the question (the only question that mattered to Diogenes): how should I live? For Diogenes, what is common to all people is precisely where the true life is not to be found. If I were to categorise myself as a creature with the generic capacity for reason, how would such an abstraction help me, concretely, to distinguish a good life from a bad one? Knowing that I can reason in principle tells me nothing about how I ought to reason in practice.

Is Nietzsche's judgement that in Plato we see the last wisps of reality evaporate deserved? It can appear as if Plato was more interested in, say, the idea of 'beauty' than in beautiful things; namely, that he was more interested in abstract sameness rather than in worldly difference. In this sense Plato has often been identified with the tendency in Western thought to prefer the one to the many, that which is identical to that which is different. But is this fair? Couldn't the search for true definitions, for what is proper to each being, rather be seen as an attempt to give difference its due – to identify that which, in enabling a horse not to be a cow for example, lets difference be?

Even when he is generalising, Plato is doing something useful. For in showing that all difference participates, equally, in being (what Plato calls 'the Good' which, like the sun, allows everything that *is* to be seen), Plato proves helpful for all those who would defend equality to this day. In his own way, Plato shared Diogenes's insight that, despite the overwhelming appearance of difference between them, both Alexander and a naked beggar equally *are*.

Plato's much criticised otherworldliness is not all it seems to be, either. It is true that Plato thinks that what is present to our senses is not all there is. In this he was following Parmenides, who argued that, since everything is One, then the appearance of change as suggested by our senses must be just that – mere appearance. But Plato's question mark about what our senses can tell us is not, like Parmenides's, an appeal to the unity of all things. Plato is saying something else; namely, that beyond what our senses can perceive there is that which, though it is not present, still *is*. Plato is therefore the first in the Western tradition to think the being of what is not. As Plato argues in the *Sophist*, each being is defined not only by what it itself is, but also by all the things that it is not. And in this sense the 'not' is as central to being as the 'is'. When we try to identify any thing (in this dialogue it is the sophist), we will have to proceed as Plato himself proceeds in his dialogues: by saying what each thing isn't. Indeed, this may well be all we can firmly say of anything.

This line of thinking also enabled Plato to say something interesting about questioning itself. What *is* the question? What gives a question its reality, makes it *be* in the world? After all, in a sense, the question is nothing. It is not like the assertion, which points some*thing* out (there is beauty). A question (is it beautiful?) is not a statement about what is in the world but something stranger. A question asks whether something is or is not. But while we can imagine something that is, how can something not be? If something is not then isn't it simply nothing? How can a question refer to something not being the case without referring to nothing at all? In this case, to answer in the negative (no, it is not beautiful) would be to talk non-sense. But it's not nonsense.

What sense can the question have given that it's not nonsensical but is dependent for its sense on that which is not – on non-being? Given that he is the first philosopher who grasped that what is present is not all there is, it is perhaps no surprise that Plato was also the first to think the conundrum of the question through to an answer. And in the process, Plato dealt with a problem that had been posed by Parmenides. Parmenides had said, not unreasonably, that there are two roads: the road of what is and the road of what is not. You will find nothing on the second road, Parmenides assured his listeners.

But Plato wasn't so sure. Perhaps what put him on to the positive power of that which 'is not' was his master's daemon. For Socrates's daemon never told him what to do – only what not to do. And this seemed to work well enough, keeping Socrates out of politics, for a start. By whatever route he came to it, Plato realised that what is not is *not* unthinkable as Parmenides had said, but rather that what is not – *is*, in some way.

For example, to say that my friend Ash is not the same person I once knew it is not enough to say that he is *not* the same person anymore. I must also say, positively, that he *has* changed. In other words, change, even though it is nothing in itself, still *is* – it isn't nothing after all. My friend is both *not* what he was and *is* different. Only in this way can we keep together the principle of change and the principle of identity.

My friend is not the same person, but he is still Ash. Ash has changed. But this means that Ash is *both* a principle of identity and a principle of change. Change is not outside Ash while identity is in him; rather, both being (as Ash) and non-being (Ash changing) are equally central to his being Ash. Every being, from Ash to Andromeda, is both itself *and* something other than itself (that which it is not).

Plato realised that if everything remained unchanged, as Parmenides had argued, then life and thinking, and with them all knowledge itself, would be impossible. You can't have life, which is defined by change, on one side and knowing as something completely separate. On the other hand, if Heraclitus (another pre-Socratic thinker) was right that being is only change, that everything is motion, then, equally, nothing could be known (there could be no self-sameness, no identity, to know). Given the impossibility of either identity or change, being or becoming, as names for what is, we are compelled to think both together. And, after all, both identity and change *are*.

Having established that what is not still *is* in some sense, Plato gives us a way of making sense of questioning. If nothing could change, if what *is* was all there is, then questions would make no sense (why ask someone why they are sad if it is impossible that they might become happy?). Equally, if there was only change then no question could stand (why ask someone why they are sad when no mood can last long enough to *be* anything?). But because things *do* change, because each thing both is and is not at the same time, our questioning is not for nothing.

Of course, Plato helps us to think about more than the being of what is not. The radicalism of Plato's questioning is that although it is sourced in Socrates's negative dialectics, it manages to say something 'positive' about being. Being is 'the Good' and, just as in Plato's famous analogy of the cave, it is like the sun in the light of which beings are revealed. Plato describes 'the Good' in his *Republic* (508b–c) as that idea which 'gives the objects of knowledge their truth and the knower's mind the power of knowing'. The Good is therefore in a real sense nothing other than 'the *cause* of knowledge and truth'. Although it is itself known, the Good therefore remains 'something other than, and even more splendid than, knowledge and truth, splendid as they are' (*Republic* 508e). Once again, the analogy of light is used. The light that illuminates beings is not itself the Good but rather the *source* of that light. As the origin of light is the sun, so the origin of intelligibility (by which we have awareness of beings) is the Good. Asking after what each being 'is', as Socrates had, presupposes the givenness of beings – that there is something rather than nothing. But why is anything given at all? The Good is Plato's answer to this question.

As well as posing the question of being, Plato does not forget his master's concern with the question of how we should live. While Platonism may have become otherworldly in its concerns, Plato's dialogues, as we have seen, are anything but. When Plato criticises writing in the Phaedrus, this has been seen (Derrida 1974, 1981) as showing a disdain for whatever is second-hand or copied – as if writing could only be a poor shadow of an original, pure speech in which the speech-giver is fully present. Writing, meanwhile, inasmuch as the author is absent from it, can only be derivative. The idea here is that living, a living in which we are never fully present to ourselves, is always more like writing than speech. In refusing writing, Plato is somehow denying life.

But it is more plausible to argue that, in fact, Plato refused to write not out of any disdain for living, but rather precisely because he valued it above all else. This is how he puts it in the Seventh Letter (314b–c):

> This much at least I can say about all writers, past or future, who say they know the things to which I devote myself, whether by hearing the teaching of me or of others, or by their own discoveries – that according to my view it is not possible for them to have any real skill in the matter. There neither is nor ever will be a treatise of mine on the subject.

Plato seems to be saying that writing down the principles of his philosophy would condemn these principles to becoming dead doctrines. Living principles have to be lived, and to write them down as if they were fixed laws or commandments would be to miss the point. Thought itself lives and breathes, primarily by way of the dialectic, in which philosophical friends continually question each other out of a shared love for truth.

Questions are the movement of thought itself, in which, together, we look to the truth of being which makes our very questioning possible.

4 Aristotle

IF PLATO'S QUESTION WAS the question of identity, of what stays the same in change, then Plato's student, Aristotle (384–322 BCE), asked about change (*kinēsis*) itself. In particular, Aristotle wanted to conceive of change without splitting the world in two as Plato had done. Instead of Plato's two worlds – a world of change and a world of ideas that don't change – Aristotle sought to think change and identity together in the same world – *our* world 'where everything comes to be from what is' (Aristotle, *Metaphysics* 12.6.1071b). After all, the world of change is not entirely in motion – things change in predictable rather than random ways. While an acorn may or may not become an oak, it cannot become a willow tree. And not only in nature is change other than flux. The block of marble does not become a statue by chance. The potential of the marble to become a statue requires a sculptor to give it form. In short, 'actuality is the *organization* (*logos*) of that which is potentially' (Aristotle, *De Anima* 2.4.415b, emphasis added).

But if everything comes to be from what is, then the question of how change is possible remains. In his *Metaphysics* (12.2.1069b), Aristotle suggests an answer: things come to be from what is, but from what is *potentially*, not from what is in actuality. This idea of generation means that, for Aristotle (*Metaphysics* 12.3.1070a), we can do without Plato's ideas. Particular human beings, for example, appear not thanks to the idea 'human' but because they are capable of generating other such beings (indeed, all living or 'ensouled' things share this capacity 'to make another such as itself' [*De Anima* 2.4.415a30]). Plato's ideas cannot explain how such change comes about (*Metaphysics* 12.6.1071b).

Rather than starting from their ideas, then, we need to question beginning from particular things: 'Because what is sure and better known as conforming to reason comes to be from what is unsure but more apparent' (*De Anima* 2.2.413a). Our questions need to be inductive (working up from particular things), not deductive (working down from first principles). Sticking with the example of particular human beings: for Aristotle (*De Anima* 2.2.414a), we need to invert Plato's approach since 'the body is not the actuality of the soul, but the soul is the actuality of some body'. Against Plato's notion that souls are fitted to bodies, Aristotle (*De Anima* 2.2.414a) insists that 'the actuality of each thing', souls included, 'comes about naturally in what has it in potentiality, that is, in its appropriate manner'. Things are the way they are not because they copy an idea, but because they have the *capacity* to be this or that.

Aristotle admits a difficulty, however. If capacity (which he calls *dunamis*, potentiality) and not actuality (*energeia*) accounts for change, then how to explain that, while everything active has potentiality, not all potentiality is activated (*Metaphysics* 12.6.1071b)? After all, since it is just as possible for an acorn *not* to become an oak, how do we account for when it does indeed become one? How do we explain the becoming actual of a potential? There is a need for something prior to potential by which it is activated. Since becoming (the activation of a potential) is a kind of motion, Aristotle infers that, ultimately, there must be a first 'mover which causes motion without being moved' (*Metaphysics* 12.7.1072a). This highest being, Aristotle tells us, is pure activity: 'For what acts is always superior to what is affected' (*De Anima* 3.5.430a). And it is eternal. As the final cause of change, it does not itself change; it 'cannot in any way be otherwise' than it is (*Metaphysics* 12.7.1072b).

Despite their different answers, Plato and Aristotle's fundamental question is therefore the same – the question of being. Indeed, even their different answers to this question have strong similarities: what does not change is more in being than what does. True knowledge, indeed, can only *be* of that which cannot be otherwise than it is. 'Of things capable of being otherwise', in contrast, 'we do not know, when they have passed outside our observation, whether they exist or not' (Aristotle, *Nicomachean Ethics* 6.3.1139b). Unlike, say, the weather, true being, necessary and therefore eternal, is not something we have to keep coming back to. Being does not require a forecast.

To hold that true being is eternal, as Aristotle does, is to reintroduce Plato's two worlds. For being in *our* world is not eternal but subject to change. So changeless being must reside elsewhere. Indeed, just how close Aristotle remains to Plato's two worlds is clear from his summary: 'That there is a substance which is eternal and unmoved and separate from perceptible things is clear from what has been said' (*Metaphysics* 12.7.1073a). This equation of being with what does not change means that, just like Plato, Aristotle distinguishes truth from opinion. Our questions must lead us beyond appearance, since 'perceiving and understanding are not the same' (*De Anima* 3.3.427b). True belief has the capacity to be right because it can also be wrong. Perception, to the contrary 'is always true, and belongs to all animals, whereas reasoning can also be false, and it belongs to nothing which lacks reason' (*De Anima* 3.3.427b). Although Aristotle thereby makes reason a condition of truth, he also refutes the sophist notion, attributed to Protagoras, that 'man is the measure of all things'. Just as for Plato, for Aristotle (*De Anima* 3.3.428b) truth does not depend entirely on us:

> Yet things do appear falsely even among those things concerning which one has at the same time a true perception: for instance, although the sun appears to be one foot across, one is convinced that it is larger than the inhabited world.

As well as knowledge relying on universal reason rather than on us, it is also the case that 'knowledge is in a way the *objects* of knowledge' rather than the subject of knowledge, the known thing rather than the knower (*De Anima* 3.8.431b, emphasis added). After all, 'one who did not perceive anything would neither learn nor understand anything' (*De Anima* 3.8.432a). Although Aristotle's emphasis on the objects of perception is different from Plato's, it is clear that the two philosophers share a more fundamental refusal to reduce truth to perception. For while Aristotle notes that there can be no truth without perception, he agrees with Plato that truth is not *reducible to* perception.

Another similarity between Aristotle and Plato is that they emphasise that philosophical questions cannot be separated, in the final analysis, from questions about the good life. In his *Nicomachean Ethics* (2.4.1105b), Aristotle criticises those who, taking 'refuge in theory', 'think they are being philosophers and will become good in this way'. Such men, Aristotle continues, are 'like patients who listen attentively to their doctors, but do none of the things they are ordered to do'. Although pre-Socratic natural philosophers such as Thales and Anaxagoras had knowledge of the cosmos, they could not be said to have practical wisdom (*phrónēsis*) because 'we see them ignorant of what is to their own advantage'. While wise men such as these may well know what is divine, this wisdom remains useless 'because it is not human goods they seek' (*Ethics* 6.7.1141b). Indeed, even Socrates, who taught virtue, assumed that virtue was the same thing as sound reasoning, missing that such reasoning requires virtue and vice versa. Like the conundrum of the chicken and the egg (which comes first?), the good person must have practical wisdom, but practical wisdom in turn demands goodness (*Ethics* 6.13.1144b).

Despite their agreement that philosophy, which questions how to live, is not like wisdom, which is indifferent to this question, a distinction between Aristotle and Plato on the role of questioning in philosophy arises in the *Ethics*. As we saw, for Plato philosophy proceeds by way of the dialectic: that questioning by which we and our interlocuters are *changed*. Aristotle's ethical ideal, meanwhile, is of a person who is constant and unchanging. Unlike the good, the bad have no principle of stability: 'for they do not remain even like to themselves' (*Ethics* 8.8.1159b). Far from being capable of change, the good person is the constant by which other, lesser, people are measured:

> For his opinions are harmonious, and he desires the same things with all his soul [...] for the same thing is always painful [to him] and the same thing always pleasant, and not one thing at one time and another at another; he has, so to speak, nothing to regret. (*Ethics* 9.4.1166a)

Unlike Plato's philosopher, who is only as good as the dialectic (mutual questioning between friends), Aristotle's ideal type is entirely self-subsistent: 'he is his own best friend and therefore ought to love himself best' (*Ethics* 9.8.1168b). Indeed, while Plato's philosophers question what is true together, Aristotle's philosopher 'can contemplate truth' 'even when by himself'. He 'can perhaps do better if he has fellow-workers, but still he is the most self-sufficient' (*Ethics* 10.7.1177a). Just as the work of the gods is contemplative speculation, so 'of human activities' the happiest is a life of contemplation (*Ethics* 10.8.1178b).

A central question of the *Ethics*, one that will reappear frequently in the chapters to come, is how to draw a distinction between what is voluntary and involuntary (*Ethics* 3.1.1109b). As Aristotle admits, the entire edifice of honours and punishments in society depends on this. Beginning with the seemingly straightforward distinction between actions that originate with the agent and those that are external to him, Aristotle soon runs into difficulty. For one thing, to the extent that all actions are dependent on the pressure of pleasure or pain, every action is compelled (*Ethics* 3.1.1110b). Of course, to the extent that agents seek to take credit for good actions and blame external influence for bad ones, to say that every action is compelled is manifestly self-interested. But this does not undermine the force of the argument as such. All that is required is for agents to take credit neither for blame-worthy *nor* for praise-worthy actions.

Echoing Socrates, who argued that nobody does evil voluntarily, Aristotle admits that 'everything that is done by reason of ignorance is *not* voluntary' (*Ethics* 3.1.1110b). He tries to get out of this by saying that there is a difference, as in the case of drunken antics, between acting *because of* ignorance and acting *with* ignorance (the drunk acts with ignorance rather than because of it). Aristotle assumes that the drinker has chosen drunkenness. Such wickedness must be voluntary since, otherwise, how will we be able to assert that people are the originators of their actions as much as of their children? (*Ethics* 3.5.1113b). It seems that the notion of attributable actions is necessary for there to be praise and blame, rather than for sound reasons of its own. Aristotle admits as much when he says that the reality of praise and blame is borne out not by any philosophical principle, but by the testimony of both private citizens and lawgivers, who all punish those who do wrong (*Ethics* 3.5.1113b). The conservative implications of Aristotle's inductive method of questioning are here laid bare: unlike Plato who, starting from ideas, can deduce a new republic that unconventionally breaks with custom, Aristotle, building on what is, must make a principle out of convention.

Aristotle acknowledges that voluntary action is connected to deliberation: 'no Spartan deliberates about the best constitution for the Scythians. For none of these things can be brought about by our own efforts' (*Ethics* 3.3.1112a). The question is whether *anything* really lies in our power to decide? Trying to avoid this question, Aristotle introduces time to his discussion of voluntariness. If it must be conceded that in the present we have no real choices (how can the drunk refuse a drink?), then it will be necessary to refer back to the way in which today's compulsion is built on yesterday's choice. The drunk cannot refuse a drink because of a history of abusing alcohol. As Aristotle (*Ethics* 3.5.1114a) makes this point: 'But perhaps a man is the kind of man not to take care [of himself]. Still they are themselves by their slack lives responsible for becoming men of that kind.'

If today's compulsion stems from yesterday's choice, as Aristotle argues, then what makes yesterday essentially different from today? Even if there was a day when the drunk first made the 'choice' to abuse alcohol, it would be easy enough to refer this 'voluntariness' back to the day when the man in question lost his job, perhaps. And so on. In the end, Aristotle falls back on bald assertion. Not to know that a bad character is produced cumulatively 'is the mark of a thoroughly senseless person' (*Ethics* 3.5.1114a).

Be that as it may, are we supposed to believe that a person chooses stupidity? In pushing back the moment of responsibility of the morally sick person to a point in time when it was 'open to him not to be ill' ('but not now, when he has thrown away his chance'), Aristotle does not overcome the argument that ignorance is an excuse, he merely ducks it by displacing it in time (*Ethics* 3.5.1114a). Suggesting that unjust people, losing all self-control, might originally have avoided becoming what they are, requires a point of origin of each person that is patently lacking (*Ethics* 3.5.1114a). Is the infant responsible for the adult? Indeed, not only is an origin lacking in the individual, but at no point in the entire chain of causes can it be found. The parents? The ancestors? Perhaps only at the end of the chain is there responsibility, but there lies the Prime Mover (Aristotle's God), and who would speak badly of God?

In the end, Aristotle admits, we can always argue that we do what we think is best. It is therefore our image of the best that is faulty rather than our actions. And how can our impression of what is best be our choice? Rather, the idea of what is best appears to each person in correspondence with their character (*Ethics* 3.5.1114b). In sum, aiming at the best 'is not self-chosen but one must be born with an eye, as it were, by which to judge rightly and choose what is truly good' (*Ethics* 3.5.1114a). Whether or not someone has this capacity is a matter of nature, not volition. Unsurprisingly, Aristotle does not like this defence. Once again, his objection to it is pragmatic rather than principled: 'If this is true, then, how will virtue be more voluntary than vice?' (*Ethics* 3.5.1114a).

As well as being more conservative than Plato, Aristotle steps back from the full force of Plato's questioning by ceasing to ask the question of what it is *to be*. It is Aristotle himself (*Metaphysics* 7.1.1028a) who notices that the verb 'to be' is ambiguous. For it means not only to be some quality – brown, say – but also to be *as such*, to exist – as does a horse, for example. Indeed, the first can only qualify the second (you can have a brown horse, but brown cannot be found in isolation as a horse can), which is why the second is primary – a substance in Aristotle's terminology. But even though brown is a quality rather than a substantial thing, it still *is*. While all things are different, that they *are* is the same. This is why the first (in the sense of highest) question of philosophy, for Aristotle, is the question of being. This (*meta*physical – meta means beyond) question is the question of why there is something rather than nothing. Aristotle, however, thinks we must begin with the (physical) question of what beings are in themselves, since what it is to be is always a matter of being *something*. Aristotle does not buy into Plato's notion that non-being also *is*. For the same reason, neither does he share Plato's preference for universals over particulars. Without individual beings there could be nothing else. Without horses there could be no species 'horse'.

Let's leave this question of being to one side for the moment and go back to the question of change. If Plato deals with the problem of change by appearing to subordinate our world of change to a world of changelessness (the realm of eternal ideas), then, as we saw, Aristotle's world, even though it is one world, retains the idea that what is changeless is loftier than what changes. A clear statement of this elevation of eternity over time is found in Aristotle's *Metaphysics* (12.7.1072b–1073a). Here, the movement of the world is described as itself moved by the stars of the 'first heaven', which, revolving in fixed orbit, are eternal. For the only movement that can be everlasting runs in a circle. But the world is not for all that uncaused, since what moves must itself be moved. That which keeps the heavens and the earth in motion must be itself eternally at rest and unchanging. Indeed, only that which is at rest can be unchanging: 'For motion in space is the first of the kinds of change' and 'all the other changes come after change of place'.

But what is always at rest? The only 'impassive and unalterable' being for Aristotle is God, the 'unmoved mover' which, as the final cause (causes do not always come first for Aristotle) of the cosmos, moves the world by being its aim – its object of love or desire. If the unmoved mover moved the world as its efficient cause – namely by starting off the movement of the world – then it would be changed by its action. God is the eternal purpose of the universe, not its big bang. This means that providence is always at work in the world, which operates according to a divine plan. The first question of philosophy, the question of being, ends up being the question of God (*theo*-logy: *theos* means God).

As we saw earlier, just as much as in Plato, for Aristotle only what always *is* can really be known. That which changes, meanwhile, is not really knowable since it will become other between the intervals in which I catch sight of it. My former view of my friend Ash is false – he is older now. Even though he is a substance (he exists in the primary sense not shared by qualities such as 'brown'), Ash is not substantial enough to be timeless. True beings, by contrast, can be known because they are always the same regardless of my view of them. While I can know God, I cannot ever fully know Ash. Old Heraclitus was right that we never step in the same river twice.

What *is* cannot be like a stream of water, which always flows away. Aristotle uses the word *ousia* ('substance') as a word for being. *Ousia* ('to be') relates to *parousia*, which means presence. Aristotle's sense of being is that being is that which is *there*. To be is to be present. More than this, *ousia* for Aristotle is constant presence – that which is fixed, stable; that which, unlike onrushing water, remains. This is why *ousia* names both being *and* property in Aristotle's Greek. Possessions are exemplary beings because of this quality of being always available. Being is solid and dependable like a house, not transient like a river. To play once again on Aristotle's term for being – beings are *substantial*.

This is why, for Aristotle, *form* is the true essence of a thing rather than the matter that makes it up – he was no materialist (somebody who thinks that there is only matter, as Democritus did). Matter, in addition to being incorporeal, is not composed randomly: it is always formed in ways that are recognisable and predictable, even if each formed thing will decompose. To be of the species horse, which is to *be* a horse, is to be a combination of form, which in nature does not change (Aristotle knew nothing of the theory of evolution), and matter, which clearly does. Particular horses die and their bodies turn to dust. But the universal form 'horse' endures with the species. Even manufactured forms, human-made forms, endure. My house has a form that would have been recognisable to Aristotle more than 2,000 years ago, even though it is also made of wood, which rots. For all this priority of form (enduring) over matter (unenduring), the form 'house' and the material of houses are inseparable, just as the form horse cannot be taken out of horses. This is different from Plato, where the idea 'horse' is somehow separate from horses. But it is also a seeming confusion in Aristotle's metaphysics – on the one hand *to be* is to be a universal form like the species 'horse', but, on the other hand, Plato is wrong for thinking that universals exist separately from their particulars.

It is perhaps this tension in his thinking that allows Aristotle to provide the first answer to the question: what *is* change? As we saw, Plato describes everything as both itself and not itself at the same time, but this is more a description of what change *does* rather than an account of change 'itself'. In Plato, ideas have no part in change, which is rather a property of perishable matter. For Aristotle, however, true change, the sort of change we find in generation (when something new is created), can only be explained by form, not matter. Given that matter is pure potential rather than anything actual in itself, only the form of a thing can explain its coming to be, just as the architectural plan of a house is first necessary if it is ever to appear. If matter did the producing, then we would never get beyond the material that makes up the house. Only the plan turns the wood into the frame of a dwelling. Only form can explain change, and while in our example the form is in the mind of the architect, in nature it is in the parent.

Without the notion of being (including coming to be) as form, Aristotle could not have distinguished himself from the relativists of his day, such as the sophist Gorgias, who argued that nothing exists and that, even if it did, it would be essentially incommunicable – the horse is only a horse *for us*. Refusing to follow Plato's response to this challenge by way of a separate sphere of ideas, Aristotle rather says that the 'measure' (form) of a horse is in the horse itself, indeed is the horse's very 'soul'. Of Aristotle's four causes (see *Physics* 2.3 and *Metaphysics* 5.2), the soul of the horse is the immediate ('efficient') cause of the horse in the sense that the horse is made by its parents who are also horses; it is also the formal cause (as outlined above); and it is the all-important final cause – that at which being a horse aims (which is why a foal can become a horse). Only the material cause (the matter of which it is composed) is outside of the horse, so to speak. In terms of Aristotle's famous distinction between actuality and potentiality, matter alone is what is potential in a horse (it could be arranged otherwise). The soul of the horse, the horse itself, is fully actual. Matter is only a potential horse, whereas a horse actually *is*.

But although a horse is not only a horse for us, and although (unlike for Plato) to be a horse is only in horses themselves, nonetheless horses only appear as horses for beings like us. For Aristotle, as we have grasped by now, true being or substance is defined as changeless because only this being can be *known*. Aristotle, like Plato, and like the Sophists too for that matter, continues to understand being (what *is*) on the basis of what can be known of it, that is on human knowing. There is an irony here. Human beings are mortal and so true being (substantial being, or the forms that do not change) ends up able to show itself only by way of that which is less in being (insubstantial human beings, who change and die).

Aristotle, maybe even more than Plato, sees what always is as more fundamental than what is perishable (recalling that being, for Aristotle, is like a house – something that is just *there*). In Aristotle's *Physics*, the cosmos itself is described as what is eternal. Impervious to time, it was not created and it will not pass away. This image of time or change as something to be suffered stretched down the centuries in Western philosophy. We can see its influence, for example, in the great chain of being of medieval Aristotelianism (the thought that descends from Aristotle). As Thomas Aquinas argued in the thirteenth century, the heavenly beings are highest because they exist in pure actuality (namely form), without any potentiality (namely matter) to take other forms. They are heavenly because they are immutable: 'The more imperfect is in potency in relation to the more perfect and so on upward to the first Form, which is act only, namely, God' (Aquinas 1959: 38).

Something starts to slip out of sight with Aristotle, something that, as we have seen, was still visible in Plato. This is the question of being. Plato's sense that there is more to being than what is present is much less apparent in Aristotle. Aristotle is also the point at which the earlier insight that everything *is* equally begins to fade – that all things bask together in the light of being that Plato named the Good. Aristotle's God, by contrast, is the highest being, which means the equality of being – that every being, even the lowliest, *is* just as much as any other – has been forgotten. Being 'itself' has been forgotten. Heidegger pointed to this forgetting as delivering us to a world in which, with no sense any longer of how everything *is* just as much as any other, human beings dominate nature and see everything as a resource to be exploited. Indeed, even human beings have become a mere resource, as Human Resources departments remind us.

We are used to seeing Aristotle as the start of a more rigorous, scientific questioning after the lingering mysticism of Plato. But did Aristotle forget the most important question of all – the question of what it is *to be*? Not entirely, it seems. In his discussion of human being in Book I of his *Nicomachean Ethics* (1.7.1097b), Aristotle briefly considers whether we are to suppose that, while the carpenter and tanner have 'certain functions or activities', human beings as such are left by nature without a function. At this point, Aristotle appears to have caught sight of the question of whether there might be nothing else for human beings to be other than – *to be*! Maybe, unlike the rest of nature, human being is potential rather than actual? Perhaps there is no human 'essence' or soul, no final cause for men and women to aim at? But Aristotle quickly draws back from the full implications of his question by answering that what is proper to human being is 'a kind of life of the rational nature'. From this point on, human being in the Western philosophical tradition has largely been defined as that of a 'rational animal'. The question of whether this animal has anything in particular *to be* seems to have been answered – it must be rational.

Yet Aristotle was by no means unaware that something unusual is going on with human being. He noted that, while other beings in nature cannot be anything else than actual (their potential is always fully actualised), human potential is also *im*potential of the same thing – the possibility *not* to be this or that. Earlier we used the example of an acorn which, although its potential need not be actualised, must be an oak tree if it is to be at all. But human being is not like this. Human potential is not used up in its actualisation: being human does not mean I have to be human in *this* and no other way. While an acorn *must be* an oak tree, a human embryo does not have to go on to be the rational animal that Aristotle said it must be.

A more contemporary example will help to make the point. Think of a chauffeur. If a chauffeur must drive, then he or she is no different from the computer that drives an automated car. Not the fact that he or she can drive (so can the computer, and better) but really only because he or she may *not* drive is the chauffer truly a driver of cars. A computer, meanwhile, lacks just this potentiality. This is why arguments about AI often miss the point. Human being is not a matter of a certain computational power in the brain, a power which has long since been surpassed by computers anyway. The difference is not the technical one of brain*power* but the ontological one that the computer *must be* all that it is programmed to be – there is nothing computer-like that it cannot be. Only human beings – and here we see the full significance of our capacity for questioning – are capable of *not* being (this or that). Or, to put the point the other way round, we are capable of not being (this or that) because we can question.

5   Epicurus

EVEN IN ANTIQUITY, EPICUREAN was a word with a pejorative sense, meaning one who thoughtlessly devotes his or her life to the pursuit of pleasure. Can Epicurus (341–270 BCE), the founder of that 'plebeian philosophy' as Cicero called it (*Tusculan Disputations* 1.55; Cicero 1985), who did indeed teach that nothing is higher than the absence of pain, tell us anything about questioning? *Ataraxia*, or freedom from disturbance, doesn't sound like a state of mind fit for posing questions. And if the Epicurean ideal is to live, as Epicurus did, in his garden, quietly and among friends, what need to question anything anyway?

Yet this Epicurean idyll was not arrived at passively. Epicurus achieved it only by finding an affirmative answer to the following question: can we live free from fear? Free, in particular, from that terrible fear of death which, in Epicurus's view, is hidden at the heart of all lesser fears and which drives us to the mad acts of violence, greed and ambition that disfigure our world.

While philosophy is not reducible to exemplary lives, for his own part Epicurus seems to have practised what he preached and to have accepted his end with calm repose. Despite a slow and painful death from kidney stones, he was nonetheless able to write to a friend:

> On this blissful day, which is also the last of my life, I write this to you. My continual struggle from strangury [the inability to urinate] and dysentery are so great that nothing could augment them; but

over against them all I set gladness of mind at the remembrance of our past conversations. ('Letter to Idomeneus' in Diogenes Laertius, *Lives* 10.22)

Epicurus lived in a time when people looked anxiously at the sky. The heavenly bodies – the sun, moon and stars – were seen as models of good order and eternity (these two principles being nearly identical in Greek mind). And yet the heavens were a source of terror, too, the place of unexpected and unwelcome comets, auguries of terrible events, and the home of the king of the gods, who hurls thunderbolts onto the earth.

Nor was there much comfort to be had from the earth. Beneath it lay the underworld, where the dead could expect to be punished at length for any impieties. Mystery religions, in which heroic figures such as Orpheus returned from the underworld, proliferated in direct proportion to a growing fear of the gods and of divine retribution. The political insecurities of Epicurus's age, when Alexander the Great's generals fought throughout the Eastern Mediterranean (Epicurus was himself expelled from his home island of Samos by the general Perdiccas), no doubt contributed much to this sense of despair for the future.

Yet Epicurus believed that he could cure people of their terror of what lay above their heads and beneath their feet, of the fear that the arbitrariness of life and the certainty of death seem to instil in most of us. The medicine? A materialist account of the world in which the gods play no part and in which there are only atoms and the void. Such an account of nature and its laws can dispel dark dread by showing, first, that the world is not an unknowable place where anything can happen at any moment and, second, that death is nothing to those who, made only of matter, do not survive it. As Epicurus's later Roman disciple, the poet Lucretius, put it in an ode to Epicurus:

> For once your reason, born of mind divine,
> Starts to proclaim the nature of the world
> The terrors of the mind flee all away
> [. . .] and headlong out of doors
> That fear of Hell be thrown, which from its depths
> Disquiets the life of man, suffusing all
> With the blackness of death.
> (*On the Nature of Things* 3.14–39)

Now free from fear, we can sit in the garden and enjoy the company of our friends.

A good example of the Epicureans' sober use of reason in order to dispel fear of the gods is found in Lucretius's *De Rerum Natura* (*On the Nature of Things*), which sets out Epicurean doctrines in verse form. Lucretius (3.420) lists reasons why people shouldn't worry that Jupiter is angry with them when lightning starts flashing from the sky. In the first place, why do these thunderbolts fall as much on the just as the unjust? And why would Jupiter bother to shoot at empty seas or deserted deserts? Does he have a grudge against the waves and the sand? Perhaps he's just practising his aim or building up his muscles! If he wants to warn us, why won't he let us see lightning strikes coming? Alternatively, if he wants to incinerate us unawares, why does he warn us with thunderclaps? Finally, why does he hurl bolts at his own temples, dishonouring 'His own fine statues with a violent wound?'

What natural explanations can we give for lightning, then? A pluralist when it came to our attempts to account for the world (many possible explanations are better than one), Epicurus was happy to admit that, while there are several ways in which lightning *might* be explained, 'exclusion of myth is the sole condition necessary' ('Letter to Pythocles' in Diogenes Laertius, *Lives* 10.104).

As Lucretius (*On The Nature of Things* 3.980–3) shows, the fear of the gods is a fear of their capriciousness. 'It is in this life that the fear of gods / Oppresses mortals without cause: the fall / They fear is that which chance may bring to them'. Jupiter can do what he wants. Epicurus, by contrast, argued that the nature of the world is set, even if it isn't fully determined: atoms occasionally swerve in the void. These atoms, invisible but still material (they're just too small to see), are eternal and unchanging. As the building blocks of all things they can endlessly assume new forms, but they cannot be destroyed. Nothing can come from nothing; and there isn't nothing, so what there is (atoms) must always have been. In short, we need not fear events of divine intervention in the world, when the predictable order of nature gives way to the wrath of the gods. As something immaterial, something that comes from nothing, divine vengeance is itself literally nothing.

Epicurus not only taught that the world and everything in it has a natural explanation, he also refused to equate these laws of nature with a divine plan. This emphasis on the absence of providence was unique to Epicurus in the ancient world. Even the Stoics, who also found themselves in a cosmos ordered by natural law, believed in providence. But Epicurus did not, and it is easy to see why. This would allow the gods back in, and Epicurus was very keen to show that the gods, having no need of anything, are not responsible for, nor involved in, our world. We should try to explain the orbits of the heavenly bodies, for example, by reference to our experience of things closer to hand, but 'the divine nature must not on any account be adduced to explain this, but must be kept free from the task and in perfect bliss'. We too have an entirely earthly origin: 'No golden chain, I think, from heaven on high / Let down the breed of mortals to the fields', as Lucretius (*On The Nature of Things* 2.1154) puts it.

Lucretius (*On The Nature of Things* 4.825–40) captures beautifully this absence of a divine plan:

> Now here's a fault you must keenly avoid,
> An error from which with great care you must flee:
> Do not suppose that the clear light of the eyes
> Was made that we might see our way before us
> [...]
> Every interpretation of this kind
> Is quite perverse, turns reason upside down,
> Since nothing is born in our body that we may use it,
> But what is born itself creates the use.
> There was no sight before the eyes were born.

This rejection of providence, of the notion that existence is purposeful, was very significant for the history of Western philosophy. In seeking to demonstrate that the world and everything in it (even that most complex thing, the eye) is the result of a profound order that is nonetheless purpose-*less*, Epicurus anticipated Spinoza, Nietzsche and others who, despite their differences, agreed with Epicurus that there is no Plan. Not any scientific investigations but rather Epicurus's overriding concern with human well-being drove him to this conclusion. Perhaps human beings feel unworthy, and their world seems inadequate, in proportion to the sense that some external power is needed to bring everything to perfection.

This instinct for liberating humanity from fear of the gods is no doubt Epicurus's chief legacy. Indeed, Stephen Greenblatt (2011) has argued that the rediscovery of Epicurean thought (by way of Lucretius's *On*

The Nature of Things) was the trigger for the Renaissance in fourteenth-century Europe. Five hundred years after the Renaissance began, Karl Marx was still taking inspiration for his materialist view of history from the atomism of Epicurus and Democritus, on which topic he wrote his doctoral thesis. In between the Renaissance and Marx, Spinoza wrote to a friend that he thought little of the authority of Plato, Aristotle and Socrates, who invented metaphysical abstractions such as 'forms' only to disparage the atomists Democritus and Epicurus, 'whose renown they so envied'.

Nietzsche (*HH* II, 227) wrote how 'Epicurus has been alive in all ages and lives now, unknown to those who have called and call themselves Epicureans, and enjoying no reputation among philosophers'. For the anti-philosopher Nietzsche, this was high praise indeed. Epicurus was as untimely as Nietzsche felt himself to be. Although Nietzsche's praise was later mixed with blame (he came to find in Epicureanism an attempt to avoid suffering that anticipated Christian otherworldliness), Nietzsche never ceased to admire the philosopher who didn't need divine purpose to find the world beautiful: 'A little garden, figs, little cheeses and in addition three of four good friends – these were the sensual pleasures of Epicurus' (Nietzsche, *HH* II, 192).

Epicurus's questioning of the world of the gods is also a questioning of the world of the spirit as advanced by the Platonists. Against the notion that the soul is of a different and higher order to the body, which in a sense is only the prison of the soul, Epicurus held that the soul is a fully corporeal (bodily) thing:

> It is impossible to conceive anything that is incorporeal as self-existent except empty space. And empty space cannot itself either act or be acted on, but simply allows bodies to move through it. Hence those who call soul incorporeal speak foolishly. ('Letter to Herodotus' in Diogenes Laertius, *Lives* 10.67)

Epicurus's garden was right outside the walls of Plato's Academy in Athens. It is tempting to see in this choice of location a deliberate signal that the world of eternal forms propounded by the Platonists is an abstraction that those in search of the good life can do without. In particular, Epicurus believed that his materialism could dispel the fear of death in a way that the Platonists, who believed that the soul survives death (a belief that they passed on to the Christians), could not.

As summarised in his letter to Menoeceus (in Diogenes Laertius, *Lives* 10.122–7) Epicurus sought to cure the fear of death with the following reasoning. Since everything that affects us is based in sensation (what can have any effect on us other than by way of the senses?), the absence of sensation that characterises death cannot affect us. Did we suffer from those countless aeons before our birth when, similarly, we did not exist? Death cannot be bad for us since 'bad' *is* only that which assaults our senses or our minds, which can no more happen from beyond the grave than it did before our birth. Death is, literally, 'nothing to us'. While we are alive death has not come; when we are dead, we are no longer there for it to come. Death can no more arrive in death than it can in life!

In understanding this we cure ourselves of the fear of death not by seeking immortality, as the Platonists do, but by taking away the craving for immortality itself. We have then cured the disease rather than treating the symptom with snake oil. 'For there is nothing terrible in life for the man who has truly comprehended that there is nothing terrible in not living' ('Letter to Menoeceus' in Diogenes Laertius, *Lives* 10.125). When today we hear people say that they fear dying rather than death, we should recognise the long reach of this argument in Western culture. For as Epicurus tells it, people in his day said the reverse: it was the being dead bit they didn't like.

Of course, some people protest loudly at life too. Yet for the most part they show no inclination to leave it. Epicurus exposes the gap between word and deed here. Such people are as scared of death as anyone else. Epicurus also points to a more life-denying confusion brought about by dread of dying. Fearing, as Lucretius (*On The Nature of Things* 3.1023) puts it, 'that after death there's worse to come / So fools make for themselves a hell on earth'. Some people are so scared of death that they make their lives too miserable to endure. They seek death as a cure for what is, at bottom, fear of death.

The right balance, as Epicurus sees it, is that in which, no longer fleeing from death, neither do we tire of life. Just as when we eat we seek neither to eat everything nor to eat nothing but rather the most pleasant portion, so also in life we should seek neither immortality nor death but the good life. And as a life defined by moderation, the good life is the same for all. We shouldn't counsel the young man to live it up and the old man to die with dignity: it is one and the same training in philosophy 'which teaches to live well and die well' ('Letter to Menoeceus' in Diogenes Laertius, *Lives* 10.126).

It might be thought that a life devoted to pleasure would need as much time as possible in order to experience more of it. But this would be to misunderstand the Epicurean division between the instantiable pleasures of the body, such as the desire for food, and the satiable pleasures of contemplation.

> ... no new pleasure
> By living longer can be hammered out.
> But while we can't get what we want, that seems
> Of all things most desirable. Once got,
> We must have something else. One constant thirst
> Of life besets us ever open-mouthed.
> (*On The Nature of Things* 3.1083)

Rather than being a matter of vainly trying to satisfy our ever-shifting desires, pleasure reaches its magnitude, but also its limit, with the removal of all pain, which requires peace of mind. For the pains of the mind are worse than those of the body, since they involve past, present and future, rather than the present alone.

This negative model of pleasure, in which pleasure is the absence of suffering rather than the satisfaction of desire, means that, far from needing eternity in which to satisfy the limitless pleasures of the body, all that is necessary is to attain peace of mind. Having reached this point of perfection, which is the true absence of suffering, 'we no longer have any need of unlimited time' (Diogenes Laertius, *Lives* 10.145). Understanding the nature of things really does make us ready to die.

If pleasure is ultimately the absence of pain, then neither do we need more pleasures than the earth easily supplies. If not eating but the absence of hunger is what is desirable, there is no need for banquets. A fig and a few small cheeses, washed down with some water, will do just fine.

We can see, then, how far the caricature of Epicurus as a decadent is from the truth. His identification of pleasure as the highest good was not motivated by the desire to justify feasting and orgies but merely by the will, common to all ancient philosophy, to tell the truth. Epicurus could not honestly see how any goal could be set above pleasure, since even virtues are chosen for the sake of it. Is anyone courageous in war except those who fear the pain of being branded a coward more? Is anyone studying until three in the morning other than those who seek the pleasure of passing an exam and the possibilities of wealth and status this brings?

Despite reducing the virtues to calculations of pleasure and pain, Epicurus did not disagree with Socrates that no good could be had in the absence of virtue. Indeed, virtue is the *only* thing necessary to pleasure, given that pleasure is peace of mind. And since peace of mind is obtainable solely by those who restrain their pleasures, prudence is the highest virtue of all. We must be able to judge what will bring pleasure and pain, even allowing ourselves some pain in the pursuit of higher pleasures. As anybody who has ever been a poor student at an all-you-can-eat restaurant knows, if you want to maximise the pleasure of food, then eating too much will not help your cause.

We can see from Epicurus's account of the pleasure principle that how to live well was his real concern, just as much as for Socrates or Diogenes. As we noted above, Epicurus's atomic theory, which he got from his teacher's teacher Democritus, sought a materialistic explanation for why things are the way they are. This has made Epicurus seem to some a father of modern science. But his concerns are not really scientific. Epicurus did not live in order to explain how the world works, he explained how the world works in order to live. Even the study of the highest beings, the heavenly bodies, is guided by this aim: 'In the first place, remember that, like everything else, knowledge of celestial phenomena [...] has no other end in view than peace of mind and firm conviction.' Given this, we need only as much accuracy in our explanations of the world 'as is needful to ensure our tranquillity and happiness' ('Letter to Herodotus' in Diogenes Laertius, *Lives* 10.80).

As Pierre Hadot (2002) has argued, not only Epicureanism but indeed all the various schools of ancient Greek philosophy need to be understood as offering philosophy as a way of life rather than as the academic exercise it is today. In as much as they competed for students, these schools vied with each other over the question of the good life. But did anyone find the good life to be as carefree as Epicurus did? And since it is the mark of the gods to live a blissfully untroubled life, inasmuch as you attain the good life, 'never shall you be disturbed waking or asleep, but you shall live like a god among men'.

Epicurus's delight in the simple life makes his philosophy seem an antidote to the Socratic injunction to care for yourself by knowing yourself, an injunction that seems to put living in question. Reclining in his garden, isn't Epicurus free from the intensity of introspection that is the examined life of Socrates or the true life of Diogenes?

Yet for all that the garden philosopher took life easy, there remains the objection that, in no longer fleeing death, he did still flee suffering. If the happy life is a life in which pain is minimised, then suffering must be avoided wherever possible. To be sure, Epicurus did not find unavoidable suffering to be an objection against life, as his last letter shows, but the principle of the avoidance of disturbance makes suffering an evil.

This was Nietzsche's objection to Epicurus. A big fan in his middle writings, Nietzsche later came to wonder if Epicurus wasn't an early prototype of the Christian who longs to escape a world of suffering in a heavenly beyond. After all, if life *is* suffering, then a philosophy that seeks to avoid it could be accused of being anti-life. Nietzsche's late Dionysian joy in existence is not his earlier Epicurean delight in it: 'I have presented such terrible images to knowledge that any "Epicurean delight" is out of the question. Only Dionysian joy is sufficient' (*WP*, 1029).

Nietzsche's rediscovery, as he saw it, of the tragic dimension of existence meant that Epicurean *ataraxia*, a bit like Buddhist detachment, had to be re-evaluated as a nihilistic failure to affirm life in all its cruel beauty. If the dismembering and rebirth of the god Dionysus becomes Nietzsche's metaphor for existence, then life calls for dangerous experiments in living, not lounging in the garden.

But in this moment Nietzsche perhaps let slip his lingering Socratism. Experiments in living are necessary only if there is something lacking in the life we already live. We are back to the unexamined life not being worth living. In fact, I will argue later that Nietzsche does indeed glimpse this, which is why he finally exchanges his injunction to 'create new worlds!' for the claim that the death of the other world is *itself* the great liberation. With this move Nietzsche comes full circle back to Epicurus, who didn't need to leave his garden precisely because he no longer feared death.

6   Plotinus

IN THIS CHAPTER WE leave Epicurus's tranquil garden, where questioning was necessary only as therapy for the fear of death. While fast-forwarding 500 years, we return to the restless philosophy of Platonism, which asks beyond the visible world for the eternal answers given by the true world. Our philosopher is Plotinus (204–270 CE), who was the main source of the revival of Plato's thought in the third century after Christ – namely of Neoplatonism (*neo* means new). We are now in the autumn years of ancient philosophy, which had to give way to Christianity from 529 CE, when the Roman Emperor Justinian outlawed the teaching of pagan philosophy.

The question asked in this chapter is whether the search for timeless answers to philosophical questions must lead to otherworldliness. Will philosophers always have their heads in the clouds? After all, if our world is (or at least appears to be) a world of change, then the idea of a world without change points us elsewhere, away from our world. In fact, things are not so simple. As we shall see when we explore Plotinus's response to the extreme otherworldliness of Gnosticism, Neoplatonism sought for ways to affirm both what does not change *as well as* our world of change. Plotinus shows that not only does what changes depend on what does not change, but even timeless truths would be nothing without those transient, temporal things that refer to them. Although Plotinus for his part did not accept the Christian doctrine of incarnation, of God becoming flesh, in many ways Christianity was able to think incarnation thanks to Plotinus's notion that higher things could not *be* higher without that which is lowly as their counterpart. What would heavenly mean without that which is worldly?

For his part, Plotinus saw his questions as being the same as Plato's 600 years before him, and his answers to be faithfully Platonic, too. Yet while Plato's 'world' of ideas, as we saw earlier, is only metaphorically a separate world, Neoplatonism has the reputation of being much more otherworldly. It is certainly the case that Plotinus's teachings, as edited by his student Porphyry in the *Enneads*, include much that whiffs of an away-from-here:

> This is the life of the gods and of the godlike and blessed among men: liberation from the alien that besets us here, a life taking no pleasure in the things of earth, the passing of solitary to solitary. (6.9.11)

What is this liberation from what is alien? It is a flight from the body, which, inasmuch as it 'partakes of matter, is an evil thing' (1.8.4). Plotinus himself recounts:

> Many times it has happened: lifted out of my body into myself; becoming external to all other things and self-centred; beholding a marvellous beauty [. . .]; acquiring identity with the divine [. . .] I ask myself how it happens that I can now be descending, and how did the soul ever enter into my body, the soul which, even within the body, is the high thing it has shown itself to be. (4.8.1)

Yet even though we must 'disengage the self from the body' in order to escape formless matter (1.8.7), even though bodies 'in their ceaseless flux are always slipping away from being' into nothing (1.8.7), this disorder can be righted by the one who forms his soul virtuously, namely the true philosopher. Thus

> the precept to 'flee hence' does not refer to earth or earthly life. The flight we read of [in Plato's *Theaetetus*] consists not in quitting earth but in living our earth-life 'with justice and piety and in the light of philosophy'; it is vice we are to flee. (1.8.6, see also 1.8.7)

Plotinus speaks of a divine One from which everything emanates in an eternal and ceaseless cascade. Just as embodied beings must follow a form which is prior to them, so even these forms are dependent in turn on that which allows them to be. But as the source of being, the One cannot 'itself' be a being since then its unity 'would be vested in something else' (6.9.5, see also 6.8.20). Nor can the One be the totality of beings, in which case it could not be One (6.9.2). The One is beyond being and this means that, taking the road beyond knowing (6.9.4), we can say only what it is *not*: 'The One, therefore, is beyond all things that are "thus": standing before the indefinable [...] you must say: "This is none of them"' (6.9.9).

As the source of being, Plotinus's God is also beyond good and evil (6.9.6). If God was good by reference to some higher standard of goodness, then God could not be the First, could not in short be God. God's activity is utterly free because it refers to nothing beyond itself. There is nothing before the will of God; indeed, God and will are 'primarily identical' (6.8.20–1). Later, the Christian doctrine of predestination as developed by Augustine would draw on this ontology and apply it to the Christian concern with salvation: God saves who he wants to and there is nothing more to say about it – certainly no good works by which we might win his favour. But Plotinus's God is not wilful in this sense. The world that emanates eternally from the One does not need to be saved because it is the very self-expression of the One.

Overflowing from the One are two lower levels of being – a second level which is effectively Plato's world of ideas, and, finally, our material world. These levels are lower not in the sense that they have fallen away from the One but in the sense that they express or unfold the One. Descent is not a tragedy, as it was for the Gnostics to whom we shall return. Understood in terms of what it is *to be*, Plotinus's three levels of being are: first, being as such (*that* there are horses); second, the being of beings (the idea 'horse'); and, third, beings themselves (horses). The first level, the One, is therefore Plotinus's name for what Plato termed the Good – that light by which all beings are made visible. 'Beauty consists less in symmetry than in the light that shines upon the symmetry, and this light is what is desirable' (1.6.1). If there were only the material world and the world of ideas then we would have an account of beings (of horses and the idea 'horse') but not of their being (that horses *are*). The One is Plotinus's way of expressing that, before there can be beings, there must be being 'itself'. To be something is, first, *to be*. And *to be* is always the same, whether we are talking about horses or God. Being is one: 'the supreme is everywhere and yet nowhere [...] He is not in the everywhere but is the everywhere as well as the giver to the rest of things of their being in that everywhere' (6.8.16).

Plotinus's One is therefore not the heavenly beyond in any conventional religious sense but rather that which is closest to us. So close, in fact, that we can never do justice the One with our words about it. We are always *in* being, never looking on. Because the One can never be accounted for, it is pure grace – a gift that is given for no reason at all (if a gift is given *for* something, is it really a gift at all?). We see this grace shining through things – there is always something 'more' to a being than its being an object, as for example there is somehow more to an old oak tree than even a complete list of its parts (roots, trunk, branches, leaves . . .) can capture.

If the One is not the beyond, then neither is the second level of being, the world of ideas, somewhere else. Plotinus insists that Plato's world of timeless ideas is not another world than our world, even though in our world everything passes away. This point comes through especially clearly in Plotinus's attack on the Gnostics (who we encountered earlier) in the ninth part of the second Ennead. The Gnostics, who were very influential in Plotinus's day, believed that their spirits (*pneuma*) were shards of divine light that came from, and sought return to, the true God. This God was understood to be beyond this world, in fact utterly alien to it. Although there were many different Gnosticisms, there was universal agreement that the creation of the world was the work not of the true God, but of a creator god (for example, Plato's Demiurge or the creator God of the Bible). Either out of ignorance of the true God or malevolence towards him, this demiurge had fashioned the world, right down to our own bodies, as a many-layered prison for the spirit. Matter is malign. To acquire *gnosis* (knowledge), then, is to understand that the world is not our home and to know how to escape it. But this knowledge cannot come from the world, which tells nothing of the true God, and in this way the confidence of Greek thought that God and nature are one is shattered (for more on Gnosticism, see Jonas 1958).

Plotinus admits that the Gnostics may have been encouraged in their world-hatred, especially in their belief that corporeality is incarceration, from a reading of Plato, 'who inveighs against the body as a grave hinderance to the soul' (2.9.17; see for example Plato's *Phaedo*, 66b). But, following Plato, Plotinus sees 'the soul's disaster' not in its fall to earth from somewhere completely alien, but in that it 'ceases to dwell in the perfect beauty' of the higher things (essentially Plato's ideas) to which its loftiest element belongs (2.9.2). Indeed, as Plato's analogy of the ascent from the cave illustrates (2.9.5), 'the measure of the soul's grace and power' is simply the extent to which it contemplates these elevated beings rather than being preoccupied with lowly things (2.9.5). Yet although earthly existence is a distraction, it is not, for all that, bad. Being, from the highest to the lowest, is One. Forced by Gnosticism to clarify in what sense mere matter is problematic (a claim he does not shy from elsewhere in the *Enneads*), Plotinus claims that, although matter is darkness, if it wasn't for that darkness, then divine light would have nowhere to shine. Absent base matter, the divine beings would be 'walled off, so to speak' (2.9.3).

As well as contesting the Gnostic claim that our spirits belong elsewhere, Plotinus also wants to defend the creator of this world, Plato's Demiurge, from the Gnostics' attack. Plotinus (2.9.4) wants to know, first, how this world-creating soul could create at all if it had fallen so far from the divine? Surely creation is an affirmative act? Also, what model would it create from if it had lost touch with the divine vision? What, moreover, could the Demiurge's motivation for creating the world have been if not a good one? Glory, perhaps? 'That would be absurd – a motive borrowed from the sculptors of our earth' (2.9.4). Finally, if the world soul had created badly, 'when will it destroy the work? If it repents of its work, what is it waiting for?' The fact that the world endures means that, at the very least, the world soul must be coming around to liking his creation, even if it did start badly. The same applies to the souls of mortals. If this world were such an irredeemably bad place, then, given the eternity of souls, these souls, 'having known in former life the evils of this sphere', would have long ceased returning to it (2.9.4).

This world should not be judged by the standards of the higher heaven, the intelligible realm where Plato's ideas reside, since it is merely the *reflection* of that loftier sphere. But as a reflection of the world of beauty, could our world be conceived as more beautiful than it is? (2.9.4). After all, 'nothing is to be blamed for being inferior to the First' (2.9.12). To be a copy of a higher original is in the very nature of our world. Besides, how could the original *be* the original that it is if it did not have a copy? There 'must, then, be something later than the Divine; for only the thing with which all power ends fails to pass downwards something of itself' (2.9.8). And what the divine passes down to our world is a true reflection of its beauty. Have the Gnostics never noticed the loveliness that is lavished even in our world of sense? Seeing the 'vast orderliness, the form which the stars even in their remoteness display – no one could be so dull-witted, so immoveable, as not to be carried away by all this' (2.9.16).

In focusing only on that which is ugly in a world so beautiful, the Gnostics are like those who would condemn a well-ordered city simply because it contains (as it must contain) lowly occupations such as pottery (2.9.7). For 'The constitution of the all' is very different from that of single, separate forms of life (2.9.7). Focusing on individual suffering, as the Gnostics do, is to be blind to how the 'larger order' will quite naturally benefit some and destroy others (2.9.7). As we might say today: it's not personal.

The presumption of the Gnostics to find their own lowly souls higher than the world soul that governs the heavens is, for Plotinus (2.9.9), risible. Even their complaints about the painful 'disorder that troubles our earth' are based on an image of order drawn entirely from 'the shapely pattern, the discipline' that, thanks to the world soul, prevails in the heavens (2.9.5). Indeed, how else to inaugurate their otherworldly vision *except* 'by some earthly correction' (2.9.15). Even the new earth that the Gnostics long for is modelled on the world of ideas which, as the model also for *our* earth, is hardly a world away from what they have already. And besides, 'Why should they desire to live in the archetype of a world abhorrent to them?' (2.9.15). If the 'Lord of providence' is indeed so absent from the world, 'then he is absent from yourselves [too], and you can have nothing to tell about him' (2.9.16).

Plotinus's evisceration of Gnostic otherworldliness is a monument to how easily the Western philosophical tradition has been able to shepherd all lost sheep back into the fold. Indeed, centuries later, Hegel would famously describe the Absolute as nothing other than the taking up of moments of negation such as Gnosticism into the larger whole. Considered, however, from our perspective of questioning, Gnosticism, as other such nihilistic interludes in Western history, looks a little different. Ultimately, Plotinus wants the Gnostics, in his own words, to be 'brought to desist from that blasphemy of majestic powers which comes so easily to them, where all should [instead] be reverent scruple' (2.9.8). Gnostic doctrine scorns 'every law known to us', cutting, in the process, 'at the root of all orderly living' (2.9.15).

A very Greek cosmos-piety which amounts to 'know your place!' seems to be the message here: 'If men rank highly among other living beings, much more do those whose office in the All is not to play the tyrant but to serve towards beauty and order' (2.9.13).

Plotinus wants nothing and nobody to disturb the cosmic harmony which, for all eternity, appoints each thing to its proper station. In this sense, we could argue, his thought reflects the ubiquitous imperialism of his time: after centuries of Roman order, disorder can only be seen in a threatening light. But what is the point of questioning such a fixed order, one to which nothing can ever really happen? Is Plotinus describing the cosmos or is he, rather, projecting the Roman Empire into the heavens?

Plotinus's exclusion of Gnostic questioning of worldly existence also expresses itself in the assumption, found to his day, that to have questions about the established order is necessarily to be a libertine: 'And while [the Gnostics] proclaim their contempt for earthly beauty, they would do well to ignore that of youths and women so as not to be overcome by incontinence' (2.9.17). By contrast with this licentious attitude, philosophy, for Plotinus, 'means continence, self-restraint, [and] holding staunch against outside pleasure' (2.9.18). In fact, far more Gnostic groups appear to have been ascetic than libertine, understanding their foreignness to the world as an injunction to *avoid* worldly contamination (Jonas 1958).

In this way, Gnosticism called forth profoundly rebellious questions concerning existence that were largely inexpressible in the terms of Greek philosophy. As Hans Jonas (1958: 88) put it:

> Ultimately the soul calls [the alien God] to account for the existence of the world as such and for its own exile there: that is, it asks the great 'Why?' which, far from being appeased by the awakening [. . .] to its origin, is powerfully stirred up by [it] and becomes a main concern of the gnosis just initiated. This query is even called 'the lawsuit concerning the world' which Adam is to present directly to [the alien God].

If the Gnostics put this world in the dock, then Plotinus reverses this by charging them with ingratitude. They are like people who living in a house which they find to be badly designed by a diabolical architect, nonetheless persist in living in it (2.9.18). If you don't like it, leave! is the familiar sentiment here. For Plotinus, all this complaining is simply evidence of a lack of fortitude, of an inability 'to bear with necessity'. The life of true philosophy, far from being ravaged by a questioning of everything, is one where we remain unperturbed by all disturbances (2.9.18).

It is understandable, however, that Plotinus, a faithful student of Plato as he saw himself to be, should be worried by the direction 'Platonism' had taken towards otherworldliness and contempt for earthly existence. In Pierre Hadot's little book on Plotinus, *Plotinus: Or the Simplicity of Vision*, the gulf between Plotinus and the otherworldliness of Gnosticism comes through clearly. As Hadot (1993) shows, the ideal world for Plotinus does not wait until after death or until the end of the world. The world of ideas is separated neither in time nor in space from our world. It is no eighth heaven, no alien realm. Indeed, 'the more we seek it the less we find' for, 'although it was right there, you will not have seen it, because you were looking elsewhere' (Hadot 1993: 46). In Plotinus, Plato's world of ideas is nothing other than this world at its deepest level, a world that can be reached immediately by returning within ourselves. What we find when we make this journey 'within' is that, at this deepest level, God is identical with the thought that thinks him while we are the same as God's thought of us. As Hadot (1993: 27) puts it, for Plotinus 'We are always in God.'

Having warned his followers that if they question after the One by looking elsewhere than where they are (as the Gnostics did) they will find no answers, Plotinus clarifies that he doesn't mean that we shouldn't question at all. Quite the opposite, in fact, because it is only when we question why we occupy just one part of the One that the One becomes visible at all. Plotinus puts it like this:

> Because you have approached the All, and have not just stayed within one part of it, you have not said, 'I am of such-and-such dimensions', but you have dropped the 'such-and-such', and have become the All. To be sure, you were already previously the All, but since something other came to be added on to you besides the All you were lessened by this addition. For this addition did not come from the All – what could you add to the All? – but from not-being. When one comes to be out of not-being, he is not the All, not until he rids himself of this not-being. Thus, you increase yourself when you get rid of everything else, and once you have got rid of it, the All is present to you. (6.5.12)

What Plotinus means by not-being is what today we call identity. Being Australian, for example, seems really to be something. But, since it introduces a division in the indivisible One, it is really nothing. Today we have become used to thinking that we find ourselves by finding our identity – what is particular to us. But Plotinus would send us in the other direction – for him, we find ourselves not in what is part but only in the One-All that recognises no distinctions.

But in this notion of the One as *in*-distinct another question arises. It is, once again, the question of otherworldliness that has also been asked of Plato. Plotinus's One is as timeless and universal as Plato's idea of the Good – it suffers no change. Meanwhile, what Plotinus calls the corporeal principle (having a body, that is) is in itself nothing. The soul longs to rise up and to be re-absorbed back into the One from which it comes, which is the experience of union that is mystical ecstasy. Mortal bodies have value only to the extent that they participate in the One, which is immortal. While he continues to question what it is to be, Plotinus seems as forgetful as Plato and Aristotle of the paradox that only mortal minds can know the immortal principle that is the One. Although time is portrayed as something bad, it is only *in* time that the timeless One is visible at all.

The true world (the world of ideas) of Plato becomes, in Plotinus, a world that is higher than our world in the sense that it is closer to the One. But our lowly world is no less important for all that. Indeed, without the living that happens down here in this world, the true world could not live at all. Our world provides the beings without which the true world would indeed be just an empty abstraction, a puff of smoke without any reality whatsoever. And so Socrates's questioning of existence reaches, with Plotinus, both its most otherworldly *and* one of its most life-affirming expressions. The One beyond being is very far from what we are here on earth, but it is also the closest to us.

7 Augustine

AUGUSTINE OF HIPPO (354–430 CE), the most influential of the Church Fathers in the development of Western Christianity, asked after God. Yet these questions, explicitly theological as they were, should not blind us to the theological drift of rationalistic questioning as such: if everything has a reason, then the question of how X was caused by Y must lead us in turn to ask what caused Y, and so on. Questioning why things are the way they are, then, leads back to a first cause. And as we saw in the case of Aristotle, it is a short step from identifying a first cause to finding God.

But if all reasons relate back to God, then does the evil in the world also originate there? Aristotle's God, being unchanging and impersonal, does not will evil. Augustine, however, believed in a personal creator God. How to absolve *this* God of evil? Even before his conversion to Christianity, while still a Manichee (Manichaeism was a Gnostic religion widespread in Augustine's day), this paradox had troubled Augustine: 'In my ignorance, I was disturbed by [this] question', for piety 'forbade me to believe that the good God had created an evil nature' (*Confessions* 3.7 and 5.10).

It wasn't only the Manichees who felt that evil must be sourced elsewhere than in God. Centuries earlier, in Plato's *Republic* (379c), we find: 'while god must be held to be the sole cause of good, we must look for some factors other than god as cause of evil'. Plato is here objecting to the stories of the gods told by the poets, which portray them as pernicious:

> 'In reality, of course, god is good, and he must be so described.'
> 'Certainly.'
> 'But nothing good is harmful, is it?'
> 'I think not.'
> 'Then can anything that is not harmful do harm?'
> 'No.'
> 'And can what does no harm do evil?'
> 'No again.'
> 'And can what does no evil be the cause of any evil?'
> 'How could it?'

Yet unlike Plato, who was able to hold that God is responsible only for good 'because he cannot be responsible for everything' (*Republic* 379c), and unlike the Manichees, who believed God 'infinite in all respects but one, namely the mass of evil opposed' to him (*Confessions* 5.10), the Christian Augustine believed in an all-powerful God. Excusing such a God of evil is not so straightforward. Indeed, according to his *Confessions*, even after he had lost faith in Manichean doctrines, this problem was the biggest block to Augustine's conversion to Christianity. He writes (7.3 and 7.7): 'I had no clear and explicit grasp of the cause of evil. Whatever it might be, I saw it had to be investigated'; 'I was searching feverishly for the origin of [it].'

What persuaded Augustine that Christianity could solve the problem of evil was the argument that believers do not *suffer* evil (as the Manichees had taught) but actively *do* evil: 'I directed my mind to understand what I was being told, namely that the free choice of the will is the reason why we do wrong' (*Confessions* 7.3). Initially, however, this answer to the question of evil only raised further questions for Augustine:

> But again I said: 'Who made me? Is not my God not only good but the supreme Good? Why then have I the power to will evil and to reject good? Is it to provide a reason why it is just for me to undergo punishment? Who put this power in me and implanted in me this seed of bitterness, when all of me was created by my very kind God? If the devil was responsible, where did the devil himself come from? And if even he began as a good angel and became devil by a

perversion of the will, how does the evil will by which he became devil originate in him, when an angel is wholly made by a Creator who is pure goodness?' These reflections depressed me once more and suffocated me. (*Confessions* 7.3)

At this point, at least as reconstructed in his *Confessions*, Augustine realised that he had been asking the wrong questions (the best way of dealing with unanswerable questions is to pose new ones). He had been searching for the origin of evil 'in a flawed way'; indeed, the search for evil was itself the flaw. For what if the search for evil is the search for something that 'has no being?' (*Confessions* 7.5). Augustine's way out of the problem of evil, then, begins with the Neoplatonic notion that evil is defined only by its *lack* of being: 'whatever things exist are good, and the evil into whose origins I was inquiring is not a substance, for if it were a substance, it would be good' (*Confessions* 7.12). God, for whom 'evil does not exist at all', makes all things substantial and that is their good (*Confessions* 7.13). It is the fall away from their true substance into insubstantial existence that gives rise to evil: 'I inquired what wickedness is, and I did not find a substance but a perversity of will twisted away from the highest substance, you O God, towards inferior things, rejecting its own inner life' (*Confessions* 7.16).

It is important to note, however, that although Augustine, like Plotinus, finds evil to be in some sense nothing, he does not find it to be nowhere. He does not find a substance, but he does locate a perverse will, and this is his difference from Neoplatonism. Augustine's identification of the source of evil in *us* avoids referring evil back to God. God is cleared of responsibility for evil. The technical name for this getting-God-off-the-hook is theodicy. Augustine's questioning after evil comes to an end not in a first cause, but in nothing: our 'own choice' (*Confessions* 4.15). The void of the uncaused will stands in for God as the source of evil. But how can something arise from nothing? The paradoxes of the free will are many. Augustine himself is forced into a circular reasoning whereby 'it is the will that commands the will to exist, and it commands not another will but itself' (*Confessions* 8.9).

If the free will evolved as the solution to a theological problem (excusing God of responsibility for evil), is the idea of causality ultimately any less theological? As Meillassoux (2008) has pointed out, the principle of sufficient reason, as formulated by Leibniz, states that everything has a reason and that, finally, all reasons lead back to God.

For if everything has a reason then the only way to avoid an infinite regression of reasons is to posit some uncaused first reason – also known as the Prime Mover (Aristotle's God, which moves but is itself unmoved). In other words, unless we accept that the way things are *has* no reason, we will be inexorably drawn to God. Inasmuch as we continue to assume that reason goes all the way down, namely that natural laws are the foundation of everything, we remain within theology. Only speculative philosophy can face the unsettling consequences that, ultimately, there is absolute contingency. Everything we take to be unchangeably law-like in the universe, according to this view, is in fact built on the void. The true atheist must accept, paradoxically, that even a god could appear at any moment – something no scientist could stomach.

Augustine, of course, did believe that a god had appeared; and not only a god, but the son of the one, true God. Living a century and a half after Plotinus, Augustine inhabited the world of late Antiquity in which not only the pagan gods but Rome itself was being eclipsed. If the Christian God had supplanted the gods of Rome shortly after Plotinus's death, then the Empire at least had stood firm. But now, in Augustine's own lifetime, the unthinkable had happened. After 1,000 years of impregnable splendour, Rome had been sacked by a barbarian army. Faced with the angry protestations of the pagans that Rome's demise should be blamed on the abandonment of its traditional gods, Augustine felt compelled to give an account of how the earthly city, even one as glorious as Rome, cannot be identical to the city of God. This became his great work, *City of God*.

The Augustine of *City of God* is, in our understanding, a theologian, but theo-*logia*, the study of the *logos* (reason) of God, is an exercise in Greek philosophy (indeed, it was Plato who coined the word theology in the *Republic*). As Aristotle says in Book V of his *Metaphysics* (1064a), 'Metaphysics is a theology of god and is primarily concerned with the divine.' Ancient Church Fathers, from Origen to Augustine, therefore wielded the concepts of Greek philosophy in order to provide their *apologia* for the new Christian religion. And what other tools could they draw on? Writing in an Empire where the literate elite were shaped by a millennium of philosophy, to give an account of the Christian God was inevitably to be drawn into the *logos* of the Greeks. When, many hundreds years later, Thomas Aquinas sought to reconcile Aristotle's recently rediscovered writings with the doctrine of the Western Church, he was so successful in his enterprise because doctrinal Christianity was expressed in the terms of Greek philosophy from the beginning. Even as early as the Apostle Paul there are clear Stoic influences, including ideas of natural law and the claim that there is individual awareness or 'conscience' of these laws (not to mention a Stoic propensity for cosmopolitanism: 'there is neither Jew nor Greek . . .'). Indeed, even a doctrine as fundamental as the Nicene Creed's statement that Jesus is 'begotten not created' of the Father is itself a piece of Greek ontology that echoes exactly Plotinus, for whom the eternal ideas of the intellectual realm also 'have a derived being but by an eternal derivation' (*Enneads* 4.4).

To say, then, that Augustine's *magnum opus* was influenced by philosophy would be a huge understatement. It *is* philosophy. The central claim of the work is that the two cities, the secular and the sacred, are differentiated above all in being. The city of men is subject, as everything mortal, to time and decay; the heavenly city, meanwhile, is immortal, being 'that kingdom whose glory is not the tottering grandeur of the temporal, but the secure stability of the eternal' (*City of God* 10.32). Indeed, the very last lines of the *City of God* (22.30) read: 'Behold what will be, in the end, without end! For what is our end but to reach that kingdom which has no end?'

Despite his reservations about the 'books of the Platonists' expressed earlier in his *Confessions* (7.13), a clearer expression of the two-worlds division at the heart of Platonist philosophy could hardly be conceived. And, indeed, Augustine praises the Platonists for 'their glorious reputation that they so thoroughly deserve', which ranks them above all other thinkers as 'the closest approximation to our Christian position' (*City of God* 8.9). For 'they realised that nothing changeable can be the supreme God'. They also recognised 'that in every mutable being the form which determines its being [. . .] can only come from him who truly *is*, because he exists immutably' (*City of God* 8.6). Asking how Plato could 'have acquired the insight that brought him so close to Christianity', Augustine speculates that he must have read the scriptures on his fabled journey to Egypt (*City of God* 8.11). The thought that Plato is close to Christian doctrine because the Fathers prior to Augustine, like Augustine himself, were essentially doing Greek philosophy seems not to have occurred to Augustine.

As we saw with Augustine's borrowing of the doctrine that evil is a lack of true being, the Platonism that particularly influenced

Augustine was the Neoplatonism of Plotinus, a fellow African. So close is Augustine to Plotinus that we need to discuss these two thinkers together in order to get a clear view of what Augustine intends. As discussed in the last chapter, Plotinus's *Enneads* are structured by a ranking in being in which only that which is eternal is fully in being while that which is mortal merely 'participates' in being. From Plotinus's Good beyond being down through the timeless beings of the intellectual realm and, finally, to the being-less (in the sense of formless) matter which underpins our world, that which truly *is* remains always and ever unchanged. That which is subject to time and becoming, meanwhile, *is* only indirectly.

In many ways Augustine's two cities, the heavenly and the earthly, are only this staple of Platonist ontology dressed in Christian costume, which means that it is presented in the form of a historical drama whereby the heavenly city eventually triumphs essentially because, unlike the earthly city, it does not pass away (Plotinus, for his part, retained the Greek notion that the cosmos is timeless). For just like Plotinus, Augustine thinks that 'the things created changeable have no real existence' (*City of God* 8.12). Indeed, he agrees with Plotinus's student, Porphyry, that, in this regard, Plato's doctrine of reincarnation needs to be reworked. Why would immortal souls, on their release from the body at death, seek to return to another corruptible body 'as if the effect of the final purification were a longing for a renewed defilement'? After all, only that which has a 'complete assurance of its eternity' can be 'completely blessed'; 'life will only be truly happy when it is eternal' (*City of God* 10.30, 14.25).

For all that Augustine seeks an escape from the predations of time in eternity, it would be mistaken to think that he does not treat time seriously. Earlier, in his *Confessions*, Augustine had devoted a whole book to questions of time in which the question 'What is time?' set his mind 'on fire to solve this very intricate enigma' (*Confessions* 11.14, 11.22). Thinking about how the past and the future are not present, and reflecting on how even the present must pass for there to be time, Augustine concludes that 'we cannot truly say that time exists except in the sense that it tends towards non-existence' (*Confessions* 11.14). Continuing with this line of thought, Augustine soon notices that far from only tending towards non-existence, the present 'flies so quickly from future to past that it is an interval with no duration' at all (*Confessions* 11.15).

If the present has no duration but still arrives, then *where* does it arise? Augustine argues that the presence of past, present and future is in us: 'In the soul there are these three aspects of time, and I do not see them anywhere else' (*Confessions* 11.20). The three divisions of time, then, are divisions in *our* capacity for, respectively, memory (of the past), immediate awareness (of the present), and expectation (of the future) (*Confessions* 11.20 and 11.28). Augustine addresses his insight to God: 'My confession to you is surely truthful when my soul declares that times are measured by me' (*Confessions* 11.24).

Just as his longing for eternity does not make him inattentive to time, neither does Augustine's devotion to immortal God lead him to denigrate mortal beings who, unlike God, must live in time. As we saw in the last chapter, Plotinus responds to the nihilistic world-hatred of the Gnostics by arguing that 'nothing is to be blamed for not being the first'. Our world is only a copy of the timeless world of the intellectual realm, but, for all that, it is indispensable. If all being is sourced in the overflowing goodness of the One then everything, even the lowest life form, not only shares in the Good but is the necessary self-expression of the Good. We find the same insistence in Augustine: 'Let these transient things be the ground on which my soul praises you', since even the 'vipers and worms which you created [are] good, being well fitted for the lower parts of creation' (*Confessions* 4.10 and 7.16). For 'all things are very good, whether they abide close to you or, in the graded hierarchy of being, stand further away from you in time and space' (*Confessions* 12.28). Fallen as our world might be, it comes from a good God. To be sure, Augustine disagrees with Plotinus that the world is itself an eternal living being and in this sense is closer to the Gnostic position whereby God and world are separated by much more than rank (*City of God* 10.29). But his idea of creation is not the Gnostic one whereby the true God neither made nor engages with the world. Augustine's God creates this world and sustains it.

But this view of the world returns us to the question of evil that obsessed the young Augustine of the *Confessions*, a question that the Gnostics' world-hatred avoided: how to account for evil in the creation of a good God? Since they are the pinnacle of creation, in *City of God* Augustine tackles this question by starting with the angles. He describes how the fallen angels abandoned God not because of any flaw in their make-up (a flaw for which God, as creator of all things, would then be responsible) but because of their ill-will alone: 'they would not have fallen away, had they not willed to do so' (*City of God* 12.9). Pushing the theodicy of his *Confessions* (where, as we saw, the human will is the source of evil) back from humanity to the angels, Augustine says that the rebellious angels fell because of a moral choice which itself had no reason: 'to try to discover the cause of such defection [...] is like trying to see darkness or to hear silence' (*City of God* 12.7). A little later, he repeats this point: 'And this evil choice consists solely in falling away from God and deserting him, a defection whose cause is deficient, in the sense of being wanting – for there is no cause' (*City of God* 12.9, see also 22.1).

The history of the free will in Western culture continues to this day in the emphasis on individual decision. When we encourage our children to make good choices, we echo an ancient angelology. Nothing could be further from Greek religion than this axiom of the unfounded decision in which an inner freedom is activated that no necessity can compel. For even in those decisive moments in the life of a hero when a Greek god manifests herself, 'everything takes its natural course' (Otto 1955: 6):

> The Greek view of divine-human operation contrasts remarkably with the view familiar to ourselves [...] The deity is one with the world and approaches man out of the things of the world if he is upon the way and participates in the world's manifold life. It is not through turning inward that man experiences deity but by proceeding outward, seizing, acting. (Otto 1955: 174)

The long shadow of Augustine's free will is cast still in European-based legal systems. The worldly causes of criminality (poverty, trauma, and so on) are bracketed out in the name of individual responsibility for the crime, a responsibility which itself must have no cause (since how else to justify the punishment that follows?). So-called mitigating circumstances, such as childhood or madness, only reiterate that personal responsibility is the underlying norm. Augustine's ill-will lives on in our courtrooms: 'when an evil choice happens in any being, then what happens is dependent on the will of that being; the failure is voluntary, not necessary, and the punishment that follows is just' (*City of God* 12.8).

Once again, Augustine is likely indebted to Plotinus for the notion that the will might be free. In the first tractate of the third Ennead on fate,

Plotinus describes the 'reason-principle' of the human soul as 'pure and detached and native to itself'. Living according to this ideal of the soul, it is possible to speak 'of personal operation, of voluntary act. Things so done may truly be described as our doing, for they have no other source.' However, differently from Augustine, who finds it in everybody, this freedom of the soul is an uncommon thing found only in the true philosopher. Moreover, such freedom is freedom only for good, since when we fail to act according to the soul's true nature (as most of us will, most of the time), it is because the necessity that determines all embodied things is having its way with us: 'In the action of our souls all that is done of their own motion in the light of sound reason is the souls' work, while what is done where they are hindered from their own action is not so much done as suffered' (*Enneads* 3.1). While Plotinus gives to us the successes and absolves us of the failures of our free choice, Augustine upends this happy formula in a misanthropic reversal – if we sin it is *we* who are sinning; if we do good it is *God* who works through us.

Plotinus is not consistent in upholding his more philanthropic formula, however. In a tractate on providence (*Enneads* 1.7), where he is seeking to establish that the world soul works for good rather than ill, he shifts his position. Individual souls must be to blame for their evil acts since, otherwise, 'the fore-planning power [providence] alone is to be charged with [their] vice'. To hold that the divine mind governs the world according to a plan, as both Plotinus and Augustine do, makes it very difficult to find any other location for evil than the bad choices of individuals. Centuries after them, as we shall see in a later chapter, it would be necessary for Spinoza to abandon the entire edifice of providence and free will in order to be able to hold that God is perfect *and* that people are innocent. As Nietzsche (*TI*, 'Errors', 7) put it: 'We know all too well what [free will] is – the shadiest trick theologians have up their sleeves for making humanity "responsible" . . . .'

Having failed to resolve the problem of how to square evil with providence by way of the will, Plotinus speculates that matter, as the form-less substrata which is then formed by the soul of all living things, might be the source of evil. As it would for Augustine after him, evil here lacks substance. It is simply that which is at the furthest extremity from the Good – so far, indeed, that its being is really that of the no-thing, where being and nothing elide: 'whence the identification that has been made of matter with the void' (*Enneads* 4.11). As in Plato, being is equated with the Good and, by extension, that which is less in being falls ever further from the Good. Matter owes its evil, then, to its own lack: 'it is utter destitution – of sense, of virtue, of beauty, of pattern, of ideal principle, of quality. This is surely ugliness, utter disgracefulness, unredeemed evil' (*Enneads* 4.16).

As he did with the two worlds of Plato (the immutable and the mutable), Augustine shifts this doctrine from the register of ontology into the register of history. Rather than the fall into the material world constituting an eternal feature of the hierarchy of being, now the fall has a beginning in time:

> When [man] turned towards himself his being was less real than when he adhered to him who exists in a supreme degree. And so, to abandon God and to exist in oneself, that is to please oneself, is not immediately to lose all being but to come nearer to nothingness [...] This then is the original evil: man regards himself as his own light. (*City of God* 14.13)

Although Augustine does not question the Platonists' identification of evil with the fall from true being, in repositioning this descent in the will he does find a way of absolving the material world as such of its association with the fall. (In Plotinus, by contrast, the claim that the world is good but that matter is somehow connected to evil seems incoherent.) For Augustine, our fall is not into matter as such but into the *perishability* of matter. 'It follows that what is needed for the soul's life of bliss is not the escape from any kind of body but the possession of an imperishable body' (*City of God* 22.26). Even the pagans largely recognise this: their gods, too, have immortal bodies.

Since, against the Platonists, it is death rather than embodiment that is the source of evil, we come to the question of how our flesh first became corruptible? Once again, Augustine's answer, given in the very last chapter of *City of God* (22.30), refers us back to the will: 'The first freedom of will, given to man when he was created upright at the beginning, was an ability not to sin, combined with the possibility of sinning.' This was a possibility that Adam, fatefully, explored. Do we really want freedom of the will when its price is set so high, when we can have its possibilities only at the cost of being guilty? Trying to be more affirmative, Augustine argues that the 'first freedom' (the ability not to sin) 'was designed for acquiring merit' (*City of God* 22.30). But where there is freedom for merit, demerit points will also be awarded.

8   Duns Scotus

WE NOW TRAVEL FORWARD eight centuries after Augustine. In Europe it is the late Middle Ages and Greek philosophy, despite re-emerging in Europe around this time, is also about to be eclipsed. Duns Scotus (1266–1308), the subject of this chapter, was part of a great shift in the Western tradition away from the confidence of Greek philosophy that our questions push on an open door, that we can know the world by way of our reason because the world wants to be known in the beauty of its order. This is the cosmos of the ancient Stoics, a world soul with 'man' at its centre sharing in the divine reason that guides the world providentially and therefore predictably.

But the Christian world, unlike the world of the Greeks, is created. And as we saw in the last chapter, what is to stop a God who can make something out of nothing doing what he wants? This wilful God haunts the Christian theology of the Middle Ages. To be sure, such a God is anticipated already in Augustine, for whom God is a 'controller of the universe' rather than its prime mover (*Confessions* 7.6). But while Augustine believed that God was identical with his will, this God had nonetheless 'made all things by a choice which in no sense manifests change' (*Confessions* 12.28). In Augustine's God there is both will and law. As God's will became ascendent in medieval Christian theology, however, questioning became ever more problematic. Our questions can only provide us with dependable answers if the world is as law-like as it seemed to the Greeks. And while Augustine still believed in a legible cosmos, hadn't he already lamented the lack of humility found 'in the Platonist books': 'Let not man say "What is this? Why is that?"' (*Confessions* 7.21, 7.6). Why should God be limited by natural law? Where would this leave miracles, including the miracle of creation, of the virgin birth, and of the resurrection from the dead?

This is not to say that Greek thought was no longer decisive for medieval theology. Far from it. Duns Scotus, like his contemporaries in the Western Church, was profoundly shaped by the recovery (via Muslim scholars who had not lost sight of him in the first place) of Aristotle, a process which began in the mid-twelfth century. Although new translations into Latin (the language of the Western Church and therefore of Western scholarship too) of Plato would also begin a century or so later, the rediscovery of Aristotle was especially significant. It would take centuries for the hold of Aristotelian scholasticism to lose its grip on the Western imagination.

A towering figure in the recovery of Aristotle was Thomas Aquinas (1225–74). Thomas attempted nothing less than a complete synthesis of Christian dogma and the teachings of 'the Philosopher' (as Aristotle came to be known): his massive *Summa Theologica* (Aquinas 2012). Picking up on Saint Paul's Stoic idea of 'conscience', whereby the laws of nature, and thereby nature's God, are accessible to individual reason (Romans 1:20), Thomas argued that we can know God naturally or intuitively. Thomas retained the Greek confidence that our questions get us somewhere.

Duns Scotus was not so sure: 'we can have no naturally acquired science about God' (Duns Scotus 1962: 12, see also 29). We cannot know of God through the evidence of our senses not only because our senses can lie (something that Greek philosophy accepted too) but, more fundamentally, because there is no analogy with what we know here on earth and what is true in heaven. After all, 'creatures only imperfectly imitate Him' (Duns Scotus 1962: 29, 32). Since the most fundamental division in being is between that which is finite and that which is infinite, knowledge of God cannot arise in us (Duns Scotus 1962: 3, 4). How can we reach up from our finite knowledge of finite things in order to grasp the infinite? Finite minds only ever consider one thing after another, never all at once (Duns Scotus 1962: 34). What's more, all 'the senses perceive only what is sensible' and 'of God there is no sense image' (Duns Scotus 1962: 17). Even Aristotle concedes in his *Physics* (Book I) that the infinite *as* infinite is unknowable.

But despite this vast, indeed unbridgeable, gulf, Duns Scotus believes that we *can* say things of God. We can talk of God because the being of infinite God and the being of finite things comes under the same concept. To be sure, 'Socrates, insofar as he is Socrates, is singular. Nevertheless, several predicates can be abstracted from Socrates. Consequently, the singularity of a thing is no impediment to the abstraction of a common concept' (Duns Scotus 1962: 36). Indeed, above and beyond even the distinction between finite and infinite being, there is the most common concept of all: being as such. *To be* is not equivocal but *uni*vocal: it *said in the same way* regardless of whether we speak of Socrates or of God. Both finite Socrates and infinite God *are*.

This means that predicates of being, such as wisdom and goodness and the like, are also common to God and creatures: 'For in so far as they pertain to God they are infinite, whereas in so far as they belong to creatures they are finite.' Both God and beings belong to being prior to any other division between them because 'being is predicated commonly of created and uncreated beings' (Duns Scotus 1962: 3, 4). The 'natural' knowledge of God that Thomas had pointed to, then, is only possible because 'being is univocal to the created and uncreated' (Duns Scotus 1962: 4). We can question after God because, first, we share with him our submission to the highest concept that there is: just as he is said *to be*, so too are we. Indeed, this shared sense of being stands regardless of what we actually *know* about God:

> Now in this life already, a man can be certain in his mind that God is a being and still be in doubt whether He is a finite or an infinite being ... Consequently, the concept of 'being' as affirmed of God is different from [these] two concepts [namely being finite or infinite] but is included in both of them and therefore is univocal. (Duns Scotus 1962: 23)

Natural knowledge is dependent on the senses, and what we can sense (the sensible) is only accidental being (*this* horse), not the necessary being that is God as eternal substance. Nothing in this finite horse tells me of infinite substance except that it *is*. As Duns Scotus puts it in the strange language of ontology (the study of being *as* being), the only concept 'that can be abstracted from that of an accident is the concept of being' (Duns Scotus 1962: 23). Being does not directly move my intellect to know it, rather I extrapolate from the existence of accidental (finite) things that there *is* (something rather than nothing). Indeed, it does not even matter whether I am wrong that this horse is a horse (maybe it's a donkey seen from a long way off) in order to know that there *is* something. And knowing that there is something contingent or finite, I can infer that there is something necessary and infinite (Duns Scotus 1962: 9). For everything that has its being by way of participation is imperfect. Only that which is entirely by its own essence is perfect (Duns Scotus 1962: 99). To be a limited being is to be a mixed being, and in this mix there must be some imperfection (Duns Scotus 1962: 100). Only where there is pure self-sufficiency is there perfection. Indeed, Duns Scotus (1962: 12) believes that this chain of being is able to infer a 'First Being' more perfectly than movement in nature is able to infer a prime mover (as in Aristotle's natural philosophy). Being is *un*-equivocal.

To say that divine and mortal existence are said in the same way (univocally) is not, of course, to deny that God's being is necessary while worldly being is contingent. Duns Scotus (1962: 10) cites the Muslim scholar Avicenna, who suggested that those who deny this should be tortured 'until they concede that to burn and not to burn, or to be beaten and not to be beaten, are not identical'.

Although eternal and temporal being is different, that it is said in one way means that something positive can be said of God. We can do more than say what God is not, since all such denial is meaningful only in the light of an affirmation (Duns Scotus 1962: 18). This is just as well, since negations cannot be 'the object of our greatest love' (Duns Scotus 1962: 18). What we would today call negative theology is no theology at all for Duns Scotus.

To say only that God is *not* this or that fails to avoid the problem that, if we can never say anything positive of God, then his very existence is put in question. Pure negation (*not*-God) can be attributed to nothing as much as it can be said of something. On the other hand, if negation is understood as modifying something (God is not X), then I must question further after that which is being modified (God). If my questions lead me to another negative notion (God is not X and neither is he Y) then I keep questioning after him. If my questions lead me to something positive, on the other hand, then I have what I seek (Duns Scotus 1962: 18): 'And no matter how far we proceed with negations, either what we know is no more God than nothing is, or we will arrive at some affirmative concept which is the first concept of all' (Duns Scotus 1962: 19).

Having found this highest concept, I will have reached beyond any distinction between *what* God is (in essence) and *that* he is (in existence). God's essence *is* his existence and his existence *is* his essence (Heidegger, as we shall see, would later apply this reduction to human being). I could not know God to exist unless I had some concept of him, namely of his essence (Duns Scotus 1962: 19). Nor could I have an awareness of existence without him existing (referring back to Duns Scotus's argument that, knowing finite being, I am led to infer an infinite being).

Duns Scotus believed that his concept of the univocity of being avoided the cul-de-sacs of ontologies that propose equivocity. If being is said *differently* of God and creatures, then a paradox occurs. If goodness, say, does not have a common meaning (common to both God and his creatures), then where is this goodness to reside? If God is said to be good in a way entirely other than his creatures, then our mundane concept of goodness can in no way apply to him. We become incapable of saying that God is good at all. Take the idea of wisdom, too: 'We would have no more reason to conclude that God is formally wise from the notion of wisdom derived from creatures than we would have reason to conclude that God is formally a stone' (Duns Scotus 1962: 28). The conundrum is this: 'we first know something to be pure perfection and secondly we attribute this perfection to God. Therefore, it is not a pure perfection precisely in so far as it is in God' (Duns Scotus 1962: 27).

Conceiving of God as an infinite being avoids these problems of predicating to God attributes such as goodness or wisdom. To say that God is infinite is not like saying he is good, since infinity is an intrinsic mode of being rather than a property of it. In place of subject (God) and attribute (goodness), I have a concept 'of what is essentially one, namely of a subject with a certain grade of perfection – infinity' (Duns Scotus 1962: 30). If we were to emphasise only the oneness, or simplicity, of God we would be identifying something that he shares with creatures. Only infinity is God's alone (Duns Scotus 1962: 31). And, indeed, what universe could 'lack the highest degree of being' (Duns Scotus 1962: 51)? Since 'to be infinite is not incompatible with being', we are compelled to agree that infinity is, and *this* is God (Duns Scotus 1962: 75).

Duns Scotus's insistence on God as an infinite (rather than the highest or most simple) being leads him to portray God as free: 'I show that the first efficient cause is endowed with will' (Duns Scotus 1963: 56). If Augustine, as we saw earlier, invented free will in order to absolve God of responsibility for evil, then Duns Scotus's ontology leads him to source this will in God. The problem, for Duns Scotus, is that it is precisely finite, natural agents that act out of necessity (the horse must do everything that horses do) (Duns Scotus 1962: 57). But if an infinite being such as God acts of necessity (as Aristotle's God does, for example), then this being is not infinite after all. For needing to be is compulsion, and this implies some higher power.

The first step in Duns Scotus's proof of God's wilfulness is to establish that God acts for the sake of nothing other than himself. If efficient causes act because they, in turn, were caused, then at the beginning of the chain of causes there must be a first cause that is itself uncaused. But to be uncaused means to act for no reason that is distinct from oneself: hence the first cause 'must act for itself' (Duns Scotus 1962: 53):

> If it were to act for the sake of any end other than itself, then something would be more noble than the first efficient cause, for if the end were anything apart from the agent intending the end, it would be more noble than the agent. (Duns Scotus 1962: 53)

If necessity implies finitude rather than infinity, then, according to Duns Scotus, only contingency can appropriately be predicated of God's acts. And this means that God possesses will (Duns Scotus 1962: 56).

Another of Duns Scotus's arguments for freedom in God is that if, as Aristotle held, God acts of necessity then, as first cause of the universe, every secondary cause would also cause necessarily, and so on. There would be no contingency in the world. But there is contingency, which must therefore be found in the first cause. Given that this contingency does not refer to God's being (his is in fact the only necessary existence), it must relate to his action (Duns Scotus 1962: 59). And where there is contingent action, there must be will (Duns Scotus 1962: 58). Inverting Aristotle, who places necessity in God and contingency in creatures, Duns Scotus (1962: 58) finds that creatures act necessarily 'and God wills things contingently'. For there are only two alternatives: 'either nothing ever happens unavoidably or contingently or the first cause immediately causes what it was also able not to cause' (Duns Scotus 1962: 59). Inasmuch as the second of these alternatives is, in Duns Scotus's view, the correct one, then not only are God's actions willed but, because God is identical with his actions, God *is* will (Duns Scotus 1962: 61).

The implications of a wilful God for theodicy (the justification of evil in the world) are, Duns Scotus believes, preferable to those of a God that acts necessarily. For don't 'the philosophers who assumed that God acted out of a necessity imposed by his nature, also admit the existence of evil in the universe?' (Duns Scotus 1962: 80). But if God acts of necessity 'then every defect, monstrosity, or evil in the universe occurs necessarily' (Duns Scotus 1962: 81). On the other hand, if God acts contingently, then 'the contingent character of the evil in the universe' does not lack an explanation (Duns Scotus 1962: 81). Because there is contingency in God there can also be contingency in us. But while contingency in God, who knows all, is pure will rather than arbitrariness, in mortals it can be very arbitrary indeed. *Our* contingency leads us into error that God is incapable of: 'Any will that is infinite wills things the way they should be willed' (Duns Scotus 1962: 92). Indeed, inasmuch as God wills on the basis of his (absolute) knowledge, the divine intellect 'is in some ways prior to the act of the divine will', but this 'prior' should be understood in terms of God's nature rather than in terms of time (Duns Scotus 1962: 133).

For Hans Blumenberg (1983), the insistence of late medieval nominalism on God's free will laid the ground for modernity, specifically for the restless spirit of scientific enquiry. For if the world is defined by will, then nothing of it can be known with certainty. We must find our own way to knowledge, including to knowledge of ourselves. This is the self-assertion characteristic of the modern age. The elevation of will to the highest principle of the universe has also been identified (Gillespie 1996) as the dawn of nihilism in Western culture. By insisting on God's wilfulness, theologians such as Duns Scotus undermined the sense that there is reason behind the world, opening up the void of meaninglessness in the process. If God acts for no reason, then how can we hope to find one?

There are strong echoes of Augustine (and therefore of Neoplatonism) in this wilful God. It is also instructive that Duns Scotus develops his metaphysics of the will in the wider context of the recovery of Aristotle. Aristotle's metaphysics of being as that which is eternal led him, after Plato, ever further away from that being which is closest to us (that we *are*), namely finite being. The thought of God as the Prime Mover that is itself eternally unmoved is very close to Duns Scotus's sense that God acts for no reasons other than his own. Each of these images of God are arrived at by the greatest possible abstraction from time and place.

In terms of the power of our questions to penetrate the highest truths, Duns Scotus marks a return to Plato's intellective approach, whereby understanding is derived from first principles (ultimately from awareness of being as given in the forms) rather than from the sensory perception of nature:

> Once we have certitude of first principles, it is clear how one can be certain of the conclusions drawn from such principles, since the perfect syllogism is [self] evident, and the certitude of the conclusion depends solely upon the certitude of the principles and the evidence of the inference. (Duns Scotus 1962: 102)

Contrary to this intellective approach, Aristotle had inferred the existence of the Prime Mover inductively from the regular movements that he found everywhere in nature. And Thomas Aquinas, although he held to the principle of divine revelation, retained Aristotle's confidence that our natural reason would corroborate the evidence of scripture.

But Duns Scotus was sceptical about this. Asking 'whether any certain and unadulterated truth can be known naturally by the intellect of a person in this life without the special illumination of the uncreated light?', Duns Scotus's answer is resounding: 'I argue that no such truth can be known' (Duns Scotus 1962: 105). For one thing, to suggest that we can know being by extrapolation from the lowest beings has the problem that, when it comes to beings, there is no 'certitude in knowing a changeable thing as unchangeable' (Duns Scotus 1962: 111). While it is true that divine light illuminates beings, because beings are constantly changing, we ourselves cannot know them 'by *any* kind of light' (Duns Scotus 1962: 111, emphasis added). Knowledge based on the study of beings, then, is uncertain and, as uncertain, will lead to scepticism.

For Duns Scotus, we know being *immediately*, without having to infer it from experience. Duns Scotus quotes Augustine approvingly, anticipating Descartes's *cogito ergo sum* as he does so: 'If anyone should say, "I know that I know or that I live", he cannot be deceived, no matter how often he reflect on this first knowledge' (Duns Scotus 1962: 113). Experimental knowledge, to the contrary, is limited just because experience is: we do not know all individual things, nor do we experience them at all times. But although we cannot know *from* experience, we can corroborate experience to the extent of knowing 'infallibly that it is always this way and holds for all instances' (Duns Scotus 1962: 117). How? Because '"Whatever occurs in a great many instances by a cause that is not free, is the natural effect of that cause." This proposition is known to the intellect even if the terms are derived from erring senses' (Duns Scotus 1962: 117).

Drawing on Aristotle for support of this thesis, Duns Scotus points to the passage in Book IV of Aristotle's *Metaphysics* where he responds to the Skeptics who say that all that appears is true. Aristotle asks these Skeptics for proof of whether they are awake or asleep. For whether what appears is true depends on whether one is dreaming or not, and this in turn needs no proof. 'The fact that we are awake is as self-evident as a principle of demonstration' (Duns Scotus 1962: 119). Against scepticism we can be confident that 'there is always some proposition to set the mind or intellect aright regarding which acts of the senses are true and which false – a proposition, note, which the senses do not cause but merely occasion in the intellect' (Duns Scotus 1962: 122). Duns Scotus gives the example of the intellectual proposition that 'the harder object is not broken by the touch of something soft'. So evident is this proposition to the intellect that we could not call it into doubt even if our senses seemed to indicate the opposite (Duns Scotus 1962: 122).

Change in things, as evidenced by the senses, is no threat to the intellect because unchanging propositions about things are available to us. To say that we cannot step in the same river twice, as Heraclitus did, does not prevent us from being able to propose that a river is something that constantly flows: 'For it is not precisely this *mutability* in the object that causes the knowledge; it is the *nature* of this mutable object that does so, and this nature is immutable' (Duns Scotus 1962: 124). The fact that we ourselves are mortal does not prevent us representing change under an immortal aspect: becoming *is*!

In the end, it is Platonism that is at work in Duns Scotus's theory of knowledge. Having awareness of being (Duns Scotus 1962: 128), we can proceed to clarify the confused evidence of the senses by discovering the appropriate definition of the thing known (Duns Scotus 1962: 129). In this way, our intellect 'concurs' in some way with the 'eternal light' by which (just as in Plato's and Plotinus's account of the Good) beings are illuminated or have their being (Duns Scotus 1962: 130). For those who grasp things as they are in themselves in this way:

> Such a one, as it were, has the sense image in the mist beneath him, but he himself is on the mountain to the extent that in virtue of the uncreated intellect, the eternal light, he knows this truth and sees what is true from above, as a more universal truth. (Duns Scotus 1962: 137)

But if there is much in Duns Scotus's theory of knowledge (epistemology) that is Platonistic, his ontology pushes against Platonism: where Platonists find only that which is most general in being to really *be* (immutable ideas), Duns Scotus thinks that singular things (mutable individuals) *are* in just the same sense. For Gilles Deleuze (2004: 44), the significance of Duns Scotus therefore cannot be underestimated: 'there has only ever been one ontology, that of Duns Scotus, which gave being a single voice'. If the task of modern philosophy is, as Deleuze (2004: 59) believed it to be, the inversion of Platonism, then Duns Scotus prepares the way for this task. Resisting the Platonism that says that the being of creatures is only *analogous* to the being of the divine, Duns Scotus shows that being must have one sense or be utterly senseless. If being is not said in the same way of God and mortals, then nothing can be said of God at all. Theology depends on the univocity of being. Although my mortal being is incomparably less than the immortal being of God, before this distinction of finite/infinite is the common sense of being as such. God can be said *to be* no more or less than me: 'Scotus therefore deserves the name of "subtle doctor" because he saw being on this side of the intersection between the universal and the singular' (Deleuze 2004: 49).

Neutralising being in an abstract concept, Duns Scotus showed a way out from the Platonism which can see only universal being, a being in which singular beings exist only inasmuch as they 'participate' in universal being (*this* horse is merely a copy of the idea horse). Showing that universal being comes under the same concept as the being of singular things, Duns Scotus prepares the way for a thinking of being in which being is *nothing other* than how it is expressed by singularities such as you, me and that horse.

9 Eckhart

A CONTEMPORARY OF DUNS Scotus, Meister Eckhart (c. 1260–c. 1328) was for centuries suspected of heresy. Today he is more often viewed as a great mystic and his questions as being among the most profound and penetrating in the history of the Western Church. As with Duns Scotus, Eckhart's questions revolve around the problem that arises when God is understood as being One-All. If God is all in all, then how do his creatures differ from him (and if they don't, then what worth could they be said to have *as* creatures)? And just as in Augustine (who Eckhart cites constantly), the question arises: if all is God, then how do we explain evil? If evil is in God, is God evil, too? We are already familiar with these thorny questions that arise from the fusion of Neoplatonism and Christian doctrine. Eckhart, however, has his own distinctive approach to them. Rather than questions being *problems* to solve, as they seem to be for Augustine, Eckhart turns them into affirmations. To question after God is to be one with him.

Eckhart's questioning therefore belongs to the mystical tradition, where the distinction between seeking and what is sought is blurred to the point of indistinction. Yet I will show that this mysticism is really nothing other than a consistent application of the axiom of Neoplatonist philosophy that being is participation in the One: 'one life and one being', as Eckhart repeats often. Working from this first principle, Eckhart rejects everything that smells of self: being nothing, I can only question away from myself and towards the oneness that is God:

> If everything corporeal [bodily or creaturely] were to be comprehended in this unity, it would be no different from that which this

unity is. If I were to find myself for a single instant in this essence [God/the One], I would have as little regard for myself as for a dung worm. (Sermon 12, Eckhart 2009: 297)

As we shall see, the paradox of mystical union with God is that a questioning that truly puts self in doubt can lead to unshakable confidence. For if 'I' am nothing outside of God, then, to the extent that I am in him, I am always being reborn as his son. Not like his son, but really *as* his son. This notion of oneness with God got Eckhart in big trouble with the Church and ultimately led to his denunciation in a Papal Bull issued by Pope John XXII in 1329. The potent mixture of self-confidence and humility that Eckhart's doctrine involves must have frightened this figure of authority. For oneness with God is undermining of religious hierarchies, which claim to mediate between God and humanity, a mediation that presupposes separation. And yet unity with God, in Eckhart's vision, is not the result of the elevation but of the sacrifice of self. Hence the humility.

Humility but not self-doubt. Contrary to the image of questioners as being full of misgivings, it was clearly the confidence expressed in Eckhart's questions that irked the Church's inquisitors, since the Papal Bull (Eckhart 1981: 77) begins with the warning that Eckhart 'wished to know more than he should'. Condemning twenty-six articles from Eckhart's writings and sermons, Pope John suspected heresy in the following claims, all of which suggest that the righteous person is indistinguishably one with God. The Bull summarises them thus: 'That the good man is the only-begotten Son of God'; '[That] the father gives birth to me his Son and the same Son [of God]. Everything that God performs is one; therefore he gives me, his Son, birth without any distinction [from the Son of God]' (Eckhart 1981: 79). Understanding that it stems from this belief in the unity of creator and creations (that the being of beings is found only in God), the Bull also condemns as 'evil sounding and rash' the following passage from Eckhart's writings: 'All creatures are pure nothing. I do not say they are a trifle or they are anything: they are pure nothing' (Sermon 4, Eckhart 2009: 226, see also Sermon 9 at 343 and Sermon 11 at 349).

The notion that creatures are nothing outside of the creator is the same as the belief that, in God, there are no distinctions. God is One. Eckhart quotes Augustine: 'the principle of everything that is one is the One alone' (Eckhart 1981: 166). All identity is found in God alone, who (unlike us) is pure self-identity where no difference can be found: 'All that is scattered among lower things is united when the soul climbs up into a life where there are no opposites' (Sermon 8, Eckhart 2009: 405). This idea that 'No distinction can exist or be found in God' is also denounced in the Papal Bull (article twenty-three), along with the related notion that all good works, as precisely *exterior* acts, are nothing compared to those 'interior acts, which the Father who abides in us makes and produces' (Eckhart 1981: 79).

Centuries before the Protestant Reformation, Eckhart is claiming that we cannot earn our salvation: 'no one performs a work that is divine and good unless he is in God', since what we are, we are from God, and what we have, we get from God and not from ourselves (Eckhart 1981: 146, 2009: 67). Either God acts in us or, acting ourselves, effectively we do nothing. For Eckhart shares the Neoplatonist view that evil is the fall away from true being (which is found only in God) into nothingness. In other words, 'sin and evil, are not things that exist', since they are 'neither seen nor known nor visible without the form of something good' (Eckhart 1981: 140, 149). Evil *is* only the absence of God.

Although it turns *our* actions into nothing, the notion of the efficacy of God's acts alone suggests that, in the bigger picture, even evil has something of God in it: 'in every work, even in an evil [...] God's glory is revealed and shines forth in equal fashion' (Eckhart 1981: 78). As Eckhart (1981: 152) puts it in his *Commentary on John*,

> darkness itself, privations, defects and evils praise and bless God [...] Judas damned praises God's justice [...] Thus, the darkness glorifies God, and the light shines in it, not so much as opposites placed next to each other, but rather as opposites placed within each other.

While from our perspective there is good and evil, from a God's-eye view all things are one; they all have a role to play, the 'good' and the 'bad'. In *The Talks of Instruction*, Eckhart (2009: 514) takes up this theme again, echoing the Stoics: 'all turbulence and unrest comes from self-will'. It is not the things themselves, not even evil things, but 'you yourself *in* the things' that hold you back: 'for you have a wrong attitude to things' (2009: 488). Working on ourselves rather than on things by resigning ourselves to them, we should learn to wish nothing to be other than it is: 'If you want to take God properly, you should take him equally in all things, in hardship as in comfort, in weeping as in joy, it should all be the same to you' (Sermon 5a, Eckhart 2009: 107, 106). This means that 'You must go right out of self-will' even to the extent of acting as if you were dead. For 'The just have no will at all: whatever God wills, it is all one to them' (Sermon 6, Eckhart 2009: 329 and Sermon 8 at 403). Inasmuch as, ceasing to will, we stop counting 'one thing more than another', we also desist from saying what is good or evil (Sermon 6, Eckhart 2009: 329). Eckhart suggests in *The Book of Divine Comfort* that we should even want our own damnation if God willed it (Eckhart 2009: 530).

What we *shouldn't* want, according to *The Talks of Instruction*, is 'that the sin into which we had fallen had never been' (Eckart 2009: 500). This belief, as expressed in *The Book of Divine Comfort*, was another of the articles censured by the Papal Bull:

> [The blessed] man is so one-willed with God that he wills all that God wills and in the way that God wills it. And so, since God in a way wills that I should have sinned, I would not wish that I had not done so. (Eckhart 2009: 531)

Not only does God somehow will my sin, but, for the same reason (that he might be all in all) 'God likes forgiving big sins more than small ones' (Sermon 4, Eckhart 2009: 225). Despite the revolutionary implications of these theses denounced by Pope John, they all stem from the simple Neoplatonist notion that God is One and that all things therefore have their being only by participation in him. Given that outside the One there is nothing, even sin must have its place in God.

Unlike the Church hierarchy, which clearly believed that the question of the being of God is not for laypeople (who must simply believe), Eckhart's sermons, preached in the German vernacular, show that he thought otherwise. What is the being of God? And how does it differ, if at all, from the being of creatures? We saw in the last chapter that Duns Scotus was so bold as to say that being in God and creatures is univocal (that is, said in the same way). Eckhart, for his part, does not go quite this far. Rather, as he writes in his *Commentary on Ecclesiasticus*, 'Being or existence and every perfection, especially general ones such as existence, oneness, truth, goodness, light, and so forth, are used to describe God and creatures in an analogical way' (Eckhart 1986: 178). To claim that being in God and creatures is analogous is to say that creatures have their being (or oneness, truth, goodness, etc.) 'totally from something outside to which they are analogically ordered, namely God' (Eckhart 1986: 178). Creatures are *like* God in having existence, but they are not in existence in exactly the same way as God is (the univocal view of Duns Scotus).

Staying closer to the Neoplatonist notion of emanation from the One adapted by Augustine, Eckhart quotes Augustine's *Confessions*: existence comes from no other source than God, 'who is the Supreme and the Highest Existence' (Eckhart 1986: 178). God's being is 'higher' than that of creatures. And so, although being is One, it is not univocal in the way that Duns Scotus held it to be: 'every created being radically and positively possesses existence, life, and wisdom from and in God, not in itself as a created being' (Eckhart 1986: 178). This point is repeated in Eckhart's *Commentary on John* (1981: 124, see also 159): 'In things that are analogical, what is produced [namely, the creaturely] is always inferior, of lower grade, less perfect and unequal to its source. In things that are univocal what is produced is always equal to the source.' Eckhart reserves univocity for the Son of God, who, unlike created creatures, 'does not just participate in the same nature [as God] but receives the total nature from its source in a simple, whole and equal manner' (Eckhart 1981: 124).

However, if not Duns Scotus's univocity of being *qua* being (being as such), Eckhart arrives at the same radical conclusion as Duns Scotus by a different route. While God's being is higher than that of his creation, nonetheless, there is a 'power of the soul' that 'seizes God naked in his essential being. It is one in unity, not like in likeness' (Sermon 13, Eckhart 2009: 161). Here, in the soul, I am not *like* God; I am *one with* God:

> I have said that the soul hates and has no love for likeness, for likeness in and for itself, but she loves it for the One that is concealed in it and is the true Father [. . .] for 'father' means birth and not likeness, it means the One in which likeness is silent . . . .
> (*The Book of Divine Comfort*, in Eckhart 2009: 537)

Put simply, the righteous soul is righteous (and good, just, etc.) in *exactly the same way* that God is, which is to say univocally. 'The humble man and God are one, the humble man has as much power over God as [God] has over himself' even to the extent that 'my humility gives to God his Godhead' (Sermon 14, Eckhart 2009: 267 and 269, see also Sermon 15). This same idea is expressed in the following passage of Eckhart's *Commentary on John* (1981: 169), a passage that constitutes one of the articles he was denounced for:

> We should not falsely suppose that it is by one son or image that Christ is the Son of God and by some other that the just and godlike man is a son of God, for [the Apostle Paul] says 'We are being transformed into the same image' [. . .] [S]o too all of us who are just and godlike are called and truly are God's sons in the same Son of God who is 'the Word made flesh' . . . .

Eckhart reiterates this point more boldly in the sermons that, being cited in the Papal Bull, can be safely attributed to him. Sermon 6, for example, contains the following condemned sentences:

> The father begets [gives birth to] his Son unceasingly, and furthermore, I say, he begets me as his Son and the same Son. I say even more: not only does he beget me as his Son, but he begets me as himself and himself as me, and me as his being and his nature [. . .] All that God works is one: therefore he begets me as his Son without any difference [. . .] He makes me his only-begotten Son with no distinction [. . .] I am converted into him in such a way that he makes me *one and alike* with his being. (Eckhart 2009: 331, see the same point reiterated in other sermons at 79, 105, 117, 227, 295, 337, 347. Eckhart also repeats it in *The Book of Divine Comfort*, see Eckhart 2009: 526 and 544)

So insistent is Eckhart that the righteous person is one with God that he pushes even beyond this metaphor of becoming-Son-of-God. The humble man remains unsatisfied even with being 'born as the only-begotten Son whom the Father has eternally borne, but he wants to be also the Father and to enter into the same equality of eternal paternity and to bear him, from whom I am eternally born' (Sermon 14, Eckhart 2009: 268). The righteous are born as the Son *and* give birth as the Father. Unsurprisingly, this also seems to have been condemned (see Article 22 of the Bull).

On closer inspection, Eckhart's radical thesis of the unity of the uncreated, intellective part of the soul with God flows over into creaturely life as such. Even 'inferior beings', he writes in his *Commentary on Genesis* (1981: 89), 'have the same primary and equal relation to and in existence that superior beings do'. In one of his sermons, Eckhart provides a helpful picture of this idea: 'In God the images of all things are alike, but they are images of unlike things. The highest angel, the soul, and the midge have an equal image in God' (Sermon 9, Eckhart 2009: 342).

This point is repeated in summary form in another sermon: 'In God, no creature is nobler than another' (Sermon 3, Eckhart 2009: 166, see also Sermon 12 at 297). Although creatures *derive* their existence from an external God rather than sharing it in exactly the same way (and some creatures are therefore 'higher' than others [see Eckhart 1981: 145]), nonetheless, God is radically 'in' them all in an undifferentiated way, too: 'what is one in many things must be above these things' (Sermon 9, Eckhart 2009: 341). Although God is 'on the outside' of creatures 'because he is above all and thus outside all', nonetheless he is also inside them since 'all things feed on him, because he is totally within' (Eckhart 1986: 179). The contemplative or intellective life, inasmuch as it takes the believer 'out' towards God, also journeys 'inwards', since God is always already within each and every creature, however lowly: 'for every creature is full of God as is a book' (Sermon 9, Eckhart 2009: 345). Hadot's summary of Plotinus's thought – 'We are always in God' – could just as well serve as a heading for the teachings of Eckhart. And just as much as Plotinus, when Eckhart says that we are within God, he is also saying that God is within us: 'God is brought down, not absolutely but inwardly, that we may be raised up. What was above has become inward' (Sermon 14, Eckhart 2009: 268).

Inasmuch as inner contemplation is contemplation of God, then everything of self must be swept away. We must 'de-form' ourselves as Eckhart puts it in *The Book of Divine Comfort* (Eckhart 2009: 527). 'Whoever shall receive him outright must have wholly renounced himself and gone out of himself' (Sermon 4, Eckhart 2009: 227). Since 'God wants this temple cleared, that he may be there all alone', only 'They who are like nothing are Godlike' (Sermon 1, Eckhart 2009: 66, and Sermon 6, at 330).

To the extent that 'I' in truth am only he, then the knowledge of God is really God knowing himself: 'The eye with which I see God is the same eye with which God sees me: my eye and God's eye are one eye, one seeing, one knowing and one love' (Sermon 12, Eckhart 2009: 298). Eckhart loves this metaphor so much that it runs like a red thread through his sermons: 'God is known by God in the soul' just as, in the eternal word, 'The hearer is the same as the heard' (Sermon 1, Eckhart 2009: 70, also Sermon 12 at 295). That which knows (God) and what is known (the soul) forms an 'essential self-identity in simple unity void of all distinctions' (Sermon 1, Eckhart 2009: 70). For just as Aristotle's God is thought thinking itself, Eckhart's God also 'knows nothing outside of himself; his eye is always turned inward into himself' (Sermon 5a, Eckhart 2009: 104):

> A master says, if all mediation were gone between me and this wall, I would be *on* the wall, but not *in* the wall. It is not thus in spiritual matters, for the one is always in the other: that which embraces is that which is embraced, for it embraces nothing but itself. This is subtle. He who understands it has been preached to enough [...] Whoever does not understand, let him not worry. (Sermon 16a, Eckhart 2009: 112)

For all its seeming mysticism, this subtle idea has practical, even political, implications. Eckhart himself draws cosmopolitan conclusions from the notion that there is no 'I' but only God. The man who achieves union with the oneness that is God has 'left behind all distinction of person, so that he is as well disposed to a man who is across the sea, whom he never set eyes on, as to the man who is with him and is his close friend' (Sermon 5b, Eckhart 2009: 109, see also Sermon 12 at 296 and 298). To favour oneself over a stranger is to 'have never for a single instant looked into this simple ground', which is One (Sermon 5b, Eckhart 2009: 109).

Another feature of Eckhart's questioning that runs counter to the usual view of mysticism as vague and woolly thinking is his confidence that the soul can arrive at true understanding: 'the soul has the potentiality of knowing all things' (Sermon 3, Eckhart 2009: 166). After all, 'knowledge and intellect unite the soul with God' (Sermon 3, Eckhart 2009: 165). The intellect can arrive at true knowledge because nothing separates what the soul knows from what is known. In this assurance we find expressed a staple of Platonism: '[B]eing and knowing are all one' (Sermon 3, Eckhart 2009: 166). How could we come to know things if we didn't *already* know them somewhere in the depths of our being? In Plato, this question leads to the myth of recollection whereby the soul recalls what it has seen prior to its descent from the true world of ideas. In Eckhart, something more Neoplatonic is being proposed: I do not know things in their truth because I recollect them, but because the highest part of my soul (the intellect), being uncreated, is indistinguishable from the Godhead. More than a memory, then, truth is the soul's very possession:

> The masters say knowledge resides in likeness. Some masters say the soul is made of all things, because she has the potentiality of understanding all things. It sounds stupid, but it is true. The masters say that for me to know anything, it must be fully present to me and like my understanding. (Sermon 3, Eckhart 2009: 166)

This notion of an uncreated, intellectual part of the soul that, one with God, can know all things, was another of the articles condemned as heretical by Pope John (Eckhart 1981: 80). We can understand why this was since, as Eckhart goes on to specify, the oneness of the intellect with God means that 'just as one little word is insignificant compared to the whole world, so insignificant is all the wisdom we can acquire here [in this world] compared to the naked, pure truth' (Sermon 3, Eckhart 2009: 166). Eckhart could easily be read as implying that the wisdom of the Church, being worldly and contingent, is really nothing. Only pure intellect can see beyond a world of time and change: 'The things we see here as mutable we shall know there as unchanging; we shall apprehend them in undivided form and close together: for that which here is distant, there is near, for *there* all things are present' (Sermon 3, Eckhart 2009: 166).

We should not be deceived by Eckhart's intimation of a 'beyond', as if true knowledge is the pursuit of what is most distant: only 'simple folk imagine they will see God as if he were standing there and they here' (Sermon 6, Eckhart 2009: 332). For Eckhart, echoing Plotinus, the outside is within and what is within is outside. This means that what the intellect knows, it knows by staying with what is closest: 'Intellect always works inward' (Sermon 9, Eckhart 2009: 345). This is why Eckhart preaches that the person who knows God, like the man who drinks wine from his own cellar, has knowledge of 'inward things': 'our Lord came to his disciples on Easter day behind closed doors. So it is with this man who is freed from all otherness and all createdness: God does not come into this man – he is essentially within him' (Sermon 10, Eckhart 2009: 335).

Knowledge as understanding of what is already within applies to all knowledge, not only knowledge of God. Take knowledge of what a human being is. Surely the man who seeks this understanding needs to encounter as many human beings as possible. No: 'The more he is detached from all things and turned in on himself, the more clearly and rationally he knows all things within himself without turning outward, the more he is a man' (Sermon 15, Eckhart 2009: 272). Rather than the intellect moving from experience of many things to knowledge of their identity, it is the identity of the intellect with the One (God) that allows us to experience 'all multiplicity' within ourselves: 'the simple intellect is so pure in itself that it comprehends the pure divine being immediately' (Sermon 15, Eckhart 2009: 272).

Philosophers often talk of the difference between an *a priori* (knowledge independent of experience) and an *a posteriori* (knowledge that follows from experience). Eckhart, like all Platonists, gives the former much more importance than the latter: 'My body is more in my soul than my soul is in my body' (Sermon 10, Eckhart 2009: 334). But Eckhart adds a Neoplatonic twist to this formula: both my body *and* my soul 'are more in God than they are in themselves' (Sermon 10, Eckhart 2009: 334). This same idea is expressed more simply in terms of a hierarchy of three kinds of knowledge:

> The first is sensible. The eye sees from afar things outside it. The second is rational, and is much higher. The third denotes a noble power of the soul [the intellect], which is so high and noble that it takes hold of God in his own being. (Sermon 11, Eckhart 2009: 349)

As with all Platonists, Eckhart's confidence in the power of the intellect depends upon the *changelessness* of truth. True being can be known because, being outside of time, it is eternal. If the One could be other than it is, if it had a beginning or an end, then it would be subject to another, and then it would not be the One. Eckhart's question is an echo of that of Parmenides at the opening of Greek philosophy: 'what-is is ungenerated and imperishable; / Whole, single-limbed, steadfast, and complete; / Nor was [it] once, nor will [it] be, since [it] is, now, all together, / One, continuous; for what coming-to-be of it will you seek?' (Parmenides 1984: *On Nature*, Fragment 8.3–6).

10 Spinoza

BARUCH SPINOZA (1632–77) IS THE first of our modern philosophers. He led the way in having the courage to question, too. For not many in Spinoza's day dared to doubt the existence of a personal God as he did. Spinoza also doubted the notion of free will and, with it, the reality of guilt. In fact, Spinoza put the entire edifice of moral law in question. Excommunicated from a community founded on religious law and living a precarious existence in a wider society that was no less legalistic, Spinoza's philosophy challenges the operation by which moral law assigns blame. As we shall see, this involves a radically new conception of ethics in which the question of responsibility (what *should* I do or not do?) is replaced with the question of capacity (what *can* I do or not do?).

Spinoza was only a generation younger than Descartes, who is traditionally considered the father of modern philosophy. Like Descartes, Spinoza had great faith in the power of reason. The question of how it is with the world is not something for the sages but has a set of precise, almost mathematical-like, answers. With reason liberated from the shackles of superstition, our fundamental questions lead us to answers. And being in possession of this understanding we can be free – not in the sense that we have any choice concerning how things are, but rather in our awareness of the order of things. As for the Stoics before and Nietzsche after him, the important thing for Spinoza is that our way of living affirms the way of the world rather than seeking solace in otherworldliness (worlds where things match up to the way we want them to be).

Though he lived in a time and place – Amsterdam in the seventeenth century – when the unfathomable providence of God was the answer to all difficult questions, explanations of things that seek refuge in the will of God were, for Spinoza (*Ethics* Part I, Appendix II), *Asylum Ignorantiae* – a sanctuary of ignorance. This was a very dangerous thought to harbour since God's freedom was central both to the Reformed Protestant faith that shaped the Dutch Republic and, in a different way, also to the Rabbinical Judaism of his upbringing (the community from which he was excommunicated).

Given the significance of the will to much of what we have seen of Western philosophy/theology since Augustine, and given its significance after Spinoza too (especially in Kant, as we shall see), it is important to understand just how explicitly Spinoza seeks to exclude the will from our thinking. To repeat: the will, for Spinoza, is a non-explanation and this means, above all, that we must expunge it from our reflections on God.

Denying that God wills is also to deny that he has a plan, and this denial of providence meant that Spinoza came to be associated with Godless pantheism. Knowing that this would be the case, Spinoza was unable to publish his great work, the *Ethics*, during his lifetime. Pantheism is the notion that God is in all things, or that all things are in God, which seems incompatible with the transcendence of God in Judaism and Christianity. God can only create the world if he is somehow separate from it. However, as we shall see, Spinoza's pantheism was an outcome of his rationalistic rejection of free will in God rather than a return to the cosmos-piety of ancient world-worship.

In addition to resisting Stoic pantheism, neither does Spinoza welcome Platonising otherworldliness. As we read in Part I of the *Ethics* (Proposition 15.6): 'I do not know why [matter] would be unworthy of the divine nature.' Spinoza's point here is that, since all things are in God, matter could not be other than God. Also, since all things are in God, then what happens to everything can happen only 'through the laws of God's infinite nature and follow (as I shall show) from the necessity of his essence' (*Ethics* Ip15.6). In short, against the whole tradition of Platonism, Spinoza cannot conceive of a separation between God and the material world, which he takes to be the same thing: *Deus sive Natura* (God *or* Nature). And if there is no separation then neither can there be any plan of salvation, since salvation implies an agent and a patient. In Spinoza's conception of God and world as indistinct, what would be acting on what?

As we saw, Duns Scotus believed that, since there is nothing above God, then neither can there be any reason for God to do one thing rather than another (since then that higher reason would be God). God, being undetermined, must be identical with his free will. Spinoza (*Ethics* Ip33s2) agrees that those who place the good outside of God, saying that he acts for the sake of it, 'seem to place something outside of God, which does not depend on God'. This makes God less than perfect for wanting 'something which he lacks' (*Ethics* I, Appendix II). But Spinoza draws the opposite conclusion to Duns Scotus from this: '[Since] there can be nothing outside him by which he is determined or compelled to act [. . .] God acts from the laws of his nature alone' (*Ethics* Ip17; see also Spinoza's *Theological-Political Treatise* 4.10.65). God, being undetermined, acts by necessity, not freedom.

That God is a free cause means, for Spinoza, that he exists 'only from the *necessity* of his nature'. And if God's existence is necessary, then so are his acts. 'Neither intellect nor will pertain to God's nature':

> [Some] think that God is a free cause because he can (so they think) bring it about that the things which we have said follow from his nature (i.e. which are in his power) do not happen or are not produced by him. But this is the same as if they say that God can bring it about that it would not follow from the nature of a triangle that its three angles are equal to two right angles; *or* that from a given cause the effect would not follow – which is absurd. (*Ethics* Ip17s1)

Spinoza's vision of God as cause of everything from the *necessity* of his nature (rather than from the freedom of his nature as in Duns Scotus's God), means that 'all things have necessarily flowed, or always follow, by the same necessity and in the same way as from the nature of a triangle it follows, from eternity and to eternity, that it's three angles are equal to two right angles' (*Ethics* Ip17s1). God could not be otherwise than he is, which means that he is eternally actual rather than potential. But this means, also, that the things that flow necessarily from God, human beings included, could not be otherwise than they are. Indeed, if they could, then God can think more things than he can create, which would render him less than omnipotent (*Ethics* Ip17s1).

Spinoza tells us that, if we must say that God wills, then it cannot be in the same sense that we are said to will. No more than a dog that barks is not the same as the constellation of stars called dog, our will and the divine will could not agree 'in anything except the name' (*Ethics* Ip17s2, see also *Theological-Political Treatise* 7.5.100). A very significant implication of God being the cause of all things immanently rather than transitively (namely, by his *being* in such a way rather than *acting* on something other than himself), is that providence is completely excluded. Given the identity of God and nature, if nature could change then God could be otherwise than he is, which is to say not-God. The idea of a divine plan introduces a separation between God and world which Spinoza has already rejected as untenable: where would beings *be* if not in God? For 'particular things are nothing but affectations of God's attributes', namely 'modes by which God's attributes are expressed in a certain or determinate way' (*Ethics* Ip25c). There is nothing contingent because all things express God and God is immutable (*Ethics* Ip29).

The connection between will and providence in Christian theology is at stake here. The Christian God wills to create, and then to save, the world, for no reason at all. The divine plan is founded in freedom. But for Spinoza (*Ethics* Ip32), 'The will cannot be called a free cause, but a necessary one.' Indeed, since God 'does not produce any effect by freedom of the will' (*Ethics* Ip32c1), so also 'will does not pertain to God's nature' (*Ethics* Ip32c2). If by will we mean free will, then such a thing does not, and could not, exist. Neither in God nor, by extension, in us: 'Things could have been produced by God in no other way, and in no other order than they have been produced' (*Ethics* Ip33).

If we do find something to have been willed freely, either by ourselves or by God, then we simply do not yet understand the true cause of it: 'a thing is called contingent only because of a defect of our knowledge' (*Ethics* Ip33s1). Spinoza is emphatic: once his readers 'have considered properly the chain of our demonstrations, in the end they will utterly reject the freedom they now attribute to God' (*Ethics* Ip33s2). In place of providence, they will find predetermination (*Ethics* I, Appendix). So insistent is Spinoza about this that he claims that *all* the prejudices that he seeks to expose are built on the idea of providence; namely, 'that God himself directs all things to some certain end' (*Ethics* I, Appendix). To the contrary, 'Nature has no end set before it, and all final causes are nothing but human fictions' (*Ethics* I, Appendix II).

The idea of divine providence leads us to perverse consequences. Spinoza (*Ethics* I, Appendix II) asks us to consider the example of a man who is killed by a slate that falls off a roof. Are we to say that the slate fell *in order* to kill the man? The fact that the wind was blowing hard at the time gives us all the explanation we need. But the defenders of providence will say that God made the wind blow in order to dislodge the slate in order to kill the man. Perhaps we will then explain that the wind was blowing hard because of a storm at sea, for which they will also provide a reason: 'for there is no end to the questions that can be asked' up until that cause of all causes: the will of God (*Ethics* I, Appendix II).

Are we then to suppose that God willed this almost infinite chain of events just in order to kill our poor passer-by? 'Men have been so mad as to believe that God is pleased by harmony', a harmony that is only harmonious *for us* (*Ethics* I, Appendix III). Our very need for an explanation of an 'evil' such as the death of the passer-by arises not from the nature of things but from our need to call things good or bad insofar as 'they please or offend' *us* (*Ethics* I, Appendix III). Spinoza's explosive claim is that, once we understand this, then we will see that there *is* no evil in the world: 'if the human mind had only adequate ideas, it would form no notion of evil' (*Ethics* IVp64c). To put the same point positively: 'by reality and perfection I understand the same thing' (*Ethics* IId6). Life seems good when things go well for me and bad when they don't. What changes here is not nature but my circumstances. I mistake the world for my own narrow perspective on it. But given that the world as such has nothing to do with my subjective experience of it, the bad I find in it is not really there. And having no evil in it, the world can only be considered perfect.

Spinoza (*Ethics* IVp68s) suggests that the Biblical story of the tree of knowledge of good and evil should be understood in this light. God prohibited the fruit of this tree to Adam and Eve not out of a jealous concern that such knowledge would make them God-like but because the knowledge of good and evil is *false* and would rob them of their contentment. Having eaten the forbidden fruit, Adam and Eve started thinking in terms of good or evil such that it now appeared as if things could be other than they are (could be either good or bad). Lacking their old certainty that things cannot be otherwise, Adam and Eve began to fear death rather than to live, and, according to Spinoza (*Ethics* IVp67), 'A free man thinks of nothing less than of death, and his wisdom is a meditation on life, not on death.'

It is not only God that is sullied by the human-centred notion that there is evil in the world. At the end of Part I of the *Ethics*, Spinoza makes the all-important link of this confused, anthropocentric theology to human ethics. For just as the doctrine of evil arises from the illusion that God is free (the world might be otherwise than it is), so also human evil is thinkable only on the understanding that we can be otherwise than we are. Indeed, it is only because we think ourselves free that the concepts central to our conventional understanding of ethics have arisen: '*praise* and *blame, sin* and *merit*' (*Ethics* I, Appendix III).

Like Nietzsche after him, Spinoza thinks that the doer is only a fiction added to the deed. The idea that behind every sin there is a 'sinner' assumes that the sin could not have occurred. This assumption is wrong, as Spinoza details in his *Theological-Political Treatise* (3.3.46):

> Given that nobody does anything except by the predetermined order of nature, that is, by the eternal decree and direction of God, it follows that no one chooses any way of life for himself nor brings anything about, except via the particular summons of God.

Before getting to everyday ethics, Spinoza turns, in Part III of his *Ethics*, to human nature. As will be clear by now, Spinoza does not think that we can understand anything apart from its nature. The problem of conventional ethics is that, in making a wrong assessment of human nature, it must also get wrong what can be expected of human behaviour. Spinoza starts with the claim that underlying this misreading of human nature is the fundamental error of taking human being to be something not subject to natural determination: 'they believe that man disturbs, rather than follows, the order of Nature' (*Ethics* III, Preface). This mistake leads, in turn, to a misdirection in ethics (and here Spinoza is targeting Greek ethics, with its idea of virtue as human self-perfectability) whereby people think that 'man' has 'absolute power over his actions, and that he is determined only by himself' (*Ethics* III, Preface). The result of this misattribution of freedom is that, when people prove to be less than angelic, *they* are held responsible for this rather than 'the common power of nature'.

The upshot of this blame game, Spinoza laments, is that those who most disdain human weakness are the ones who are thought to be most godly (*Ethics* III, Preface). Yet the hellfire and damnation announced by the religious leaders who bewail human weakness is not only in error but is likely to rebound on the one preaching it: 'those who know how to find fault with men, to castigate vices rather than to teach virtues, and to break men's minds rather than to strengthen them – they are burdensome both to themselves and to others' (*Ethics* IV, Appendix XIII).

Finding fault with humankind is to find fault with yourself. Spinoza's whole effort, to the contrary, is no longer to condemn but to *understand*: 'not at all to consider men's vices, or to disparage men' (*Ethics* Vp10s). Since nothing happens in nature which is undetermined, then human actions, too, must follow the laws of nature. Vice, no more or less than any other natural thing, must always and everywhere be the same: 'the affects, therefore, of hate, anger, envy, and the like, considered in themselves, follow with the same necessity and force of Nature as any other singular things' (*Ethics* III, Preface). Instead of questioning after human appetites by assuming that they could be otherwise, as the philosophers and preachers do, 'I shall consider [them] just as if it were a question of lines, planes, and bodies' (*Ethics* III, Preface). In place of an ethics (classical and Christian) of morality, Spinoza proposes an ethics akin to geometry.

Spinoza (*Ethics* IIId2) begins this geometrical ethics by specifying that human actions are those actions for which we are the 'adequate cause'. But in place of the void of the will in us being the location of this causality, Spinoza finds our causal actions to follow *'from* our nature' (*Ethics* IIId2, emphasis added). We cause as we are caused. Given that our nature is to have minds, we cause things as these mental causes cause us. But minds can have more or less adequate ideas. Directed by inadequate ideas, our actions are likely to be directed by passion rather than reason, as, for example, when I get angry with my neighbour when he offends me. But if we keep in mind 'that men, like other things, act from the necessity of nature, then the wrong, *or* the hate usually arising from it, will occupy a very small part of the imagination, and will easily be overcome' (*Ethics* Vp10s). Motivated by the (adequate) idea that my neighbour is caused rather than free, I will be able to forgive him. Driven by the (inadequate) idea that he is free, I will shout and scream in my turn. In other words, the affect of anger (or its absence) needs to be referred to the ideas that predominate in my mind, not to some will or decision on my part. Indeed, guided by reason (adequate ideas in the mind), we will not even feel the need to have our neighbour apologise for his actions. For even repentance presupposes 'some deed we believe ourselves to have done from a free decision of the mind', and there *is* no such free decision (*Ethics* III, Definitions of the Affects XXVII).

The notion that people will their actions is an easy mistake to make. After all

> the infant believes he freely wants the milk; the angry child that he wants vengeance; and the timid flight. So the drunk believes it is from a free decision of the mind that he speaks the things he later, when sober, wishes he had not said. So the madman, the chatterbox, the child, and a great many people of this kind believe that they speak from a free decision of the mind, when really they cannot contain their impulse to speak. (*Ethics* IIIp2s)

Ignorant of the causes by which our actions are determined, we see 'decision' where really there is only the expression of an appetite. Even our notions of what is good are implicated here, since we call good whatever it is we strive for, rather than what we strive for being in itself good (*Ethics* IIIp9). Today, for example, we might call exercise good, when really it is just what we desire. Appetite, rather than reason, is what is really driving us to the gym. Going to the gym, the passion for exercise in my mind passes to a greater degree of perfection. This Spinoza (*Ethics* IIIp11s) calls joy but, as we shall see, joy is very different from blessedness and is not something to aim at.

Just as the increased passion for exercise brings me a certain endorphin-fuelled joy, so this joy, in as far as it attaches to the gym, makes me love the gym. For love, '*is nothing but joy with the accompanying idea of an external cause*' (*Ethics* IIIp13s). Hope, too, is born here, since (to stay with our example of exercise) sometimes the gym is unexpectedly closed, and so hope arises that it will be open soon.

Spinoza is telling us that affects like joy, love and hope (and their opposites of sadness, hate and fear), although they *seem* to arise freely within us, are in fact as regular as the lines and planes of geometry. We need not be tossed around by these emotions since, in reality, they are entirely predictable. But we cannot escape them, since desire 'is the very essence of man', who strives above all else 'to preserve in his being' (*Ethics* IVp18). It is more a matter of coming to understand this predictable striving, rather than escaping it. Failing to understand, most people are unable to moderate and restrain affects such as joy or sadness, hope or fear. This Spinoza (*Ethics* IV, Preface) calls bondage. How, then, can we escape these chains and live according to what reason demands?

Spinoza reminds us that reason wants nothing that is contrary to our nature, which means that his ethics, unlike conventional Christian ethics, allow for us loving ourselves and seeking our own advantage (*Ethics* IVp18s). However, guided by reason as free people are, we will want nothing for ourselves that we do not also want for others (*Ethics* IVp18s). I strive for my own advantage, and why shouldn't others too? After all, they share a common nature with me.

But where did this talk of 'free people' arise from suddenly? Hasn't Spinoza told us that we are determined from head to toe? And yet earlier we saw Spinoza (*Ethics* IVp67) write 'A free man thinks of nothing less than of death', so he obviously thinks that people *can* be free. Freedom, for Spinoza, being the same as virtue, does not mean escaping natural necessity. Rather the free man, unlike the man in bondage, is 'determined to do something from the fact that he understands' (*Ethics* IVp23). Note that Spinoza writes '*determined*' to do something. In other words, 'freedom' is not lack of determination (free will) but rather being determined in one's actions by *understanding*. Freedom is not freedom for whatever but freedom for that which the free person understands *must be*. It is not freedom for X or Y but a freedom for X that arises from an understanding that X is how the world *is*. Freedom, virtue and understanding all say the same thing: 'only insofar as the mind understand does it act, and can be said absolutely to act from virtue' (*Ethics* IVp28).

Acting from reason, then, is not a matter of prudence, as it was for the ancients, but really nothing other than 'doing those things which follow from the necessity of our nature'. To follow reason is first to understand the nature of things, not merely to calculate on the basis of experience. It follows that the 'free man' 'strives most of all to conceive things as they are in themselves' (*Ethics* IVp73s). Indeed, striving to conceive things truly will lead us to 'want nothing except what is necessary' (*Ethics* IV, Appendix XXXII). Striving for understanding can therefore end our striving. While there is more than a hint of ancient Stoicism here, Stoicism emphasised the need to moderate our (free) inner responses to (caused) external events – for example not to let grief overwhelm us at the death of a loved one. Spinoza aims at something different. *Understanding* the nature of things is what is important, not Stoic indifference (*apatheia*) to them.

For Spinoza, the source of all true joy or sadness is that things are the way they are. To the extent that we understand our own nature, we will be liberated from that false hope which, as precisely an unclear vision of what we can do, is not where our blessedness lies. Like the ancients, Spinoza does not share our contemporary notion that hope is a fine thing. Hope is the only thing left in Pandora's box (once all the other bad things have flown away) not because the gods are kind but because they love to toy with us. Hope is cruel because it is a deceiver. Only contemplation of things as they truly *are* leads to freedom. On the other hand, emotions that arise from things being *other* than they seem or than we want them to be are false. In other words, what matters is not joy or sadness as such, but that these affects are *true*. This is why, from a Spinozist perspective, questioning is so much more important than the feelings which, today, we are increasingly encouraged to display.

It seems strange that a philosopher who emphasises necessity in all things, including in human-all-too-human creatures such as ourselves, should restore our blessedness. But in returning us to what is necessary, Spinoza (*Ethics* III, Definitions of the Affects III) believes that he enables us to overcome the sadness that is being cut off from what we can do. Sadness is the loss of the *power* of acting rather than anything external lost. By the same token, the opposite of sadness – joy – 'is not perfection itself, but *passing* from less to more of it' (*Ethics* III, Definitions of the Affects III). Perfection is not something apart from our existence, but on the contrary asserts it. The more truth there is in our lives the more perfection we find; just as the more perfection there is the more truth will abound. Our questioning really can set us free.

11 Kant

UP UNTIL LATER LIFE there was little indication that the eighteenth-century German philosopher Immanuel Kant (1724–1804), well-regarded as he was, had any original questions. But then he encountered a problem that placed everything he thought he knew in doubt. This was David Hume's problem as set out in *An Enquiry Concerning Human Understanding* (1748). Hume had pointed out, not unreasonably, that our knowledge of the world is founded on the relation of cause and effect. If asked how we know about this relation, we point to experience. But what experience do we have, *can* we have, of causality as such? In noticing that we only ever *infer* causality rather than being able to experience it directly, Hume posed the wider question of whether our knowledge of the world can ever go beyond our experience of it.

Kant's response (*Prolegomena* 4:260–1) to this challenge, which 'first interrupted my dogmatic slumber', was decisive in the development of critical philosophy. Indeed, as Kant wasn't shy to point out, his critique of dogmatic metaphysics led to a Copernican revolution in philosophy. Given that the original Copernican Revolution had turned the European universe inside-out by showing that the earth moves around the sun rather than the reverse, this was no small boast. But what did Kant mean by it?

Before Kant, Western philosophy had assumed that we can have true knowledge of things. While Descartes and Spinoza believed that error was commonplace, they held that reason could sort truth from falsehood and that, in this way, we could gradually attain complete knowledge of the world and God. Even sceptics of rationalism like Hume did not doubt that our senses give us access to the world. Hume believed that we know only through empirical experience, and therefore know much less than we think we know – as we saw, he doubted that we really *know* causality because this is unavailable to the senses. Causality is only the *habit* of associating one thing with another, no more. But though we can't know relations between things, Hume didn't doubt that we can still know things themselves through our experience of them.

While Kant came to accept Hume's argument against the rationalists (himself included) that we can only know what is given empirically, that we can't go beyond experience, it dawned on Kant that even empiricism had misplaced its confidence. There is no reason why things that we have experience of should be experienced as they really are. All we can ever say is *how they appear to us*: 'What the things may be in themselves I do not know, and also do not need to know, since a thing can never come before me except in appearance' (*Critique of Pure Reason* A277/B333). The thing as it is in itself and the thing as it is intelligible to me are not the same thing, and we can have no access to the former. This is true of everything, even other people and the world taken as a whole. While reason *compels* me to believe that there are other minds besides mine and an outside world beyond us all, because these other souls and the totality can never be objects of my experience, I can never know them. Radicalising Socrates, Kant holds that reason *necessarily* deceives us into thinking that we know what we in fact do not know.

The opening lines of the first edition of the *Critique of Pure Reason* (Avii) read:

> Human reason has the peculiar fate in one species of its cognitions that it is burdened with questions which it cannot dismiss, since they are given to it as problems by the nature of reason itself, but which it also cannot answer, since they transcend every capacity of human reason.

Questioning the sovereignty of metaphysics, the 'queen of all the sciences' (Aviii), Kant notes that, spurred on to ever more questions, metaphysical speculation must lead to 'obscurity and contradiction'.

'[B]ecause the questions never cease, reason sees itself necessitated to take refuge in principles that overstep all possible use in experience' (Aviii). But having sought shelter from the storm of questions in this way, metaphysical questioning steps out beyond 'any touchstone of experience. The battlefield of all these endless controversies is called **metaphysics**' (Aviii). The whole tradition of questioning that descends from Greek philosophy is, for Kant, a questioning to which there *could never be* any definite answers. Metaphysics is pure speculation.

For all Kant's rejection of metaphysics, he retains a very Platonic conception of the distinction between truth and opinion: 'As far as **certainty** is concerned, I have myself pronounced the judgment that in this kind of inquiry it is in no way allowed to **hold opinions**' (Axv). Kant's critique of pure reason is Plato's conception of truth turned from the *objects* of knowledge to knowledge as an object of enquiry itself. Just as our reason should not be satisfied with mere opinions about beings, neither should we settle for reason itself when it becomes a matter only of opinion. And when it comes to what reason can know, Kant (Axvii) does not see himself as offering an opinion concerning which the reader is free to come to another opinion. Kant sees himself as offering us the truth about questioning, not mere speculation.

Kant's rejection of speculative metaphysics is not aimed at the tradition of Greek philosophy in particular. As we saw, in Kant's understanding, *reason itself* deceives. This perversity of reason Kant calls the 'transcendental illusion' (A297/B354). The troubling implication of this illusion is that we are compelled to overstep the limits of reason. Needing to connect *our* concepts, we mistake these subjective connections for objective 'determinations of things in themselves' (A297/B354). For example, forced to find a reason for the world I must necessarily infer God. But just because my reason compels me to posit God does *not* mean, as I am tempted to think, that my reason can know God. Reason trips me up: it makes me mistake my merely mortal perspective for a God's-eye view.

If reason taken on its own terms, '*pure reason*', is a dead-end for questioning, then what terms can we find that will offer a surer path for our questions? For Kant, it is necessary that reason come to awareness of itself and, thereby, to an awareness of its limits:

> reason should take on anew the most difficult of all its tasks, namely, that of self-knowledge, and to institute a court of justice, by which

reason may secure its rightful claims while dismissing all its groundless pretensions, and this not by mere decrees but according to its own eternal and unchangeable laws; and this court is none other than the critique of pure reason itself. (Axi–xii)

Rather than using reason unquestioningly, Kant proposes for the first time to question the faculty of reason. Instead of reason offering us understanding of the world, reason will now become an object of understanding itself. In Kant, the medium of thought becomes the message. But Kant is confident that, in this way, questioning can secure for itself a true road for knowledge:

> It is on this path, the only one left, that I have set forth, and I flatter myself that in following it I have succeeded in removing all those errors that have so far put reason into dissension with itself in its nonexperiential use. I have not avoided reason's questions by pleading the incapacity of human reason as an excuse; rather I have completely specified these questions according to principles, and after discovering the point where reason has misunderstood itself, I have resolved them to reason's full satisfaction. (Axii)

Kant (Axiv) admits that the results of his enquiries into reason are not what dogmatists would wish. By setting reason's limits in experience, he will disappoint those who want to speculate about the soul and the origins of the world, for example. On the other hand, Kant's comprehensive account of reason may be accused of being immodest; yet it is much more modest, he believes, than speculation on those topics, such as the nature of God, which go far beyond human experience.

Kant's question, then, is not so much what we can have knowledge of but what we *can't* know: 'the chief question always remains: "What and how much can understanding and reason cognize free of all experience?" and not: "How is the faculty of thinking itself possible?"' (Axvii) The philosophical word for this concern with the limits of knowledge is epistemology, but Kant is also doing ontology (asking what it is *to be*), since he is saying that what *is* is what appears *for us*.

Kant himself did not question that there is a world beyond appearance, since then nothing could appear at all, but he cut us off from knowledge of this true world. In limiting the powers of our reason,

Kant is the beginning of the end of the humanist tradition which, stretching from the ancients all the way up to the early modern rationalists such as Spinoza, had made human reason God-like in its reach. Taming the hubris of overreaching reason, Kant believed that he had made 'room for faith' (Bxxx). And, indeed, Kant *did* create space in Western thought, although not for the Christian God as he intended, but for that unfathomable Other which is still a major strand of European philosophy today (see, in particular, Levinas 1969).

Kant's realisation that we only ever know things as we experience them led him to develop a formidable account of the conditions of all possible experience. This was Kant's famous transcendental method, and it added a new level of self-awareness to a philosophical tradition that had somehow missed the inescapable role of our minds in all our experience of the world (A94/B126). Given that we can never get outside of our heads, what is it in our heads that allows for experience? What 'faculties' (capacities) must our minds have in order for anything to appear at all?

> There are, however, three original sources (capacities or faculties of the soul), which contain the conditions of the possibility of all experience, and cannot themselves be derived from any other faculty of the mind, namely **sense**, **imagination**, and **apperception**. (A94/B127, see also A115)

Without sense nothing could be perceived. Without imagination I could not bring to mind things not, or no longer, present to the senses. I could not create anything, nor could I have memory. Without 'apperception', a sort of inner sense, I could not be aware that my perceptions are mine: 'The **I think** must **be able** to accompany all my representations' (B131).

When we think about what necessarily conditions experience, another problem arises: given that appearance is always the appearance of something recognisable, which is to say something somehow rounded out and whole, what in us *unifies* how things appear? For example, how do I know that this wall is part of a house given that I see it from one side only? Kant's answer to this question is very complicated, but it involves time and space, which 'contain *a priori* [prior to experience] the conditions of the possibility of objects as appearances' (A89/B121–2).

Time and space are not properties of the world, but of our consciousness of it (A143/B182). Take time: 'Time itself does not elapse, but the existence of that which is changeable elapses in it' (A144/B183). In other words, time is the sense that *we* bring of what persists (identity) in that which changes (difference). My slow, aged dog is connected to the eager puppy of a decade ago by a time concept that I summarise with the name Waldi. Without the time concept that enables me to bring identity (the name Waldi) to a creature that is never the same, Waldi *as* Waldi could not appear at all. We do not acquire the sense of time and space from experience but rather the reverse: without them we could not experience anything, at least nothing coherent.

Time and space, then, are those inner senses by which I am able to unify my experience. Without the sense of space, I could not understand the wholeness of my house – I could not put together the wall of the house that I see with the rest of the house in order to have the understanding that this is indeed a house. As we saw with the example of Waldi, time is crucial too, this time to constructing identities from what always changes (A138–9/B177–8). More fundamentally still, time gives me *me*. Time is that inner sense that identifies me to myself: 'There is only one totality in which all of our representations are contained, namely inner sense and it's *a priori* form, time' (A155/B194). Time is that inner sense which refers all my experiences back to me. When somebody loses her memory, she loses herself.

Space and time can't unify our experience on their own, however. They are necessary for intuition to be possible, but intuition is passive (just as our sight doesn't produce anything, but merely receives what is given to it in the visual field). The role of unifier of experience can't be given to the faculty of the understanding either, since the understanding is unable to intuit anything on its own (recalling that Kant accepts Hume's argument that we cannot go beyond experience). Another faculty must take a leading role, one that *combines* intuition and understanding. Kant suggests that the faculty of the imagination plays this part:

> I perceive that appearances succeed one another, i.e., that a state of things exists at one time the opposite of which existed in the previous state. Thus I really connect two perceptions in time. Now connection is not the work of mere sense and intuition, but is here rather the product of a synthetic faculty of the imagination, which determines inner sense with regard to temporal relations. (A189/B233)

I know this wall to be part of a house because my imagination furnishes my mind with an image that links the different aspects of the house into a whole. The house becomes an object for me not because I sense all of it at once (I can't do this), nor because I can understand it (the understanding has to have something to work with), but because the image 'house' brings together what I can sense of the house with my capacity to think it. Time is inseparable from the role of imagination here. The image brings to mind the resemblance of a new house with one that I have encountered before.

That the imagination unites my intuition with my understanding means that experience is not in direct contact with the world, with things in themselves. Rather, to the extent that it *synthesises* intuition and understanding, everything passes through the imagination. My experience of the world is synthetic. It is *made* – by me. This does not mean that my experience of the world is subjective in the sense of peculiar to me – only that the synthesising role of mind is necessary for the experience of anything whatsoever.

Much later, Heidegger (1990) would argue that Kant was really onto something here – we do not experience things and then order them in imaginative ways; rather imagination is what makes things intelligible in the first place. Heidegger calls this primary role of the imagination 'Being' (which is usually capitalised to differentiate it from beings or things – Being is not a thing, but the context within which things appear). We encounter things only in the wider context that makes sense of them. For example, a hammer, can only *be* a hammer where there is building (which itself presupposes human dwelling). Taken out of this context, as for example when the head of the hammer flies off, it is only a piece of wood and a lump of metal – namely, not a hammer at all.

For all the explanatory power of his emphasis on the role of the imagination, in the second edition of his *Critique of Pure Reason*, Kant (B223–4) came to doubt that the imagination can synthesise our experiences into a unity. The imagination, linked as it is to intuition, must remain 'blind' without the power of concepts to bring it to knowledge. While the image 'house' synthesises my partial impressions of any empirical house, it does so only in the sense of calling to mind what a house is, which depends first on having the *concept* house. In the end, the understanding rules. Does Kant thereby return to the Platonist fold, reneging on his philosophical revolution in the process?

That the imagination fails to mediate fully between intuition and understanding, sliding back into intuition, means that the division between intuition and understanding remains in Kant's critical philosophy. This problem isn't solved by making the understanding mediate, since Kant has already shown that the understanding and intuition are entirely different, and mediation requires some common ground. Kant's turn to the understanding is akin to asking a wife to mediate with her husband in relationship counselling. There needs to be a marriage counsellor who can work with both parties without being identified with either.

Kant's failure to resolve this problem gave Salomon Maimon his opportunity. Unlike Kant, Maimon was an unconventional figure from the Russian Empire who spoke German badly and who spent whatever money he had, which was never much, on beer – indeed, he would sell his conversation for a jug. But Kant (Ak. 11:48) wrote that 'none of my critics understood me and the main questions as well as Herr Maimon does'. This was generous given that Maimon had pointed to a major blind spot in Kant's system: if we can't know things in themselves, then how can they become objects of experience? As we have seen, Kant drew a sharp distinction between the faculty of the understanding, which thinks, and the faculty of the intuition, which passively receives data from the senses (or, in the case of pure intuition, from my encounter with, say, a mathematical proof). As Kant himself said (A51/B75), 'thoughts without content are empty, intuitions without concepts are blind'.

It was Maimon (2010) who first objected that these two faculties must be more closely related than this. If thought can't intuit anything then not only can it not know the thing in itself but it can't know anything at all. Similarly, if intuition is unthinking then how can sensory data be anything other than utter nonsense – mere white noise? Maimon makes this point as follows. Given that 'the business of understanding is nothing but **thinking**', understanding can produce unity in the 'flow' of the object it thinks. But it cannot think (intuit) that object as 'having already arisen' (2010: 22):

> An object requires two parts. First, an intuition [. . .]; second, a rule thought by the understanding, by means of which the relation of the manifold in the intuition is determined. This rule is thought by the understanding *not as flowing* but all at once. On the other hand,

intuition [...] is such that the object can *only be thought as flowing*. (Maimon 2010: 22–3, emphasis added)

To intuit something is to perceive it as arising, that is to say, as coming to be. To *think* that thing, on the other hand, is to arrest this movement in a grasping of its being. But how can awareness of becoming, which is movement, and the understanding of being, which arrests movement, relate to one another? In fact, being thoughtful and being intuitive can't be divided as they are in Kant's account. Experience is always unified.

This conviction that experience is indivisible led Maimon to suggest that although what is given in experience is not something we can know in itself, nonetheless there is no reason to think, as Kant did, that it comes from outside our minds. The material that we think about comes to us from our own minds, which are *productive* of our experience. When we think, we become conscious of that small part of the divine mind that, knowing everything, is thinking in and through us. Like Plotinus and Spinoza before him, for Maimon we are always in God. Our thinking is not cut off from knowledge of God – our thinking *is* God.

There is a sense in which Kant, too, makes our thinking God-like. Kant's Copernican Revolution in philosophy is usually seen as placing limits on human knowledge. But we could equally say that in making finite human minds the condition for anything to appear at all, Kant makes thinking everything. Nothing could *be*, in the sense of appear, if we did not think it.

But is this really where Kant wants to take us? As Heidegger (1990) observes, that things can appear only for our finite minds should be contrasted with divine knowledge for which nothing can appear because everything is already known. God's knowledge, being infinite, is not dependent on anything. The divine mind is what brings things into existence, not what is brought to an awareness of them. Thinking, in other words, is already an indication of human finitude since it depends on thinking things that I did not create. Something has to appear, to show itself, and thinking is dependent on that thing. God, by contrast, thinks everything in advance.

Kant's questions were not limited to 'what can I know?'. In his own words (*Critique of Pure Reason*, A805/B833), 'what must I do?' and 'what may I hope?' were questions that were equally pressing for him.

While the question 'what may I hope?' will not concern us here (the interested reader should refer to Kant's essay 'Perpetual Peace' for more on this), the question 'what should I do?' is the central question of ethics. And Kant's answer to this question refers him to the will. Given the significance of the will to our earlier discussions of Plotinus, Augustine and Duns Scotus, it will be useful to address this topic in the context of modern philosophy (especially given the influence of Kant on contemporary ethics). In particular, I intend to show that Kant's moral law, an idea of pure willing, builds on Augustine's notion that a void lies at the heart of human being. Just as in Augustine the will was created in order to absolve God of responsibility for evil by locating free choice for wrongdoing in us, so in Kant, too, human freedom for good and evil requires the will. Kant's morality, in other words, is unthinkable without Christian theodicy.

Significantly, Kant (1991: 55) starts his *Groundwork of the Metaphysics of Morals* by connecting morality to the sphere of freedom rather than nature. If physics concerns the causality of natural necessity, then ethics is a question of what, being free, must be uncaused. Kant's account of the moral law, even though it goes beyond the practical or applied aspect of moral philosophy to provide a metaphysics of morals, begins here. Like Augustine before him, Kant is staking everything on there being something that escapes the chain of determination, something he admits is not a feature of the natural world. Like Augustine, Kant is looking for this place of non-determination because he is seeking a location for human responsibility: 'the ground of *obligation* must be looked for, not in the nature of man nor in the circumstances of the world in which he is placed, but solely *a priori* [prior to experience] in the concepts of pure reason' (Kant 1991: 58).

Where is this 'ground of obligation' to be found? Like Augustine, Kant finds this ground (which, as undetermined, is more like the absence of ground), to be the will. Only the pure will can *choose* the moral law for the law's own sake rather than out of forced conformity with its commands. Kant (1991: 59) is seeking 'such a will as is completely determined by *a priori* principles apart from any empirical motives and so can be called a pure will'.

Kant's pure will alone has the possibility of being a *good* will (since how can something subject to natural determination be deemed either good or evil?). Indeed, 'It is impossible to conceive of anything at all in the world, or even out of it, which can be taken as good without qualification, except a *good will*' (1991: 63). This good will is not good because it choses some good external to itself, but 'is good through its willing alone – that is, good in itself' (1991: 64). If the good will was good because it submitted to some higher good, then it would not be free and could not be either good or bad. It would be beneath good and evil.

In what sense is the good will good, then? Kant (1991: 65) admits that the idea 'of the absolute value of mere will' is very 'strange'. But it is nonetheless the case that the good will is good not because it submits to a higher code but because it acts according to *reason*. The true function of reason, then, is 'to produce a will which is *good*, not as a *means* to some further end, but *in itself*' (1991: 67). But if reason has the function of producing a good will, then isn't reason the highest good rather than the will?

It isn't. Will 'must be the highest good and the condition of all the rest' (1991: 67). For reason, being purely formal, has no content. Reason can only establish a good will, it cannot be that good itself. The difference here is a question of duty. Reason can tell us what is in conformity with duty, but it cannot act '*from the motive of duty*' (1991: 68). Only the good will can do this. Kant (1991: 68) uses the example of a grocer. If the grocer refrains from overcharging his customers because he reasons that he might get caught, then he acts in conformity with the law. But he cannot in any way be said to be good since his motive for such conformity is purely practical – presumably, if there was no chance of being caught then he would overcharge. The grocer's actions are meaningfully good only if they stem from the motive of duty itself. In other words, a morally good grocer does not overcharge for no other reason than that it is the wrong thing to do. His motive is not fear of punishment, but doing the right thing, also known as duty.

Indeed, so central is the will to goodness, says Kant (1991: 69–70), that our grocer cannot be said to be morally good even if his actions stem from his being a good character (and in this way Kant rejects the whole edifice of Greek ethics, built as it was on virtue). A grocer who does not overcharge because he is a nice guy is no more an example of the good will than a grumpy grocer who would overcharge if he could get away with it. The moral rightness of not overcharging for groceries is not a matter of character but of duty. After all, actions in conformity with character, which is determined (either by birth or experience), cannot be said to be free. Only if our grocer's actions arise from a pure willing of duty can they be said to be morally good: 'It is precisely in this that the worth of character begins to show [...] that he does good, not from inclination, but from duty' (1991: 69–70).

The centrality of duty in Kant's account of morality clearly requires something like Augustine's will, where evil is chosen for no reason at all. Really all Kant does with Augustine's will is to switch the emphasis from un-determined evil actions to un-determined good ones. But the will that does the work remains the same throughout this shift in emphasis. If Augustine has the fallen angels choose rebellion against God for no reason, then Kant, too, emphasises that we must do good for no reason.

Acting without reason is pure willing, as when we say that we did something simply because we could. As Kant (1991: 71–2) acknowledges, if the moral worth of a right action is not any goal sought *by* that action but only the choosing of the action for its own sake, then moral actions rest 'solely on the principle of *volition*': 'Where then can this [moral] worth be found if we are not to find it in the will's relation to the effect hoped for from the action? It can be found nowhere but in *the principle of the will* . . .'.

The famous 'categorical imperative' (the thing that must above all be done) that Kant (1991: 74) extracts from these considerations on will and duty he expresses as follows: I should act only 'in such a way *that I can also will that my maxim should become a universal law*'. The categorical imperative has the appearance of a universal maxim, one that applies in all places and at all times. After all, our grocer only has to ask himself: 'can I will that others should overcharge me as I overcharge them?' in order to know that he can't. The 'do unto others' of Jesus has become 'don't do unto others what you would not have them do to you'. But the appearance of timeless wisdom here should not deceive us: Kant's categorical imperative, the capstone of the entire edifice of his moral law, is thinkable only if there is freedom of the will (the pure will that wills for no other end than willing itself). But the freedom of the will is an idea that emerged because of the requirements of theodicy in the theology of Augustine. Kant's moral law, far from being timeless, has a history, and a strange one at that.

12 Kierkegaard

KANT QUESTIONED WHETHER WE could know things in themselves. But he didn't doubt that we could know the moral law, since that law, while it has a timeless and universal form, has no particular content. To act morally is not a matter of learning a code (for example the Ten Commandments in the Bible). Rather, moral acts are those which any rational person could repeat (what Kant called the 'categorical imperative'). For example, I don't need the Ten Commandments to tell me that murder is wrong since I couldn't reasonably murder anyone. Reasonably here means: will that others should do the same. If I commit murder, I most likely wish to get away with it in my case; but I cannot will that murder in general goes unpunished. I act in a way that my principle of action cannot be made into a general rule. I act only as an individual.

The idea that our actions are ethically significant only if they transcend our individual perspectives was one that Søren Kierkegaard (1813–55) questioned passionately. Kierkegaard does not mean by this that we should depend upon our everyday morality: 'one does what one can' is a phrase that is entirely empty for him (Kierkegaard 2004: 345). Rather, for Kierkegaard, the acts that matter are precisely those in which the individual knowingly abandons the guidance of general principles and *decides* for something that, in other circumstances, would indeed be wrong. Even murder.

We shall look into Kierkegaard's case for murder in a moment. But, for now, it is worth reflecting that Kierkegaard has a point. Can *general* principles of action such as Kant's 'categorical imperative' really help us other than *in general*? For example, while murder as such is undoubtedly a problem, would killing a Nazi collaborator in occupied France be the wrong thing to do if you were a resistance fighter? Indeed, would there be anything else *to do* in such difficult and dangerous circumstances?

Kierkegaard's case for murder is for a murder that, at the very last moment, didn't happen. But the would-be murderer was in the process of plunging the knife into his victim before he was stopped. And he didn't stop on his own behalf but because God intervened. That man was Abraham. His victim? His very own son, Isaac. In his book *Fear and Trembling*, Kierkegaard (1985) takes a close look at this strange and compelling Bible story. Genesis 22:1 tells us that an aged Abraham was told by God: 'Take your son, your only son, whom you love – Isaac – and go to the region of Moriah. Sacrifice him there as a burnt offering on a mountain I will show you.'

Kierkegaard is gripped by the faith that Abraham showed in response to this awful command. For the Bible tells us that Abraham neither shied away from his terrible task, nor resigned himself to his fate, but simply expected God to remain true to his promise to bless all nations through Isaac. While there have been many 'knights of faith', 'greater than all was Abraham, great with that power whose strength is powerlessness, great in that wisdom whose secret is folly, great in that hope whose outward form is insanity' (Kierkegaard 1985: 50).

Although *Fear and Trembling* is an essay on faith, Kierkegaard had the idealist philosophy that followed in the wake of Kant in his sights (especially Hegel's philosophy, which was dominant in Kierkegaard's day). Kierkegaard wants to know what has become of the individual, and the agony of individual decision, in the all-embracing philosophical systems erected by German Idealism. This is why Kierkegaard has had an enduring influence on so-called existentialist philosophy, from the early Heidegger (about whom more later) to Sartre. Existentialists think that human life is defined by freedom, such that questioning is something we have to do for ourselves rather than by finding the answers in a philosophical system.

In Hegel (1991), the direction of ethical life is one that moves *away* from the individual in the direction, first, of the family, second, civil society and, finally and most completely, the state. Not unlike Kant, Hegel thought that individual actions are redeemed of their particularity (their self-interestedness) only when they are brought into relation with the universal, which for Hegel (1991: 276) is the state. The state reconciles the competing interests of civil society, just as civil society reconciles the competing interests of families and families the egoism of the individual. We can see that ethical life, in Hegel, must leave the life of the individual behind.

Shortly before writing *Fear and Trembling* Kierkegaard had studied in Berlin, a city steeped in the philosophy of Hegel, who had died there only ten years earlier. Kierkegaard knew Hegelian philosophy well. And he would have none of it. Of the Hegelians, Kierkegaard (1985: 90) wrote:

> They live in their thoughts, secure in life, they have a *permanent* position and *sure* prospects in a well-organized State; they are separated by centuries, even millennia, from the convulsions of existence; they have no fear that such things could happen again; what would the police and the newspapers say?

The Hegelians, secure in the System, have forgotten the only question that really matters, the question of existence. Hegelian philosophy sees only the ways in which inner life is shaped by the world. In other words, it finds that every life is equivalent to (commensurable with) every other. Kierkegaard (1985: 96) asks: 'is there nothing incommensurable in a human life?' The paradox of faith, in truth of every real decision, is that, at the moment of decision, that lack of equivalence is indeed found. Then, 'interiority is higher than exteriority'. Nobody can decide in my place.

> Living as the individual is thought to be the easiest thing of all, and it is the universal that people must be coerced into becoming. I can share neither this fear nor this opinion, and for the same reason. No person who has learned that to exist as the individual is the most terrifying thing of all will be afraid of saying it is the greatest [...] To think that existing as an individual is an easy enough matter implies a very dubious indirect admission with regard to oneself. ...
> (Kierkegaard 1985: 102)

The question of existence is the question of how to *live*. It is a question that most people avoid. In *Concluding Unscientific Postscript* (2009: 512), Kierkegaard uses the cultural Christianity of his day as an example of this avoidance strategy. Kierkegaard contrasts the notion that one is a Christian because one lives in a Christian culture, with Christianity as 'an existence-communication':

> The task is to become a Christian and to continue being one, and the most dangerous of all illusions is to be so certain of being a Christian that one has to defend the whole of Christendom against the Turk – instead of protecting one's own faith against the illusion about the Turk.

Not abstractions like 'Christendom' but my *own life* is what is at stake in existence. Christianity, as something that must be lived, is not identification with, nor even becoming a member of, the Church. It is decided 'not by that which has gone on *in* the individual, but by what has gone on *with* the individual'; not by outward baptism but by inwardness (Kierkegaard 2009: 513).

If religion overlooks that no one can live my life for me, then so does philosophy. In *Fear and Trembling*, Kierkegaard wonders repeatedly how it is possible that the philosophical questions of his day all 'go further' than the question asked by Abraham: what am *I* to do? If Abraham is remembered as the father of faith it is because this alone was his question, a question that he could receive no help with because, in his case, it was a question that already has an irrefutable answer: murder is wrong! Indeed, how could Abraham even *ask* for help with his question? If someone asked you whether or not they should sacrifice their son, what would you say to them? If morality is closely related to transparency (I only do that which I could wish all others to do in my place), Abraham's question is by contrast completely opaque and he must remain silent. For nobody could possibly understand. Abraham must decide entirely alone.

While the questions that go further than faith are questions that can have timeless answers, Kierkegaard saw that the living of a life is not much helped by this. Kierkegaard compared the fixation on eternal truths to King Midas's wish for his touch to turn everything to gold. When this wish was granted, Midas grew immeasurably rich while slowly starving to death (since even his food turned to gold). Conventional wisdom 'believes it is enough to have knowledge of large truths. No other work is necessary. But then it does not get its bread, it starves to death while everything is transformed into gold' (Kierkegaard 1985: 57–8).

'Large truths' cannot judge for me in the moment of decision. For example, just because Hegel has told us that ethical life goes beyond the individual in the direction of family does not help *me* to decide whether to marry. Indeed, Kierkegaard broke off his engagement to his beloved Regine, a decision that preoccupied him for the rest of his life (not least in *Fear and Trembling*, where it simmers between the lines of his discussion of Abraham).

Having agonised over Regine, Kierkegaard was intent on bringing the much greater agony of Abraham's decision to our attention. We know that Abraham's story has a happy ending, which makes us forgetful of his experience, of the three terrible days during which he has to make the long march to Moriah under the burden of God's death sentence on his son and himself as the executioner. Kierkegaard insists that Abraham's decision to trust the outcome to God, to have faith, is based on nothing other than the absurd. How could God, having promised him this son, now demand his sacrifice? And if God's command makes little sense, how much less does the hope that he will rescue Isaac from it. Abraham really has no *reasons* for his faith in God.

The *madness* of every true decision is that, if it really is a decision, then we can have no grounds for deciding either way. If we have these grounds, then there is not really a decision to make. Decisions are made in the void. While the stakes in our decision-making are rarely of the magnitude of Abraham's, the same is true of them too. If I had guarantees that my prospective marriage would be a long and happy one, for example, then would I really be choosing it? Faith is a leap into the unknown; Abraham 'believed the absurd'.

As Kierkegaard emphasises repeatedly, the paradox of Abraham is that he is remembered as a hero of faith because he really, truly contemplated (and very nearly carried out) a monstrous act that no ethical code or moral law could countenance. Abraham was willing not only to murder, but to murder his own son! If he had been ethical in a Kantian or Hegelian sense then Abraham, knowing that God's command was only a temptation to sin, would have turned away from it in horror. After all, the only distinction between Abraham's willingness to sacrifice Isaac and his willingness to murder Isaac is in Abraham himself. Only Abraham's faith changes murder into sacrifice. There is nothing of ethics, with its indifference to individual context, here at all. Given this, Abraham would perhaps have done well to reject God's command. But then we would never have heard of him. For to 'decide' ethically is not really to decide at all but to let general principles do the work for us. And if Abraham had done this then he could not have been the father of faith.

Abraham's decision to carry out God's monstrous command not only ignores the Kantian imperative to do only that which all others could do the same, it actively suspends it. Abraham places himself *above* morality. His act is possible only to the extent that he has great faith, a faith that other people lack. Abraham knows that just because God wouldn't ask this of other people does not mean that it isn't being asked of *him*.

To the extent that philosophy replaces this painful awareness of questions that are particular to me (what Kierkegaard calls 'the shudder of thought') with the anaesthetising certainty of universal answers, it betrays its own roots in questioning. Socrates, by contrast, went no further than doubting everything.

> What those old Greeks, whom one must credit with a little knowledge of philosophy, took to be the task of a whole lifetime, doubt not being a skill one acquires in days and weeks [. . .] is where nowadays everyone begins. (1985: 42)

Even Descartes's injunction to doubt everything was one he gave to himself rather than offering it up as a categorical imperative: 'for Descartes was a quiet and lonely thinker, not a bellowing street-watch' (Kierkegaard 1985: 42). True philosophy does not seek to provide an example for others but only to question itself.

Kierkegaard distinguishes the shudder of questioning from world-weary resignation, where, once again, the *un*-decidability of the true decision is ducked. If Abraham had journeyed to Moriah in head-hanging submission then he would have been very brave, but he would not have been a hero of faith; 'for it is great to give up one's desire, but greater to stick to it having given it up' (Kierkegaard 1985: 52). This is also the distinction between the 'knight of faith' that is Abraham and the tragic hero. Even though Agamemnon must sacrifice his daughter Iphigenia in order for the Greek ships to set sail for Troy, everyone will understand his decision and admire his bravery. For although most people are incapable of such an act, it is an act taken for the common good rather than for self and in that sense it remains universal like all ethical actions. Agamemnon does not give *everything* up, since he becomes the hero even because of his tragedy.

Abraham, by contrast, not only decides alone but also knows that the future will abandon him. The agony of his decision to sacrifice his child will not be offset by a glorious posterity such as Agamemnon can hope for. With Isaac's death, Abraham's future dies also. Not only does his terrible act not save his nation, neither does it even save his family. Nothing wider is at stake in Abraham's actions than his own faith. From the perspective of ethics it is a profoundly selfish act, even if it is not mad. Universal condemnation is the only fate that those who 'overstep the ethical' in the name of some higher goal can expect.

Abraham's faith is a rebuke to philosophy's pretensions to be able to think everything. Kierkegaard admits that his thought stumbles on Abraham and that, while he can admire him, he cannot claim to fathom his faith. The faith of Abraham 'begins precisely where thinking leaves off' (Kierkegaard 1985: 82). As Kierkegaard (1985: 75) portrays it, it is faith in the absurd, which is another way of saying that it is faith in that which goes beyond our understanding: 'The absurd is not one distinction among others embraced by the understanding. It is not the same as the improbable, the unexpected, the unforeseen.' Faith presupposes complete resignation as far as the understanding is concerned – Isaac must die, and the dead stay dead – even as it continues to hope for the impossible – God will raise him up again.

Kierkegaard seems to be making more than just a religious point here. As he says, faith is not an 'inclination of the heart' but really 'the paradox of existence' (Kierkegaard 1985: 76). Unlike the Hegelians, who merely secularise the religious idea of a providential plan, I must resign myself to the loneliness of existence. I must let go of any idea that my life will be taken up in some larger purpose. Nevertheless, on the strength of the absurd, my complete resignation in the face of existence is the first step towards *winning* my existence. I exist more passionately than ever now that I have loved existence even despite its indifference to me: 'to exist in such a way that my opposition to existence expresses itself every instant as the most beautiful and safest harmony'. A little further on, Kierkegaard (1985: 79) returns to this theme of grasping 'the whole of existence on the strength of the absurd':

> To live joyfully and happily in this way every moment on the strength of the absurd, every moment to see the sword hanging over the loved one's head and yet find, not repose in the pain of resignation, but joy on the strength of the absurd – that is wonderful.

As we shall see in the next chapter, this thought is close to heart of what Nietzsche wanted to say, too.

Very unlike Nietzsche, however, Kierkegaard insists that the 'I' that must grasp its existence is something that only Christianity can give us. Beyond the empty abstraction of the Greek concept 'man', Kierkegaard sees the doctrine of sin as the individuating element in Christian culture: *I* am guilty before God, not generic humankind.

Kierkegaard lays out this argument in *The Sickness unto Death* (1989). In this text we find some of the earliest elements of an 'existentialist' philosophy as developed by Heidegger, Sartre and others in the twentieth century. Early in his discussion, Kierkegaard once again implicitly challenges the notion, central to the Hegelian philosophy of his time, that everything is decided at the level of the totality, concretely embodied in the state. It is only at this level, for Hegel, that individual, not to mention social, contradictions are reconciled in a higher unity. From the lofty perspective of this System, however, 'The biggest danger, that of losing *oneself*, can pass off in the world as quietly as if it were nothing; every other loss, an arm, a leg, five dollars, a wife etc. is bound to be noticed' (Kierkegaard 1989: 63, emphasis added). Taking your appointed place in the whole is, for Kierkegaard, a living death. In the System, it is only by losing oneself that one 'gains all that is required for a flawless performance in everyday life, yes, for making a great success out of life'. Ground 'as smooth as a pebble' in this way, the System-man is 'as exchangeable as a coin of the realm' (Kierkegaard 1989: 64). Bureaucrats, teachers, lawyers, social workers: none of them needs to be *me*.

What the person of the System lacks is *possibility*. And while possibility can itself be a problem, 'A self that has no possibility is in despair' (Kierkegaard 1989: 65). For only possibility saves:

> When someone faints, people shout for water, Eau-de-Cologne, Hoffman's drops. But for someone who is on the point of despair it is: get me possibility, get me possibility, the only thing that can save me is possibility! A possibility and the despairer breathes again, he revives; for without possibility it is as though a person cannot draw breath. (Kierkegaard 1989: 69)

This emphasis on the self and its possibilities sounds very contemporary. But it bears repeating that Kierkegaard, a Christian, believed that the 'I' emerges only as a sinner before God. The self will find itself solely by losing itself in repentance.

Where does this sin come from? Echoing Augustine, Kierkegaard is in no doubt that it emerges in the will which, knowing what is right, nonetheless does wrong. Discussing the Socratic definition of evildoing as actions based on ignorance of what is right, Kierkegaard (1989: 122) writes: 'What then is the missing component in Socrates' specification of sin? It is the will, defiance.' Socratic 'sin', as mere ignorance, gives to sin no positive content at all: I act badly only because I *lack* knowledge of what is good. For Kierkegaard, such a conception of sin is too abstract. While it may be true that, taken generally, 'men' do what is wrong because they lack awareness of what is right, 'In the actual world, on the other hand, where we do bring in the individual person, there is this tiny little transition from having understood something to doing it' (Kierkegaard 1989: 126). If this moment of transition is very quick, nonetheless, 'a very lengthy story begins at this point' (Kierkegaard 1989: 126).

The story that begins at this point is the story of the will. What the will *thinks* of the knowledge that a person has is decisive. Since, following Augustine, Kierkegaard believes that the will sits atop 'the whole of man's lower nature', there is always a struggle between a person's knowledge and her base desire (Kierkegaard 1989: 126). The will is far from guaranteed to obey the former. This is especially true over time. For if the will does not like the knowledge that it possesses, it does not have to disobey, only to delay. Subject to this delay, 'the knowing becomes more and more obscured, and the lower nature more and more victorious. For, alas!, the good must be done immediately, directly it is known' (Kierkegaard 1989: 126).

For Kierkegaard, this insight explains the problem with ethical life when it is abstracted from individual existence. Wanting always to *know* more, the Greek mind endlessly defers the moment of real ethical decision. The libraries full of philosophical knowledge are, ethically speaking, only 'a distraction' (Kierkegaard 1989: 127).

Unlike the Greek concept 'man', the category of sin particularises. 'Sin cannot at all be thought speculatively' in the manner of philosophy since 'the particular human lies below the level of the concept' (Kierkegaard 1989: 152). In this sense, the individual begins with Christianity, specifically with the doctrine of sin (Kierkegaard 1989: 153). In saying that not 'man' but *you and I* are the sinners, this doctrine alone 'splits up "the crowd"' (Kierkegaard 1989: 154). The individual is first an offender before God, namely an individual *sinner*, before she is an individual as such.

None of our categories, not even those we cherish the most (and who doesn't want to be an individual today?), lacks a history. And that history, as Nietzsche said, is often of the most shameful kind.

13 Nietzsche

LIKE KIERKEGAARD'S, FRIEDRICH NIETZSCHE'S fundamental question concerns individual existence. Unlike Kierkegaard's, it is a test of strength rather than of faith. Nietzsche (1844–1900) wants to know whether it is possible to say an unreserved 'yes!' to life, though he doubts that anyone is strong enough for this in his own day (*A*, 'Preface'). In place of otherworldliness, other worlds where we have it all (even eternal life), Nietzsche wants to affirm *this* world and *this* life that we suffer in. This means ceasing to pretend that there is another world. Indeed, for Nietzsche, such otherworldliness is the very nihilism that has eaten away at the soul of European culture. The more truth has been linked with the elsewhere of eternity, the more mortal life has been cursed by its identification with falsehood. Even wise Socrates (who started this whole business of asking after what does not change) was tired of life and grateful for the balm of approaching of death – why else would his final act be to ask for a sacrifice to the Greek god of medicine? (*TI*, 'Socrates', 1) And as for Plato, his desire for death was surely even stronger, as Seneca (2007: 79) suggested in his *Consolation to Marcia*:

> And great souls are never happy to linger in the body: they long to depart and to burst forth, and feel resentment at their narrow confines, accustomed as they are to roving on high over the universe and to looking down with scorn from their lofty seat on the world of men. This is what lies behind Plato's cry that the man of wisdom makes death the focus of his whole mind, desires it and dwells on

it in his thoughts and, because he yearns for it, passes through life striving for what lies beyond.

Why is it so difficult to affirm mortal, earthly existence? Nietzsche is unsure how to answer this question; unsure whether it is difficult for *all* people to affirm change, or whether it is a particularly European disease. No doubt it is a temptation of all mortals to cling to what does not change:

> We have projected the conditions of *our* preservation as *predicates of being* in general. We have taken the fact that in order to prosper we have to be stable in our belief, and made of it that the 'true world' is not one which changes and becomes, but one which *is*. (*Writings from the Late Notebooks*, note 9[38])

For all that it is a universal problem, however, Nietzsche observes that the denigration of change, which he often calls 'Platonism', is very ancient in European culture. Even the pre-Socratic philosopher, Parmenides, claims that the appearance of change is only an illusion:

> Grant me, ye gods, but one certainty . . . if it be but a log's breadth on which to lie, on which to ride upon the sea of uncertainty. Take away everything that comes to be, everything lush, colourful, blossoming, illusory, everything that charms and is alive. Take away all these for yourselves and grant me but one and only, poor certainty. (In *PTAG*, 11)

Meanwhile, a cryptic fragment from another pre-Socratic philosopher, Anaximander, reads:

> Where things have their origin,
> There also their destruction happens,
> According to necessity;
> For they give to each other justice and recompense
> For their injustice
> In conformity with the ordinance of Time.

Nietzsche (*PTAG*, 4) interprets this fragment as evidence that Anaximander saw existence as an illegitimate emancipation from eternal being, a wrong for which destruction is the only way to atone. Life is in debt to eternity.

Nevertheless, despite this evidence from the pre-Socratics, the identification of the world that does not change as truer than our world of change becomes decisive in Platonism. For Nietzsche (*BGE*, Preface), then, the 'true world' appears first with Plato: 'the worst, most prolonged, and most dangerous of all errors to this day was a dogmatist's error, namely Plato's invention of pure spirit and the Good in itself'.

Platonic ideas are truer, because unchanging, than their mundane copies, and the 'world' where these ideas reside, even if it is not yet the heavenly beyond of Christianity, points the way to otherworldliness. This is why Nietzsche famously quips, in the Preface to *Beyond Good and Evil*, that Christianity is merely Platonism for plebs. Christianity absorbed the two worlds of Greek metaphysics, which it then passed on to European culture as the heaven-earth distinction and the increasingly explicit condemnation of everything earthly. For Christianity radically breaks apart the two worlds of Greek metaphysics, where access to the true world (albeit only for the true philosopher), is still possible in *this* life. Now access to the true world is given fully only in death (to those who are saved, that is). The true world is not only other than our world – it is utterly beyond it. The true world has become the other world.

This genealogy of the true world, which is effectively the history of otherworldliness, explains why, in most of Nietzsche's writings, there is a strong identification with precisely what is earthly, as *Thus Spoke Zarathustra* (Prologue, 3) makes clear:

> I beseech you, my brothers, *remain faithful to the earth* and do not believe those who speak to you of extra-terrestrial hopes! [. . .] Once the sacrilege against God was the greatest sacrilege, but God died, and then all these desecrators died. Now to desecrate the earth is the most terrible thing, and to esteem the bowls of the unfathomable higher than the meaning of the earth!

From the perspective of the other (true) world, our (false) world seems intangible and lightweight, passing away at every moment. It only *appears* to be. And in one sense, Nietzsche's entire project, and his answer to nihilism, is to reverse this and to say: No! The true world is what is appearance, and our world of appearance is what is true. This is a consistent theme in Nietzsche's work, as can be seen from the following sample, in that order, of two earlier works (*Human All Too Human* and *Daybreak*); two mature works (*Zarathustra* and *On the Genealogy of Morality*); and two late works (*Twilight of the Idols* and *Ecce Homo*):

> When we hear ingenious metaphysicians and [*Hinterweltler*, otherworldly ones] talk, we others may feel that we are 'poor in spirit', but we also feel that ours is the kingdom of Heaven of change, with spring and autumn, winter and summer, and that theirs is the [otherworld] – with its grey, frosty, unending mist and shadow. . . . (*HH* II, 17)

> World of phantoms in which we live! Inverted, upside-down, empty world, yet dreamed of as full and upright! (*D*, 118)

> But 'the other world' is well hidden from humans, that dehumaned, inhuman world that is a heavenly nothing. (*Z* I, 'On the Hinterworldly')

> Away with this "world turned upside down"!' (*GM* III, 14)

> The 'apparent' world is the only world: the 'true world' is just a *lie added on to it*. (*TI*, 'Reason', 2)

> The concept of the 'beyond', the 'true world', invented to devalue the *only* world there is. (*EH*, 'Destiny', 8)

Turning the tables on the metaphysicians and theologians, Nietzsche calls the true world false and the false world true. The change-less world is not and the world of change *is*!

A question therefore confronts Nietzsche: if the true world is a curse on life, what should we do with it? At first glance the answer to this question is obvious: just get rid of it. The other world is false. We have no more need of it. We've grown out of it. Nietzsche, as we have seen, follows something like this reasoning himself for a while: the true world is a lie! But then he starts to have some doubts. Is *denial* of this other world really the answer to nihilism?

In *The Gay Science* (published 1882), Nietzsche begins to acknowledge that the 'false world' that he has been affirming (a world of chance and contingency) is only a shadow cast by the true world. He notices that it is 'only against a world of purposes' that the world 'accident' has any meaning (*GS*, 109). He also admits that the true world cannot be torn down through an account of its origins in human needs and drives. The 'misty shroud of delusion' by which the true world came to count as real will be dispersed not by more reality but by new creations: 'Only as creators can we destroy.' 'There is another world to discover – and more than one! On to the ships, you philosophers!' (*GS*, 289). This is also why Nietzsche's Zarathustra does not want *the* meaning of the earth but the *creation* of 'a meaning for the earth!' (*Z* I, 'On the Hinterworldly'). There is no true world; rather, those who invent new values are the axis around which the world turns (*Z* I, 'On the Flies of the Marketplace').

But isn't the creation of new worlds still an away-from-here, still otherworldliness? It dawns on Nietzsche that not only is the true world something to be overcome, but that the true world was *necessary* to the possibility of other worlds. Nietzsche senses this as early as *Zarathustra* (published 1883), where we read:

> I ever sat jubilating where old gods lie buried, blessing the world, loving the world, next to the monuments of old world maligners – because I love even churches and God's graves, once the sky's pure eye gazes through their broken roofs. (*Z* III, 'The Seven Seals', 2)

In *Zarathustra*, the blue sky stands for chance or contingency and is to be contrasted with the heavy clouds of providence – what Nietzsche calls the 'spirit of gravity' (*Z* I, 'On Reading and Writing'). Zarathustra loves even churches, and not just because they now have holes in their roofs, but because it is only *through* these very holes that the blue sky of possibility first gazes with its pure eye. Even the true world is to be loved, for only its death has given us the possibility of new worlds.

It is in *Twilight of the Idols* (written in August 1888) that Nietzsche most emphatically breaks with the idea that the true world can be answered by exposing it as a lie. In a section entitled 'How the True World Finally Became a Fable: The History of an Error', Nietzsche describes ridding ourselves of the true world as only the penultimate stage of this error: 'The "true world" – an idea that is of no further use, not even as an obligation, – now an obsolete, superfluous idea, *consequently* a refuted idea: let's get rid of it!'

However, the *final* stage by which the true world is overcome is described as follows:

> The true world is gone: which world is left? The illusory one, perhaps? ... But no! we got rid of the illusory world along with the true one! (Noon; moment of the shortest shadow; end of the longest error; high point of humanity; INCIPIT ZARATHUSTRA.). (*TI*, 'World')

The death of the true world kills off the false world, too. After all, the latter was only a shadow cast by the former. What are we left with? Nietzsche implies that we are left with nothing. But, looking more carefully, Nietzsche does not describe this nothing as nothingness. It is rather the noontime of humanity! For the nihilism that the death of the true world ushers in is the opportunity for something beyond the human: enter Zarathustra, who announces the overman (*Übermensch*) (*Z* I, Prologue, 3).

So far, I have summarised Nietzsche's thought under the heading of the true world in order to give an impression of the arc of that thinking. Nietzsche starts by affirming this world and denying the true world; but he ends up affirming even the true world, or at least the history of the true world.

But Nietzsche did not think that affirming our history, or fate, was the only thing we need to say yes to. Central to Nietzsche's attempt at an affirmative thinking is the affirmation of suffering, also. Indeed, Schopenhauer, the philosopher who was revered by the young Nietzsche, is rejected precisely because, in Nietzsche's opinion, he cannot do this. Schopenhauer (2004) teaches that life is suffering, but he holds this *against* life. Nietzsche views this as a pessimism of weakness. Nietzsche's pessimism of strength, by contrast, sees suffering as no objection to life: 'Was *that* life? Well then! One More Time!', as Zarathustra puts it (*Z* III, 'On the Vision and the Riddle', 1). Nietzsche (*EH*, 'The Birth of Tragedy', 3) therefore sees himself as the first truly *tragic* philosopher, where tragic philosophy is the antipode of pessimistic philosophy:

> My new version of *pessimism*: willingly to seek out the dreadful and questionable sides of existence: which made clear to me related phenomena of the past. 'How much "truth" can a spirit endure and dare?' – a question of its strength. The *outcome* of a pessimism like

this *could be* that form of a Dionysian *saying Yes* to the world as it is, to the point of wishing for its absolute recurrence and eternity: which would mean a new ideal of philosophy and sensibility. (*Writings from the Late Notebooks*, note 10[3])

Nietzsche believed that what he called the 'Tragic Age' of the Greeks was, to date, the only moment in European history when suffering was affirmed. In the plays of the ancient Greek tragedians such as Aeschylus, for example, we are presented with an image of life as tragedy. Nietzsche admires an epoch which did not hide from the suffering of mortal existence.

But the Tragic Age is long gone. Indeed, in keeping with his assessment of the slow decline of European culture towards contemporary nihilism, Nietzsche dismissed the values of this culture as decadent in precisely the same sense as pessimistic philosophy: they are based in flight from the suffering of existence, a flight which takes the form of revenge against life itself. Particularly in *On the Genealogy of Morality*, Nietzsche argues that the Christian morals that continue to dominate European culture are based on what he calls this great 'slave revolt' of resentment against life:

The beginning of the slaves' revolt in morality occurs when ressentiment itself turns creative and gives birth to values: the ressentiment of those beings who, denied the proper response of action, compensate for it only with imaginary revenge. Whereas all noble morality grows out of a triumphant saying 'yes' to itself, slave morality says 'no' on principle to everything that is 'outside', 'other', 'non-self': and this 'no' is its creative deed. (*GM* I, 10)

The slave revolt that lies behind morality involves those who suffer the most from life turning all the values of life on their head. All that works *against* life's creative force (for example humility) is now celebrated as good while all that works for it (for example pride) is deemed evil. But there can be no values higher than life. Indeed, the idea that there are moral laws that stand over us is what first made God necessary (*A*, 25). Lacking any foundation in this world, another world was needed (the true world), where these morals could issue from.

The driving force behind morals such as 'love you neighbour' and 'the first will be last' is resentment of the healthy by the sick (Nietzsche, himself very sickly, does not mean physical sickness but, more classically, sickness of the soul). Driven by bitterness at the strong, morality makes the 'healthy' feel sick, and the sick healthy:

> here, the web of the most wicked conspiracy is continually being spun, – the conspiracy of those who suffer against those who are successful and victorious, here, the sight of the victorious man is *hated* [. . .] [A]s though health, success, strength, pride and the feeling of power were in themselves depravities for which penance, bitter penance will one day be exacted: oh, how ready they themselves are, in the last resort, to *make* others penitent, how they thirst to be *hangmen*! (*GM* III, 14)

While the poor in spirit pretend, as much to themselves, that they want to bring the strong to account, actually they want power for themselves: 'The will of the sick to appear superior in *any* way, their instinct for secret paths, which lead to tyranny over the healthy, – where can it not be found, this will to power of precisely the weakest!' (*GM* III, 14) This, for Nietzsche, is Christianity in a nutshell. He finds it genuinely baffling that the mighty Roman Empire, an Empire of the strong if ever there was one, was turned on its head by an itinerant preacher from dusty, dirt-poor Judea, an outpost of the Empire. And yet who is worshipped in Rome today? Caesar or the crucified one?

A common misunderstanding of Nietzsche arises at this point, one that was even exploited by the Nazis to make Nietzsche seem like their philosopher. Nietzsche a Nazi? This is a man who called for anti-Semites to be shot! While it might seem as if Nietzsche is calling for a return to a slave-based society in which the strong rule over the weak, Nietzsche's work, taken as a whole, easily rebuts this simplistic misreading.

What sustains this misreading more than anything else is the idea that the 'overman' (who Nietzsche's Zarathustra sets as a goal for humanity) is a kind of proto-fascist strongman: '"I teach you the overman." Human being is something that must be overcome' (*Z* I, Prologue, 3). Given the parodic style of *Thus Spoke Zarathustra*, it is very possible that Nietzsche intends Zarathustra as the parody of a prophet and his teachings as anti-teachings (Zittel 2000). This reading has Zarathustra teaching nothing other than the end of all teachings. The concept of the overman, collapsing in on itself (true self-overcoming finds 'itself' with no self at all), encourages us to abstain from doctrines altogether (Stegmaier 2006). But even if this form of anti-teaching is not what Nietzsche intends, that the overman is anything *but* a fascistic ideal is made clear in Part IV of *Zarathustra*. In this part, which concludes the work, Nietzsche's Zarathustra meets a range of 'higher men' – people such as kings, scientists, creative geniuses, popes and the like – who are clearly 'above' the common herd. Zarathustra invites these higher types, who are characterised as sick themselves, to convalesce in his cave in the mountains. Here he tells them that even the higher man is something that must be overcome.

The higher type is not the overman. Nietzsche does not want masters who sacrifice the weak at the altar of their strength, but people who are able to sacrifice (in the sense of overcome) *themselves*. This is the overman. Nietzsche's idea of life as a vital, creative force, means that those who would preserve themselves are the problem – as much the higher as the lower types. Nietzsche wants to deliver us all to the childlike innocence of being able to become *other* than we are: 'Do the majority not *believe* in *themselves* as in complete *fully-developed facts*? Have the great philosophers not put their seal on this prejudice with the doctrine of the unchangeability of character?' (*D*, 560)

In his late works, Nietzsche returns to a Greek divinity that had obsessed him in his youth – Dionysus. As the god who suffers death and rebirth in *this* life (rather than being raised to heaven in the manner of the Son of God), Nietzsche is making Dionysus the god of those who would overcome even themselves. Indeed, the last line of Nietzsche's last work, *Ecce Homo* ('Destiny', 9), reads: 'Have I been understood? – *Dionysus versus the crucified* . . . .' If there be any doubt that overcoming Christianity was Nietzsche's ambition, note that he wrote a book with the title *The Antichrist*. What is Nietzsche's chief objection to the crucified one? It is that Christ *pities* humanity's suffering and offers a way out of it – eternal life. As we saw, only the affirmation of life's suffering will suffice for Nietzsche. The question of whether we are capable of this Nietzsche poses as follows: could we will that *this* life recur eternally ever the same? This is the question of all questions. In *The Gay Science* (341), he sets out this question as follows:

> *The heaviest weight.* – What if some day or night a demon were to steal into your loneliest loneliness and say to you: 'This life as you now live it and have lived it you will have to live once again and

innumerable times again; and there will be nothing new in it, but every pain and every joy and every thought and sigh and everything unspeakably small or great in your life must return to you, all in the same succession and sequence – even this spider and this moonlight between the trees, and even this moment and I myself. The eternal hourglass of existence is turned over again and again, and you with it, speck of dust!' Would you not throw yourself down and gnash your teeth and curse the demon who spoke thus? Or have you once experienced a tremendous moment when you would have answered him: 'You are a god, and never have I heard anything more divine.' If this thought gained power over you, as you are it would transform and possibly crush you; the question in each and every thing, 'Do you want this again and innumerable times again?' would lie on your actions as the heaviest weight! Or how well disposed would you have to become to yourself and to life *to long for nothing more fervently* than for this ultimate eternal confirmation and seal?

The heaviest weight for Nietzsche, the thing that he found the hardest to wish to repeat eternally, is Christianity. In the end, though, Nietzsche realises that the test of eternal recurrence means affirming even the Christian otherworldliness that he had spent years denouncing. This is why, as we saw earlier, Nietzsche claims that the 'true world' (also known as God) is finally overcome *not* by calling it a lie but by recognising the possibilities opened up by its death.

Much against the trend of what today goes by the name of 'New Atheism', Nietzsche is acknowledging that one cannot merely denounce God in the name of a world without God. To denounce a history of God, for Europeans, is to denounce themselves, who share in that history. This is why future Europeans are faced with a 'terrible Either/Or: "Either abolish your venerations [Christian in origin] or – *yourselves!*" The later would be nihilism; but would not the former also be – nihilism? That is *our* question mark' (*GS*, 346). Besides, once we understand that God has a history, we no longer need to prove that he does not exist:

> *Historical refutation as definitive refutation.* – In former times, one sought to prove that there was no God – today one demonstrates how the belief in the existence of God could *come into being* and by what means this belief attained its gravity and importance: thus, a counterproof that there is no God becomes superfluous. (*D*, 95)

But a genealogy of God can only get Nietzsche so far. Yes, God is only a history, but he is Nietzsche's history. Even the history of God, the history of the 'greatest error' no less, must be loved. If Nietzsche can do this, then the purposelessness of life to that point acquires a purpose. Life's meaninglessness becomes life's meaning when it is affirmed as such (*Writings from the Late Notebooks*, note 5[71]). Everything returns, eternally the same, but with the arrival of one who can say yes to all of this, something new appears.

The first to really affirm the tragic nature of existence is fated *not* to be repeated. Rather, he will be the one who breaks the history of the world in two. In place of the eternal return of all things there is now a before and an after. There is a lot of evidence that Nietzsche came to see himself as this break, and that it was the terrible burden of this role that pushed him into madness. His last work, *Ecce Homo*, reads:

> The *uncovering* of Christian morality is an event without equal, a real catastrophe. Anyone who knows about this is a *force majeure*, a destiny, – he splits the history of humanity into two parts. Some live *before* him, some live *after* him . . . . (*EH*, 'Destiny', 8)

Nietzsche's question – can I love my fate (*amor fati*)? – was a question that, inasmuch as it overwhelmed him, he could not answer himself. But if to really say yes to the world is no longer to consider oneself apart from it, then perhaps Nietzsche's insanity was really his final affirmation. For the dissolution of the self into its history could only present itself as madness.

14   Heidegger

IT IS OFTEN SAID that the key to Martin Heidegger's epochal book *Being and Time* (1927) is in the title. Rather than wading through hundreds of pages of difficult philosophy, the reader who knows that being *is* time can get on with something else. But what does it mean to say that being is time? For one thing, it means that being is always a question. There cannot be *an* answer to the question of what it is to be because being, for Heidegger (1889–1976), is time and time is nothing abstract but something historical, something that concerns *us* (Heidegger 1996: 306; 350). Time is only ever my time or our time (Heidegger 2002: 90).

As early as his lectures from 1920–1 on *The Phenomenology of Religious Life*, Heidegger notices this difference between the timeless world of the philosophers and historical time as something that is lived. Heidegger observes that the Apostle Paul's sense of time is not the cosmic one of, say, Aristotle or Plotinus. Rather, in Paul 'The present time has already reached its end and a new age has begun since the death of Christ. The present world is *opposed* to the world of eternity' (Heidegger 2004: 48, emphasis added). If eternity is the metaphysical sense of time and the world, then Paul's world is *now*.

Building on this early insight, one of the central themes of Heidegger's mature work is that, when we experience time merely as a chronological succession of nows, then we paradoxically lose time itself (Heidegger 2000: 389). Time is ours only as finite beings; time is mortal time. For Heidegger (2000: 390), the time that passes, chronological time, is known to us only from the knowledge that we will die. We question starting from where we are. Indeed, even the Greek idea of time as eternity is conceivable only because we know that we are mortal: 'finitude completely determines the human being from the ground up' (Heidegger 1990: 50).

In keeping with this theme of finitude, in *Being and Time* to be is always to be *somewhere* (indeed, Heidegger's preferred term for human being is **Da-sein**, being-*there*) – thrown into the world in a particular place and time (Heidegger 1996: 164–8). And to be historical in this way is also to share a history with others. As I cannot help but notice as I write this book by reading books written by other people, being is always **Mit-sein**, being-*with*: 'the world is always already the one that I share with the others. The world of Da-sein is a *with-world*. Being-in is *being with* others' (Heidegger 1996: 111–12).

Heidegger (1996: 49) brings together the being-*there* and the being-*with* of mortal existence under the heading 'being-in-the-world' (*In-der-Welt-sein*). As the hyphens of being-in-the-world suggest, Heidegger does not see our being and the world as separate entities that are put together at birth. Rather, this compound expression 'stands for a *unified* phenomenon' (Heidegger 1996: 351). *To be* is to be worldly, to be 'dependent on a "world," and [to] exist factically with others' (Heidegger 1996: 351). The abstraction 'man' has no real existence outside of dusty philosophy books.

As well as beginning with being-in-the-world, the question of being will also have to take account of *who* it is that questions after being in the first place. Questioning, after all, is one of 'the modes of being of a particular being, of *the* being we inquirers ourselves in each case are. Thus to work out the question of being means to make a being – one who questions – transparent in its being' (Heidegger 1996: 6). The question of being turns out to be inseparable from the question of what we questioners ourselves *are*: 'The being whose analysis our task is, is always we ourselves' (Heidegger 1996: 39). This 'we', however, is not an abstract entity; rather, 'the being of this being is always *mine*' (Heidegger 1996: 39). Put otherwise: '*The "essence" of Da-sein lies in its existence*' (Heidegger 1996: 40, see also 1998: 248).

Heidegger believed that in asking the question of being he had revived the only question worthy of philosophy, a question that metaphysics, focused on eternity and therefore ignorant of time, *could not even ask* (Heidegger 1998: 246). The very first line of *Being and Time*, under the heading 'The Necessity of an Explicit Retrieve of the Question of Being', reads: 'This question has today been forgotten' (Heidegger 1996: 2). And yet this forgotten question of being is surely 'the most basic and at the same time most concrete question' (Heidegger 1996: 7).

Before all other questions, the one that should strike us the most forcibly is: 'Why are there beings at all, and why not rather nothing?' (Heidegger 1978b: 57) What, put otherwise, is it *to be*? Even when it has engaged with topics as weighty as the highest being, philosophy has busied itself only with beings, with things. But the lowliest thing *is* as much as the highest being (Heidegger 2003: 292). And even nothing *is* in some way! Heidegger calls this difference between being and beings ontological difference, and for him it is the riddling answer, not yet discovered, to the question of existence, as *Being and Time* makes clear: 'What does it mean that being "is" where being is, after all, supposed to be distinguished from all beings? [. . .] The answer to the question of being is still lacking' (Heidegger 1996: 211, see also Heidegger 1990: 258–9).

Years later, in his 'Letter on Humanism' (1947), Heidegger will still see the question of being as a question that, dependent as it is on this *difference* between being and beings, is a question without an answer. Metaphysics 'does not think being as such, does not think the difference between being and beings' (Heidegger 1998: 246). This difference is, once again, not an abstract philosophical concept but something that defines us. Mortals are the only beings for whom being – what it is *to be* – can be a question. In introducing his notion of Da-sein twenty years earlier, Heidegger had made this feature central: 'Da-sein is a being that does not simply occur among other beings. Rather it is ontically distinguished by the fact that in its being this being is concerned *about* its very being' (Heidegger 1996: 10). Questioning is not simply something that we are capable of; we *are* a question through and through. This is why our existence cannot be reduced to that of mere beings and is the reason why Heidegger never refers to us as human beings. 'Human being' is an *answer* to the question of what those who question are. And Heidegger does not think an answer is so forthcoming.

Although being is that which is closest – so close that we are always already in it and cannot catch sight of it – this does not mean that it is what is most generic. Heidegger criticises the philosophical tradition for making this mistake. Hegel, for example, had argued that our verb 'to be' intends something particular (there is a horse) but says something universal (there *is*). And, in antiquity, Aristotle defined metaphysics as the study of what is most abstract: being is what is left when all predicates (such as large and red) are taken away. But, for Heidegger, this concern with things taken in abstraction is still a concern with *things*.

The question of being, for Heidegger, is *not* a question of beings – of things. Nor is it a question even of the totality of beings – of the cosmos (Heidegger 1998b: 120–1). Recall that Kant had asked how beings appear holistically (I know there is a house even though I see only one wall). But Kant didn't ask how it is that not only beings but also the totality of the beings that we encounter is somehow a whole:

> As surely as we never comprehend absolutely the whole of beings in themselves we certainly do find ourselves stationed in the midst of beings that are revealed somehow as a whole. In the end an essential distinction prevails between comprehending the whole of beings in themselves and finding oneself in the midst of beings as a whole. The former is impossible in principle. The latter happens all the time in our existence [. . .] No matter how fragmented our everyday existence may appear to be [. . .] it always deals with beings in a unity of the 'whole', if only in a shadowy way. (Heidegger 1978b: 49–50)

Being is neither a thing nor everything, which is why in a sense it is nothing. But in Heidegger's use of the word nothing we should hear no-thing. Being, as essentially time, is not a thing, but not for all that nothing. To be aware of being is to be aware not of nothing but of *the* nothing (therefore of something!).

How can we become aware of this no-thing that is not nothing? *Being and Time* specifies that we come to this awareness only in the fundamental mood of anxiety:

> That *about which* fear is afraid is the fearful being itself, Da-sein. Only a being which is concerned in its being about that being can be afraid. Fearing discloses this being in its jeopardization, in its being left to itself. (Heidegger 1996: 132)

Boredom seems similar to this but really isn't. Think about when you are profoundly world weary (the French word *ennui* captures better

Heidegger's sense of an existential boredom). You can't find anything to hold your attention, let alone to interest you – even the things that usually captivate you. All things slip away into indifference. 'Boredom reveals beings as a whole' (1978b: 50). But, for the same reason, it doesn't reveal the nothing 'in' which those beings are found.

Only angst does this. I am not fearful of this or that (any*thing*), rather my anxiety arises from my sense of nothingness:

> The receding of beings as a whole that closes in on us in anxiety oppresses us. We can get no hold on things. In the slipping away of beings only this 'no hold on things' comes over and remains.
> Anxiety reveals the nothing. (Heidegger 1978b: 51)

While other animals can be scared of something that threatens them, Heidegger claims that they cannot know anxiety, which is not about anything. Only mortals, aware of the nothing, can be anxious.

Our awareness of this nothing is, at bottom, an understanding of the possibility of *not* being, or death. In *Being and Time*, Heidegger (1996: 240–6) argues that being-towards-death, an unflinching recognition of mortality, is what separates authentic from inauthentic everyday existence. While an inauthentic life flees from the knowledge of its death, authentic life owns it. Heidegger is often criticised for this concern with authenticity (*Eigentlichkeit*) – indeed he later distanced himself from it – but it is worth pointing out that authenticity is not a matter of being this or that, rather of our *relation* to what we are. The authentic, for Heidegger (1996: 244), is existentially 'only a modified way in which the [inauthentic] is seized upon'. A carpenter can live authentically while a philosopher may not (indeed, in Heidegger's world, the carpenter *is* more likely to lead an authentic existence than the philosopher).

It is easy to see how these concerns led Heidegger to be identified with the existentialist tradition that began with Kierkegaard. Indeed, the great French existentialist, Sartre, got his notion that our existence precedes our essence (that our existential choices shape who we are) from reading *Being and Time*. But Heidegger (1998) always refused existentialism. In a letter from 1946 he writes that it is a mistake to see human existence and essence as separate. Our essence *is* our existence. Differently from the existentialist sense of authenticity, Heidegger highlights that we *have to be*, to exist. Existence is not something we chose. Authenticity, then, is not so much choosing our mode of being as rather an *awareness* of being. If we could really choose our way of being then it could not really matter. For if I can choose something than I can equally well choose something else. 'Thrown-ness' (*Geworfenheit*), even though it is not a 'finished fact', is nonetheless fateful (Heidegger 1996: 167).

This emphasis on our being thrown was no doubt at the heart of Heidegger's conservatism, and even of his fateful flirtation with the revolutionary conservatism of the Nazi party, of which he was a member. Although he seems to have quickly become disillusioned with Hitlerism, Heidegger initially liked the idea of a movement which believed in a specifically German destiny, against what he saw as the soulless cosmopolitanism of both Soviet and capitalist society. To be thrown is to be caught up in the fate of a people, not to be a citizen of the world.

As we saw with the idea of being-towards-death, finitude is an abiding concern of Heidegger's. Indeed, in his later writings Heidegger takes to calling human beings 'mortals' in the manner of Homer. Awareness of finitude is what enables things to have significance for us. Human being is defined by care (*Sorge*): 'Da-sein is a being which is concerned in its being about that being', as *Being and Time* puts it (1996: 179).

Heidegger (1995: 282) thinks that this awareness of being is what separates us from other animals. While my dog Waldi is aware of the cat that runs across the yard, he is aware only in the instinctive sense of having to chase it (he is, Heidegger would say, 'captured' by it). Waldi is not aware of the cat *as* a cat – the being of the cat is invisible to him. This means that he could never decide one fine day *not* to chase the cat. Waldi cannot come to *care* about his existence in a way that could ever make him think about becoming a cat-lover, for example.

How, unlike Waldi, *do* I become aware of the being of beings, of the cat *as* a cat? Through language (Heidegger 1998: 248). And yet Heidegger thinks that language is not what first shows us the being of the cat, rather that we can point to a cat (or anything else for that matter) because first we have an awareness of being. An awareness of being comes *before* language. To put the point another way: we have language *because* being is opened to us. The later Heidegger (1998: 254) acknowledges that 'language is the house of being', but there remains a sense that awareness of being is ultimately a mystery that no philosophy of language could solve (Heidegger 1998: 253).

This lingering mystery of being stems from a deep and abiding ambiguity in Heidegger's philosophy: is mortal existence an outcome of the revelation of being, or is the revelation of being an outcome of mortal existence? Heidegger equivocates, at one moment suggesting that being is primary (since *nothing* could be without it), at other times acknowledging that, absent mortal existence, being could not be revealed at all. If the early Heidegger emphasises that the 'clearing of being' is available only by way of mortals, then the later Heidegger tends towards the view that mortal existence is the gift of being. But Heidegger always brings the one back to the other, as if to say that it is a false dichotomy.

There has been a recent trend in philosophy, named speculative realism, to break out of this circle whereby being is somehow dependent on us. Meillassoux (2008), the leading representative of this movement, terms it the problem of the correlationist circle, and traces it back to Kant's Copernican Revolution. As we saw earlier, although Kant claimed that there are things in themselves, all that can ever appear are things as they are given by our minds. Kant opened up a question, one that Heidegger's question also descends from, about the nature of objective reality. Given the subjective quality of all experience (although neither Kant nor Heidegger think that this is individually subjective), on what basis can we any longer speak of the 'real world'? If Kant felt that the structure of our minds is what provides the possibility of experience, then Heidegger argued that it is rather being or 'world'.

Take the example of a hammer, an example which Heidegger himself uses in *Being and Time* (1996: 65): 'The less we just stare at the thing called hammer, the more actively we use it, the more original our relation to it becomes and the more undisguisedly it is encountered as what it is, as a useful thing.' The less we think about the hammer the more of a hammer it can be. For the hammer to appear as what it is (*as* a hammer rather than a piece of wood affixed to a hunk of metal), we need to *use* it (it's a tool after all), which in turn presupposes that we have a sense of what the hammer is *for*. We do not first comprehend the hammer and then understand its use. Rather, it is only by comprehending the hammer's use that we can see the hammer for what it is. *Being* – in this case the context of human dwelling within which tools like hammers are meaningful – is what gives the hammer to us, not the thing itself.

Heidegger does not think that being is at stake only in the individual things, such as hammers, that we perceive. Much more extensively than this, being is what illuminates everything that makes up our world. For Heidegger, even that seemingly most objective thing, nature, is discovered in the use of useful things. *How* we discover nature depends on what we are doing. The forest might be a dwelling place of the gods for the ancient Celts, but for modern Europeans it is more likely to be a source of timber. Ultimately, however, being is not just one context such as the forest but the *total* context given by an entire way of life.

Like Kant's objects of experience, Heidegger's being is always somehow rounded out and whole. Indeed, we only notice this totality of reference, which Heidegger calls 'world', when something in that world no longer works. When the hammer breaks, I become aware that I am building; when I have a question that my faith seems unable to answer, I become aware of my faith. Our worlds are revealed to us only when we have *questions* about them.

For all his emphasis on recovering the question of being in *Being and Time*, Heidegger later came to doubt that we *can* question after being. The famous 'turn' (*die Kehre*), by which Heidegger (1963) himself described how his thought changed direction after *Being and Time*, consisted in an inversion of his earlier emphasis on how mortals have *forgotten* the question of being to the formulation that being has *abandoned* beings such as us: 'The *abandonment by being* is the ground of the forgottenness of being' (Heidegger 2012: 91). In this work (*Contributions to Philosophy*) from 1936–8, the agent and patient of *Being and Time* (1927) have switched places – now it is being that is doing the work, as it were, rather than mortals.

The implications of this reversal for questioning are profound. If 'we' have forgotten being then we can question after it. If, on the other hand, being has abandoned 'us', then where could questioning lead us other than down dead ends? We need to listen *to* being (as the late Heidegger's shift towards poetics indeed sought to do), not strive after its meaning with our questions.

Heidegger (1998: 249) came increasingly to believe that his earlier emphasis on forgetting had too much of subject-centred metaphysics about it. It is being that gathers us, not we that gather evidence of being, as his *Letter on Humanism* makes clear: 'Metaphysics closes itself to the simple essential fact that the human being essentially occurs in his essence only where he is claimed by being' (Heidegger 1998: 247). Indeed, this way of putting things is in many ways merely the culmination of Heidegger's insistence in *Being and Time* that mortals do not stand apart from the world looking on. We are always already in-the-world:

> the essential worth of the human being does not consist in his being the substance of beings, as the 'Subject' among them, so that as the tyrant of being he may deign to release the beingness of beings into an all too loudly glorified 'objectivity'.
>
> The human being is rather 'thrown' by being itself into the truth of being, so that ek-sisting in this fashion he might guard the truth of being [. . .] Human beings do not decide whether and how beings appear [. . .] The advent of beings lies in the destiny of being. But for humans it is ever a question [. . .] of guard[ing] the truth of being. The human being is the shepherd of being. It is in this direction alone that *Being and Time* is thinking. . . . (Heidegger 1998: 251–2)

But there is a problem with Heidegger's reversal of his earlier, still metaphysical, understanding that being is a question: by his own lights, 'the reversal of a metaphysical statement remains a metaphysical statement' (Heidegger 1998: 250). If this is right, then it is not clear how Heidegger's thought after his 'turn' remains any less metaphysical than it was before, either. For in reversing the claim that we can question after being to say that being abandons us, Heidegger does not escape the assumption that being is a question. He does not avoid the, frankly metaphysical, implication that, in our abandonment, something has abandoned us.

15   Weil

SIMONE WEIL (1909–43) WAS ONLY thirty-four when she died. Yet the writings of this young French woman are perhaps the purest distillation of Neoplatonism in modern Western thought. In Weil, this Neoplatonism took the form of a stringent Christian mysticism, the insights of which were lived quite as much as they were thought.

In Weil's view, 'Since Greece disappeared there hasn't been such a thing as a philosopher' (Weil 1952b: 254). Reviving the concern of ancient Greek thought with philosophy as a form of life, Weil never doubted that truth is only for the few and that the way is hard. But the condition of access to divine truth (the need for which 'is more sacred than any other need' [Weil 1952b: 36]) is not questioning as such but poverty of soul:

> The true road exists. Plato and many others have followed it. But it is open only to those who, recognizing themselves to be incapable of finding it, give up looking for it, and yet do not cease to desire it to the exclusion of everything else. (Weil 1958: 148)

The implication of Weil's thought for questioning, as we shall see, is that the Socratic injunction to recognise that we *know* nothing is radicalised to the point where the one who questions must *herself* be nothing.

If Socratic questioning is insufficient, then Weil sees something more profound in Plato. From Plato comes the insight, which she finds also at the core of Christianity, that worldly necessity and the good can have no relation to each to each whatsoever (Weil 1958: 158). The good is 'situated outside the world' (Weil 1958: 148). Catching sight of this good, then, is not a matter of mundane questioning; rather, 'a light, as it were, is kindled in one soul by a flame that leaps to it from another' (Plato: 1966: 341b). As Weil (1958: 156) makes the same point in her more Christian terms: a person sees the good only 'in so far as he is freed by the supernatural operation of grace'. Not reason but revelation is what we need. Weil, then, confronts questioners with a challenge: left to our own devices, are we capable of questioning after truth? Indeed, to the extent that we have only our *own* thoughts, are we even thinking?

> So long as man submits to having his soul taken up with his own thoughts, his personal thoughts, he remains entirely subjected [...] But everything changes as soon as [...] he empties his soul so as to allow the conceptions of eternal Wisdom to enter into it. (Weil 1952b: 288)

Given her affinity with Plato, Weil was fascinated by the influence of Neoplatonism on Christianity. Writing about Porphyry (Plotinus's student), she notes that the Christian theologian, Origen, had been reported by Porphyry as using Greek philosophy in order to interpret the Hebrew scriptures. Why then, Weil asks (1953: 49–50), does Origen try to refute Greek philosophy when he is clearly so dependent on it? Is he trying to hide something?

Wanting to acknowledge the true significance of the cross-fertilisation of the Greek and the Christian for Western culture, and indeed for her own thought, Weil (1953: 56) writes:

> For since all the profane life of our countries is directly derived from 'pagan' civilizations, as long as the illusion persists of a break between so-called paganism and Christianity, the latter will not impregnate the whole of profane life as it ought to do [...] How our life would be changed if we could see that Greek geometry and the Christian faith have sprung from the same source!

From a Jewish background, Weil saw her vocation as 'to be a Christian outside the Church' (Weil 1953: 3). What held her back from being baptised into the Catholic Church was, at heart, that she was captivated by the passion of Christ rather than with the doctrine of his resurrection:

> Hitler could die and return to life again fifty times, but I should still not look upon him as the Son of God. And if the Gospel omitted all mention of Christ's resurrection, faith would be easier for me. The Cross by itself suffices for me. (Weil 1953: 34)

Weil identified strongly with the God that sacrificed himself on a cross. Writing to a priest, she insisted that, 'For me, the proof, the really miraculous thing, is the perfect beauty of the accounts of the Passion.' '"He was made accursed." That is what compels me to believe' (Weil 1953: 34–5).

Christ refrained from intervening in a world ruled by brute necessity ('for I came not to judge the world, but to save the world', John 12:47) and we imitate Christ by imitating his powerlessness – what Weil (1952: 34) called 'decreation':

> He emptied himself of his divinity. We should empty ourselves of the false divinity with which we were born.
> Once we have understood we are nothing, the object of all our efforts is to become nothing. It is for this that we suffer with resignation, *it is for this that we act*, it is for this that we pray.
> May God Grant me to become nothing.
> In so far as I become nothing, God loves himself through me.

Decreation is defined as making 'something created pass into the uncreated'. It is differentiated from the pure negativity of destruction, which makes created things 'pass into nothingness' (Weil 1952: 32). Weil accepts the Neoplatonic claim that God's creative act is perpetual and that, having emanated from God, this life-giving force seeks return to its source. In short, God loves himself *by way* of his creations. He loves himself through us. The implications of this ontology, which strongly echoes Eckhart's, are taken to their radical limit in Weil's hands: since our being is really nothing (remember that we are only the *by way of which* God loves himself), God must love in us only the *acceptance* of this not-being (Weil 1952: 32). We love God by denying ourselves: 'Our existence is made up only of his waiting for our acceptance not to exist. He is perpetually begging from us that existence which he gives. He gives it to us in order to beg it from us' (Weil 1952: 32).

That being consists in accepting our nothingness means, for Weil, that we should be grateful for suffering. If God did not withdraw from us then we would not be called away from ourselves to love of him. Indeed, if God did not abandon us then we would be overwhelmed by his presence, evaporating 'like water in the sun' (Weil 1952: 33). If God did not hide his face from us, all would be God indifferently. Just as God 'renounces being everything', so should we 'renounce being something': 'We participate in the creation of the world by decreating ourselves' (Weil 1952: 33).

In keeping with her central theme of decreation, ego is something Weil fled from, never ceasing in her attempts to die to self. Even her early death seems to have stemmed, in part, from her punishing schedule and general indifference to caring for herself. This indifference was intentional. Everything that is good in us comes from elsewhere to the extent that, if we appropriate that good for ourselves (which happens even when we feel joy in it), it immediately becomes useless. Worse than useless: since only evil makes distinctions, when I say 'I', I sin. Anything that 'prevents God from being equivalent to all' is a lie, just as Plotinus had argued against the Gnostics centuries earlier (Weil 1952: 30). Only wretchedness – the absence of God – truly individuates, just as only the Passion of Christ personalises God: 'my God, why have you forsaken me?' (Matthew 27:46).

Weil's association of personhood with abjection, although it is sourced in Plotinus's One beyond being, goes further in that direction than anything a Greek philosopher could have accepted. Radicalising Neoplatonic ontology in keeping with Christian humility, Weil suggests that even action itself (recalling that Aristotle in his *Nicomachean Ethics*, 1.7.1098a, defined human being as 'concerned in some way with action') is something to be renounced. Weil describes 'the extreme difficulty which I often experience in carrying out the slightest action' as 'a favour granted to me', praying: 'May I endure [my sufferings] in a completely passive manner' (Weil 1952: 35). Love, the only worthy 'action', is itself a work in which 'all that I call "I" has to be passive' (Weil 1952: 118).

Weil believed that the sense of self – seemingly the surest of things – is in fact a seductive illusion. What we take for the reality of self is only the result of our worldly attachments, of how we transfer the self into things. To live as an individual is be led away from the truth, which is always *im*personal (like Plato, Weil saw no relation between truth and opinion): 'We have to be nothing in order to be in our right pace in the whole' (Weil 1952: 36). We can access the truth only through annihilating ourselves. Indeed, even the idea of the immortality of the soul is, for Weil, a distraction from this deeper truth. The belief that my soul will live on after death is, after all, the belief that *I* will endure, a belief that 'robs death of its purpose' (Weil 1952: 37). Again, Weil remains close to Plotinus, who differed with Plato (in Plotinus's own understanding at least) only on this point: death is not the occasion for the soul to be reborn but rather the moment of its reabsorption into the One from which it came.

Just as in Plotinus, for Weil worldly appearance, including the appearance that the self is substantial, is only an image of true being. 'Appearance clings to being' but, in truth *is* not (Weil 1952: 39). But where Plotinus would separate appearance from being by way of the understanding, Weil (1952: 39) is convinced that 'pain alone can tear them from each other'. Not philosophy but mortal suffering will divide what *appears to be* (individuation) from what *is* (oneness or in-distinction). 'Time in its course tears appearance from being and being from appearance by violence. Time makes manifest that it is not eternity' (Weil 1952: 39):

> It is necessary to uproot oneself [. . .]
> It is necessary not to be 'myself', still less to be 'ourselves'.
>> The city gives us feeling of being at home.
>> We must take the feeling of being at home into exile.
>> We must be rooted in the absence of place.
> To uproot oneself socially and vegetatively.
>> To exile oneself from every earthly country [. . .]
>> But by uprooting oneself one seeks greater reality. (Weil 1952: 39)

The way to self-annihilation is to live in that 'extreme and total humiliation' by which we no longer doubt that everything that we have – indeed everything that we are – can be taken away from us at any moment (Weil 2015: 27). Reaching this point of access to the truth requires that we pay supreme *attention* to this affliction, both in others and ourselves. After all, 'he who is forgiven little, loves little' (Luke 7:47). This is why Weil (1952: 118) names attention *love*. What love, or attention, reveals to us is only the truth of our wretched condition. But even being afflicted with this knowledge of our wretchedness is not enough. 'Unconsoled affliction is necessary', an affliction in which there is no consolation, no expectation of future compensation for past wrongs (Weil 1952: 12). Weil had no time for heaven in the usual sense of the word, namely the pie-in-the-sky-when-you-die kind.

Weil identifies this unconsoled affliction with Platonic desire for the absolute good, the extinction of desire in Buddhism, and with Nietzsche's *amor fati*. Each of these paths seek to empty desire of any content; to desire 'in the void', or without any wishes (Weil 1952: 13, see also Weil 1952b: 262). Once we have done this, all we can do is wait. The good that we now will is so far beyond our comprehension that all ordinary willing is suspended. We cease even to will any good thing, since the good is not thing-like: 'but this nothingness is not unreal. Compared with it, everything in existence is unreal': 'We must leave on one side the beliefs which fill up voids and sweeten what is bitter. The belief in immortality ... The belief in the providential ordering of events – in short the "consolations" which are ordinarily sought in religion' (Weil 1952: 13).

From this maxim follows the truth that 'in proportion to the hideousness of affliction is the supreme beauty of its true representation'. This is why, for Weil (2015: 29), the *Iliad* is bettered only by the accounts of the Passion in the Gospels. Truth, then, has nothing to do with intelligence but everything to do with bravery; it is *parrhesia*, the courage of truth. Weil (2015: 27) compares an intelligent man to a lifer who is proud of his large cell. Meanwhile a less intelligent lifer in a smaller cell, if he does not turn away from his enclosing walls but rather beats his head against them, is starting to pay attention. If this man continues, day after day, to bash his head against the walls of his cell then, one day, he will wake up on the other side of the wall. This new location will no doubt remain within the larger confines of the prison, but no matter: he has found the key, 'the secret which breaks down every wall. He has passed beyond what men call intelligence, into the beginning of wisdom' (Weil 2015: 26). Questioning *hurts*.

To experience in the depth of one's soul, by way of love, the humiliating truth of one's captivity is to experience non-being. And this death of the soul is nothing less than 'the condition for passing over into truth' (Weil 2015: 27). God is beyond being. Weil has what is called a negative theology, which allows itself to state only what God isn't: 'We can only know one thing about God – that he is what we are not' (Weil 1952: 121–2). Indeed, our love for God must not be dependent even on his existence! All our words for God such as truth, justice, love and good must in no way refer to anything humanely conceivable. Even as we love, in fact *in order to* love, we must not flinch from acknowledging that the human condition is one of abandonment: 'Sin is nothing else but the failure to recognize human wretchedness' (which is why it is easier for a camel to go through the eye of a needle than for a rich man to enter the kingdom of God) (Weil 1952: 22). God's love in no way protects 'the soul against the coldness of force, the coldness of steel' (1952: 63).

Like Nietzsche, Weil thought that the tragic age of the Greeks was capable of this unvarnished truth of the human condition in a way that our modern age is not. The beauty of the *Iliad*, a beauty Western culture is no longer capable of, is its unflinching gaze at the impersonal fate that rules mortal lives: 'The bitterness of such a spectacle is offered us absolutely undiluted. No comforting fiction intervenes; no consoling prospect of immortality; and on the hero's head no washed-out halo of patriotism descends' (Weil 1965: 6).

Homer's Greeks and Trojans, despite being mortal enemies, are defined by their common subjection to cruel fortune. This is why Homer, a Greek, in no way takes his own side in telling of the Trojan War. Greek and Trojan warriors are equal in a way that they could never be according to some abstract universal measure of what it is to be human. What is sacred about the warriors of the *Iliad* is only that *nothing* can compensate for their deaths. As Achilles says: 'Nothing is worth my life, not all the goods / They say the well-built city of Ilium [Troy] contains'. In human rights culture, by contrast (a culture Weil was highly critical of), children are taught that they are special precisely for being unique – just for being them. Echoing Kant's kingdom of ends, modern individuals are ends in themselves. Weil's world knows no such crumbs of comfort: 'It is impossible for me to take myself as an end or, in consequence, my fellow man as an end' (Weil 1952: 164). Rather than personhood, 'what is sacred in a human being is the impersonal in him' (Weil 2015: 13). Indeed, the mystic has never sought anything other than that state in which 'there is no part left in his soul to say "I"' (Weil 2015: 14).

Weil's Platonism comes through clearly here. Perfection, or the good, is essentially anonymous. Weil borrows Plato's analogy (see the *Meno*) of the slave boy who, lacking any education, is nonetheless quickly compelled to accept a geometric proof: 'If a child is doing a sum wrong, the mistake bears the stamp of his personality. If he does the sum exactly right, his personality does not enter into it at all. Perfection is impersonal' (Weil 2015: 14). This impersonality of truth means that love of truth is necessarily accompanied by humility. To personalise truth is to substitute truth for pride.

Just as the good in people is that which is not theirs, so the good 'itself' (or God) is defined by its absence rather than its presence. Like the alien God of the Gnostics, Weil's God is entirely uninvolved in the world. Unlike the Gnostic God, he is not even present in the spirits that are imprisoned in earthly matter: 'Pure good from heaven only reaches the earth in imperceptible quantities' (Weil 2015: 32). The world *is* only matter – the blind force unveiled in the *Iliad* – and in accepting this world without God (something the Gnostics could not do) we find that we love it all the more precisely because it has no purpose. God is somehow more present because he is absent – is present *in* his absence: 'For the absence of God is the mode of divine presence which corresponds to evil – absence which is felt' (Weil 1952: 27).

The notion that our world is structured by absence rather than presence is not unique to Weil (we find it also in Heidegger and, later in the twentieth century, in Lacanian psychoanalysis and in Derrida's theory of language), but it is clearer in her work precisely because she did not hide the theological aspect of this way of thinking.

As her example of the two lifers in their cells illustrates, Weil was much less interested in our illusions of freedom than in our courage to face our imprisonment. What matters is not willing but attention, or love. The will controls only 'a few movements of a few muscles' – I can will to put my hand on the table, and that's about it (Weil 1952: 116). Attention has little to do with the will but everything to do with consent – if I seek the truth then this is not because I will to but because the good in truth makes me desire it. All 'I' can do is give way to this desire. Similarly, attention alerts me to the fact that the widow and the orphan really exist as much as I do; 'that is enough, the rest follows' (Weil 1952: 119). True questioning arises only when we pay attention, that is to say when we love.

The quest for truth leads us away from fantasies of free will (how big my cell is!) and towards that which determines the will (but there are walls!). This is especially clear in Spinoza, who Weil quotes approvingly on this point. And in Weil's essay (1965) on the *Iliad* she emphasises that the fates, aided and abetted by the gods, decide everything. The battle ebbs and flows between the Greeks and the Trojans, but each warrior hurries towards his doom – even mighty Achilles. Indeed, in knowing his fate more clearly than the others (thanks to his goddess mother, he knows that he will die at Troy), Achilles is even more keen to accomplish his destiny.

Death is that destiny, since finitude is the fate of every mortal. As Weil (1952: 107) says,

> The beings I love are creatures. They were born by chance. My meeting with them was also by chance. They will die ... I have to know this with all my soul and not to love them the less. I have to imitate God who infinitely loves finite things in that they are finite things.

Imitating God's love for mortal things means that we must not wish for them to be eternal. Indeed, the vulnerability of things is the mark of their very existence and also that they are irreducible to their existence. The destruction of Troy, the blossom that fell from the tree; they still *are*, even though they no longer exist. 'That is beautiful. Why? It projects the soul beyond time' (Weil 1952: 108). Even my thought of God, which for Weil is everything, has to be referred back to contingency: 'Stars and blossoming fruit trees: utter permanence and extreme fragility give an equal sense of eternity' (Weil 1952: 108).

An awareness of blind fate leads us to act in ways that illusions of free will never can. Free will must be sacrificed not only in the name of truth but also in order to clear the way for those actions that *do* matter – namely those that we cannot choose because they choose us. Loving actions, in particular, have the quality that they are compelled. Our love for our children, for example, is strengthened rather than weakened by its not being a choice on our part. If we are to be capable of love then this will not be because we *must be* loving but because we *are* loving: 'May the eternal light give, not a reason for living and working, but a sense of completeness which makes the search for any such reason unnecessary' (Weil 1952: 181).

The search for reasons presupposes that things should be otherwise than they are. But this condemns the way of the world when, in fact, 'The order of the world is the same as the beauty of the world' (Weil 1952b: 291). Wanting nothing else than what we find means that there is no place for a plan of salvation. Indeed, there is much that echoes Spinoza in Weil's rejection of a personal providence: 'The ridiculous conception of Providence as being a personal and particular intervention on the part of God for certain particular ends is incompatible with true faith' (Weil 1952b: 279).

As we saw, for Spinoza too providence is a refuge of ignorance – the explanation we grope for when we don't understand and can't face the way of the world. Chastising orthodox Christianity for its providential order, Weil (1952b: 260) points to the Gospels: the sun rises and the rain falls as much on the unjust as the just (Matthew 5:45). 'The non-intervention of God in the operation of grace is expressed as clearly as it can possibly be' (Weil 1952b: 260). As in Spinoza, the 'sum of the particular interventions of God is the universe itself' (Weil 1952b: 280), which is the same as to say that there *are* no interventions, that the world simply *expresses* God at every turn: 'Divine Providence is not a disturbing influence, an anomaly in the ordering of the world; it is *itself* the order of the world' (Weil 1952b: 281, emphasis added).

To love the world, then, is not to love this or that which occurs in it, but to love its *order*. The Stoic conception of *amor fati*, Weil writes, teaches nothing else than this (1952b: 285, see also 1958: 158). Once we love the order, the way, of the world then we will love 'everything, without any exception, joys and sorrows alike'; *all* 'ought to be welcomed with the same inward attitude of love and thankfulness' (Weil 1952b: 286). To the extent that Christianity opposed itself to Stoic insensibility to pain (namely *pride*), then Christianity and Stoicism appear to be opposites. But once we see that Stoicism is really love of the divine order of the world, then Christianity and Stoicism intend the same thing (Weil 1952b: 286).

Weil's thought is a fascinating and unique blend of what seems like contradictory impulses: on the one hand a certain Stoic (and Spinozist) love of worldly fate and, on the other hand, a reaching beyond fate to the good that lies above worldly necessity. This is the Neoplatonist, even Gnostic, element in her thought. In Plotinus, the world of the spirit is higher than the material world and yet, for all that, 'nothing is to be condemned for not being the first'. In the Gnostics, meanwhile, this world is merely the prison house of souls that long to escape it. Weil, like Plotinus, refuses to judge the world (indeed proclaims her love for it in the manner of the Stoics) even as she invokes a good somehow beyond it. Denigrating the world is a sign of an excessive weakness that isn't even capable of showing pity or doing harm to others: in this sorry state, 'every good or beautiful thing is like an insult' (Weil 1952: 6). Love, to the contrary, needs reality just as the beautiful is only 'that which we cannot wish to change' (Weil 1952: 65). This is 'why beauty and reality are identical. That is why joy and the sense of reality are identical':

> Every desire for enjoyment belongs to the future and the world of illusion, whereas if we desire only that a being should exist, he exists: what more is there to desire? The beloved being is then naked and real, not veiled by an imaginary future (Weil 1952: 66).

But for all her refusal of Gnostic world-hatred, Weil still echoes the Gnostics in her lament at the spirit's helplessness in the face of the violent necessity of the world. Of the *Iliad* she writes: 'Its bitterness is the only justifiable bitterness, for it springs from the subjection of the human spirit to force, that is, in the last analysis, to matter' (Weil 1965: 27). Yet where Gnosticism found an escape from this subjection for the elect few, Weil was more egalitarian: 'This subjection is the common lot, although each spirit will bear it differently, in proportion to its own virtue' (Weil 1965: 27). Given Weil's own definition (1952: 122) of purity as 'the power to contemplate defilement', it is tempting to say that Weil's spirit, which looked unblinkingly at the darkness even while finding itself full of love, was more virtuous than most. But this homily she would surely have rejected. Only an ill will personalises that which is indifferently in God.

16   Arendt

ONE OF THE CONTRIBUTIONS of Hannah Arendt's (1906–75) thought to our understanding of questioning is the way in which she seeks to put questioning in its place. You might think that a German Jewish philosopher who narrowly escaped the Shoah (Arendt fled to New York in 1941) would call for less politics and more philosophy. But in many ways, as we shall see, it was the other way around.

Heidegger, one of Arendt's professors when she was an undergraduate and a lifelong influence, had already dethroned philosophy. But Heidegger's commitment to a certain kind of questioning (being open to being) remained undimmed, identifying it as he did with the essence of human being itself. Indeed, the elevation of this kind of questioning made the later Heidegger seem to be suspicious of any form of action. He found too much 'subjectivism' in the idea of humans acting on the world as if from the outside.

Although she remained in many ways close to Heidegger, Arendt could not have disagreed more that the passive life is closer to the truth of existence than a life of action. Although she was at pains not to be understood as saying that politics is *all* that a human life should aim at, she did not hide her belief, which she shared with the ancient Greeks, that the active life of politics is the uniquely human vocation.

A question therefore haunts Arendt's work: is the 'striving for immortality' (Arendt 1958: 20) which she took to be the wellspring of politics in the ancient Greek city-state capable of being recovered, or at least reactivated in new forms, in the modern world? If not then her work must be seen as being tinged with nostalgia. If yes, then what forms could such a politics take today?

This question is pressing for us also since, to repeat, for Arendt the life of action that is the political life is the only uniquely human life. As she argued in *The Human Condition* (chapter 3), labour, by contrast, merely reproduces the necessities of life that ceaselessly return day by day and season by season. Animals have their labours, too. Even what Arendt terms 'work', that making or fabricating that adds something to nature (as when a lump of stone is worked into a statue), for the same reason fails to *escape* nature (Arendt 1958: chapter 4). Only human action can constitute freedom in a world defined by necessity:

> In order to be what the world is always meant to be, a home for men during their life on earth, the human artifice must be a place fit for action and speech, for activities not only entirely useless for the necessities of life but of an entirely different nature from the manifold activities of fabrication by which the world itself and all things in it are produced. (Arendt 1958: 173–4)

Only human action really begins, indeed it defines beginning as such, since escaping the natural cycle of cause and effect is possible only insofar as there is speech. Only speech allows actions 'which cannot be expected from whatever may have happened before' (Arendt 1958: 178).

The originality made possible by speech is itself a gift of what Arendt calls 'natality' (1958: 178). Being capable by way of speech of the unexpected, each individual is a beginning, a unique person who, *as* unique, in one sense has no precursors (though she will of course have ancestors). Speech, then, 'is the actualization of the human condition of plurality' (Arendt 1958: 178).

So important is a shared space for this speech which is the actualisation of the human condition, that, in *The Origins of Totalitarianism* (1948), Arendt is dismissive of the modern attempt to establish human dignity on the basis of human rights. Such rights, divorced as they are from citizenship, are not rights to appear in a (always particular) space of action, but purely abstract notions of human equality. Equality, for Arendt, is something that is given only by the right to address one's peers as an equal – 'the right to have rights' as she calls it (1948: 296).

The tragedy of those who lack this right of belonging (namely citizenship) is that their

> treatment by others does not depend on what [they] do or [do] not do. This extremity, and nothing else, is the situation of people deprived of human rights. They are deprived, not of the right to freedom, but of the right to action . . . . (Arendt 1948: 296)

Separated from this right of action, human rights appeal only to the bare, animal life that human beings have in common, indeed have in common with all other sentient creatures (see Aristotle's *Nicomachean Ethics* 1.7). This shared animality has no connection to freedom and, indeed, debases those who have nothing else to appeal to. Writing in the shadow of the Shoah, Arendt (1948: 299) notes that

> The conception of human rights, based upon the assumed existence of a human being as such, broke down at the very moment when those who professed to believe in it were for the first time confronted with people who had indeed lost all other qualities and specific relationships – except that they were still human. The world found nothing sacred in the abstract nakedness of being human.

As well as being inseparably linked to freedom and dignity, human action endures in ways that works never can. While the statue may well outlive its sculptor, as a work it has not transcended the world of things. And all things, even rocks, are perishable. Actions, unlike works, are *deeds*. They are not thing-like at all, appearing only by way of agreement between free people in the context of political life. The great Athenian political leader, Pericles, didn't add any-*thing* to the world and yet his immortal words, which should be considered as his deeds, echo down the ages (Arendt 1958: 205–6). Reading Pericles's famous funeral oration, one is struck by the fact that Pericles lives on far beyond the Olympian gods he worshipped, who did not survive the coming of Christianity.

What has happened to this politics that is the expression of a uniquely human capacity for speech and action? Arendt's thesis is that it began its decline long ago with the rise of the contemplative life – that is with Greek philosophy:

> Since Plato, and probably since Socrates, thinking was understood as the inner dialogue in which one speaks with himself [. . .]

[They] considered this dialogical thought process to be the way to prepare the soul and lead the mind to a beholding of truth beyond thought and beyond speech – a truth that is incapable of being communicated through words. (Arendt 1958: 291)

From Plato onwards, solitary reflection on timeless eternity substituted for those great deeds that lend their doers a certain immortality (although it lasts forever, immortality, unlike eternity, is a creation *in* time – humans, god-like in this sense, are capable of it).

The death sentence handed down to Socrates by a popular court in Athens had already convinced Plato that truth and politics could not be bedfellows; but the imminent demise of the self-governing city (Aristotle was Alexander's tutor, and Alexander's father, Phillip II of Macedon, defeated the alliance of the last free Greek city-states) led to a turning away from political life altogether. What use political immortality when politics itself – understood as the self-government of free citizens – had proved short-lived? Now came 1,000 years of Empire (first Hellenistic and then Roman) and the philosophical contemplation of eternity suitable to a political wasteland in which nothing could ever really happen. While politics had sought to leave behind private natural necessity in the name of collective political freedom, philosophy tried to leave even this common world behind. But in flying, Icarus-like, above political life, philosophy lost the world too. Otherworldliness, the archenemy of worldly politics, had gained a foothold.

Did things improve with the demise of Rome and the rise of Christianity? Not at all. Indeed, Christianity was only an intensification of the attempt to disentangle oneself from worldly affairs that started with Greek philosophy. Modernity, meanwhile, although it appears to have renounced otherworldliness in fact has not rediscovered that only truly worldly thing that is political life. Indeed, modernity has closed down the possibility of politics even further. What Arendt (1958: 38) calls the 'rise of the social' in the modern world means that the life-process which is the concern of labour has moved out of the private sphere that it was previously consigned to and has colonised the public sphere. Now domesticated, this sphere is further from being a space for politics than ever. In place of the speech and action (as we saw, these terms are virtually synonymous for Arendt) that made up political life in the Greek *polis*, the public sphere is today taken up with domestic chores on a massive scale:

The emergence of society – the rise of housekeeping, its activities, problems, and organizational devices – from the shadowy interior of the household into the light of the public sphere, has not only blurred the old borderline between private and political, it has also changed almost beyond recognition the meaning of the two terms and their significance for the life of the individual and the citizen. (Arendt 1958: 38)

Living through the Covid-19 pandemic, we understand that Arendt was not wrong about this. Social distancing and other public health decrees isolate and separate citizens to the point where the idea of citizenship as making oneself understood in the public sphere seems to come from another world. This shift in the nature of politics whereby life itself becomes the business of the sovereign is what the French philosopher Michel Foucault (2010b) called 'biopolitics' (after *bios*, the Greek word for life). Yet even while the public sphere is filled increasingly with the government of the life-process, Arendt (1958: 50–1) pointed out that this process itself remains stubbornly resistant to any real political expression. For example, while Pericles's speech can still communicate something to me and my students two and a half thousand years later, the pain I felt on stubbing my toe just now is essentially *in*communicable – all I can really say is 'ow!'

The fact that the life-process is mute while politics is speech means that a 'politics' fixated on life is, for Arendt, incapable of realising freedom. And it is true that, as Foucault noted, questions posed to the sovereign in the modern era tend to be questions of its effectiveness rather than questions of its legitimacy. The epidemiologist's question 'will lockdown last long enough to slow the spread of disease?' is today much more posable politically than 'can a free people be confined to their homes indefinitely?' Few Greek citizens, committed to ruling and being ruled in turn, would have accepted such a biopolitical approach to politics.

But Arendt sees a deeper problem with the eclipse of the political in modern 'social' regimes. No longer having to think for themselves in the manner of citizens (who after all must appear before each other), individuals in the modern age are tempted to trust that the state will do their thinking for them. We settle for obedience. The extreme of this process of socialisation is, for Arendt (2006: 90), the 'banality of evil' displayed by senior Nazi Adolf Eichmann, the chief organiser of the Shoah. Sent by *The New Yorker* to report on the trial of Eichmann in Jerusalem in 1961, Arendt (2006: 27) was struck by how this man, surely a monster if ever there was one, seemed actually to be entirely ordinary, even a bit of a clown. It was clear to Arendt (2006: 9) that, terrible as Eichmann's crimes were, he had carried them out not from any deep personal animosity towards the Jews but because he did not have the imagination to see that moral personality goes beyond obedience to orders. Eichmann's 'evil' was the entirely everyday refusal to think for oneself put to the service of a monstrous crime.

Writing as she did about Eichmann, as well as her famous book on totalitarianism, tempts us to place Arendt's abiding concern with the eclipse of the political in the context of the turbulent political events of her lifetime. But this would be to overlook that it was just as much a philosophical context. Understanding this requires that we begin where she herself began – a doctoral dissertation on love in Saint Augustine started before the events of the 1930s and 1940s with which she is now so readily identified. A strange topic for one of the greatest political philosophers of the twentieth century? On closer inspection, this turns out not to be the case.

The first thing to note about this doctoral thesis is that it is in many ways an analysis of how otherworldliness took root in Western culture (recalling that Arendt identifies politics with worldliness, indeed suggests that politics is the only truly worldly thing). As the most influential of the Fathers in the Western Church, the significance of Augustine, in Arendt's view, is that with him the Greek concern with eternity was married to the Christian concern for love. Not only should the world beyond be what our understanding aims at, it should even be the object of our true desire. Arendt (1996: 17–18) quotes Augustine: 'Love, but be careful what you love.' 'Just as temporal life is cherished by its lovers [pagans], thus we [Christians] should cherish eternal life.'

In keeping with the influence of Heidegger, Arendt is keen to emphasise that this looking beyond the world of mortal life to the timeless true world is really to miss human being itself, since human being *is* only the short span of life that opens up before us once we have the knowledge of death. Indeed, even the very idea of a heavenly beyond is dependent on mortal humans. Given that the world as such endures whether we are in it or not, it is only our mortal love for the world that turns the earth into a place that suffers from time. In truth, only *we* suffer from time. For the same reason, only mortals long for eternity. Augustine's condemnation of our love for the mundane (in the name of love for eternity) is therefore an understandable rejection of mortality. But its consequence is a rejection of ourselves, of the only time we have, of the (short) time that we *are*. And Augustine did not shy away from this, arguing that only in self-negation do we find ourselves; that only by being strangers to the world do we find a home in it.

Arendt's growing frustration at this otherworldliness bubbles up in the following passage from her dissertation:

> Given that, for Augustine, this world is what the desert was for the people of Israel, 'Would it not then be better to love the world in *cupiditas* (earthly desire) and be at home?' Why should we make a desert out of this world? The justification for this extraordinary enterprise can only lie in a deep dissatisfaction with what the world can give its lovers. (Arendt 1996: 19)

Arendt wants, by contrast, to be worldly, and all the things that Augustine finds problematic in pagan existence are things she identifies with the political: thrown into the world, we make ourselves at home, and this making is never something we do alone. Together with others we establish something that we share in common. Indeed, coming after those who have gone before us, we not only establish the human world but that world establishes us. Augustine calls men and women to return to God from the world; Arendt calls men and women to return from God to the world. And the making or dwelling – the action – that this requires is the political itself. Cities are not founded by builders but by those who speak them into existence.

Although she is years from developing her famous analysis of totalitarianism, the young Arendt finds in her reading of Augustine the building blocks of that later work. Since the Christian must reject the world, the injunction to love your neighbour can only mean to love what is least worldly about her. The neighbour is loved only for what identifies her with all the other sons and daughters of Adam, namely that she is made in the image of God. She is loved, in short, only for what is universally human in her, losing in the process any distinctiveness, for example that she might be a friend or an enemy. The command to love your enemies indifferently to your friends is a command not only to love them but to be indifferent to them. While they are to be loved, they are to be loved for what in them is like everybody else, not for what makes them singular. Arendt (1996: 95) cites

Augustine: 'For you love in him not what he is, but what you wish that he might be.'

The outlines of Arendt's later scepticism about human rights are visible here in this reading of Augustine. The rights of man, as she still termed them, point only to that which is most abstract, and therefore empty, in human existence. When German Jews such as Arendt were stripped of their citizenship and had only their human rights to fall back on, they found, to their horror, that these rights were useless. Not belonging to any state, there was no one to come to their aid. The bare fact of being human motivated nobody to admit them. Indeed, at the war's end even the surviving European Jews themselves disdained to rely on human rights, committing themselves instead to establishing a state of their own. The rights of man and citizen, as the French revolutionaries referred to them, turned out to be the rights of citizens only. In a republic those who have citizenship can enjoy the rights of man; by contrast, those who have the rights of man because they lack citizenship have nothing. To have a world is to belong to a political community.

Years later, in *The Human Condition*, Arendt returns to the theme of worldliness, and indeed to Augustine. While for us moderns the public sphere is the private household writ large, Arendt identifies the public sphere proper with 'the world itself' as opposed to our private place it. This 'public realm, as the common world, gathers us together'. Arendt (1958: 53) continues:

> Historically, we know of only one principle that was ever devised to keep a community of people together who had lost their interest in the common world and felt themselves no longer related [...] by it. To find a bond between people strong enough to replace the world was the main political task of early Christian philosophy, and it was Augustine who proposed to found not only the Christian 'brotherhood' but all human relations on charity.

Arendt goes on to contrast this bond of love with the political bonds established by a shared world. While ties of love are suited to carrying an essentially world-less people through the world, such a people leave nothing behind them, and why would they when the world itself is doomed to end? Ties of love are essentially familial, and no family has ever established a public realm.

For anything (and anybody) to be remembered in its singularity, for it to gain that immortality that even the gods fail to find, it is necessary that there be a public sphere into which such things can first appear and then be recalled, generation by generation. This is the only escape from mute existence, which, animal-like, is fated to return the same as before. To escape this darkness of 'sheltered existence', whether that sheltering be in the familial home or, increasingly in our day, in our entirely individuated lives, requires a public sphere in which men and women can appear, not as private individuals, but as free citizens (Arendt 1958: 51).

The human condition is not the same as human nature because human beings, unlike animals, do not exist only as members of a species. As mortals, beings aware of death, human lives move in a line and thereby escape the cyclical order in which all other beings are forever caught. And although this line of flight is short, due to their speech – their deeds and their words – mortals can establish a common world in which they can be remembered. This is the task of politics and, when that task is achieved, it transforms that most mortal of creatures into an immortal. Human beings have an almost divine nature; but only where there is politics is that nature expressed.

17 Badiou

QUESTIONING ARISES FROM A sense that things might be other than they are. This is why the French philosopher Alain Badiou (born 1937) is significant, for his is the most systematic answer to the question: how can anything new happen? What Badiou means by new is not variation on a theme, for example the sort of normal change involved in processes such as ageing, but New – a genuine creation. Can the normal ways of the world be subject to transformation such that what was previously counted possible is no longer all there is?

Take love, for example. When I fall in love, it feels like something really unique is happening. There was my life before I met my lover; now everything has changed. But is this feeling anything other than just that – a feeling? Most experts would say no – psychoanalysts might dismiss my feelings as at bottom issues with Daddy and Mummy. Anthropologists, meanwhile, would point to the inconvenient fact that my seemingly unique love affair is conducted in much the same way as everyone else's in my culture: I buy roses; send a valentine's card. Maybe not so unique after all. Neuroscientists, for their part, could identify that part of my brain that is activated in love – my life-changing encounter is just a state of mind.

Against the naysayers, Badiou (*In Praise of Love*) is convinced that love can be New – in other words that it can be true. Denouncing the 'safety-first' concept of love – a love 'insured against all risks' – love, for Badiou, must be 'something that innovates' (Badiou 2012: 6; 11). A true love affair really does break with the previous order of my life.

Once I was one in the sense of being alone in the world; now the one of love is made up of two. Badiou does not deny that nothing *objective* really changes in love, but to the extent that two people remain true to their (purely subjective) declaration of love for each other, their lives really can change beyond recognition. Things they were incapable of before (thinking of somebody other than themselves, perhaps) become possible, while things that were previously nothing (living without the person they love, especially) become everything. Although no love affair can have any guarantee of success, to the extent that both of the lovers remain true to the conviction that something really happened (that it wasn't just a fling), then it remains indestructible. Something really has come from nothing – something eternal, even. For although a love affair is an ongoing creation rather than some soppy destiny, to the extent that true love can always begin again in each new generation, it is an experience of eternity in time. When I love, I partake of that same truth that inspired Anthony and Cleopatra over 2,000 years ago. When I love, I become an immortal.

Another example of the possibility of the New is found in the field of politics. Most of what we call politics today is merely administration – not real change. Indeed, what goes by the name politics is largely directed at making sure that fundamental change *can't* happen. What is all that money spent on security (the US government splashed nearly $800 billion on its military in 2020) if not a massive investment in everything remaining the same? As an unrepentant 1960s radical who was centrally involved in the revolt of May 1968 in France, Badiou (2008: 31) is also contemptuous of the idea that voting in modern democracy offers the possibility of real change:

> If we posit a definition of politics as 'collective action, organized by certain principles, that aims to unfold the consequences of a new possibility which is currently repressed by the dominant order', then we would have to conclude that the electoral mechanism is an essentially apolitical procedure.

Deciding which suit should administer capitalism is hardly the possibility of the New, is it?

But Badiou reminds us that real political change *is* possible, as we know from those revolutionary moments (Spartacus's revolt against Rome in 73–1 BCE; the Paris Commune of 1871; and the Russian

Revolution of 1917, for example) when the wretched of the earth rose up against their masters. People who were literally nothing under the old regime (slaves, workers, peasants) became everything. While the powers-that-be would like to say that these revolts were nothing but minor disturbances, with normal order soon restored, Badiou points to the incalculable consequences of such political events. After Spartacus, for example, no slave ever need think that rising up against even the mightiest empire is impossible. Indeed, as Badiou (2009: 52) notes in *Logics of Worlds*, the appeal to the name Spartacus inspired both the Haitian slave revolt of 1796 and the revolutionary uprising in Germany of 1919: 'the subject whose name is "Spartacus" travels from world to world through the centuries. Ancient Spartacus, black Spartacus, red Spartacus.'

Similarly, after the Paris Commune, workers will always know that they don't need bosses (2008: 35, 2007b: 148). While the political struggles of each age are unique to their own time and place, the possibility of revolt is universal and enduring – always ready to begin again. This, of course, is a cause of dismay to political elites, who protest too much that radical politics can never really change anything (if they really believe this, why bother denouncing radical movements so vociferously?).

Badiou thinks that the sceptics (cynical about the possibility of the New in love and politics, not to mention in science and art, also) miss something. While, objectively speaking, there *is* only the world as it has always been, this is to miss the subjective power of truths. There is nothing but the given way of the world – except that *there are also truths*! While there is no such *thing* as love, to the extent that I love, then love *is* (even though it is nothing other than my loyalty to it). Similarly, while in the ordinary run of things there is no such thing as politics (only administration), inasmuch as we remain faithful to our revolutions, then political change *does* happen.

Perhaps the most significant example of something really New appearing in history is, for Badiou (2003), the Apostle Paul's declaration (Galatians 3:28), at the dawn of Christianity, that 'There is neither Jew nor Gentile, neither slave nor free, nor is there male and female, for you are all one in Christ Jesus.' As Badiou (2003: 5, 9) points out, for anyone who knows anything about the rules of the ancient world, where the difference between free men and slaves, and between men and women, structured everything, this is a 'genuinely stupefying statement'; so stupefying, in fact, that Paul 'is, strictly speaking, the inventor' of universalism. Paul provoked, 'entirely alone', 'a cultural revolution on which we still depend' (Badiou 2003: 5, 15, see also 107).

Who is this 'we' that Badiou refers to? As a Marxist, Badiou is clearly dependent on the idea of human equality. But so, too, would anyone who appeals to human rights, for example. After all, what *are* human rights other than the secularisation of the idea that, despite their differences, human beings have equal worth. As Badiou sees it, Paul invents the notion of indifference to difference, which remains the foundation of universalism to this day.

What allows this possibility of subjective truths changing the objective world? After all, if the world really is given, then change must remain at the level of appearance only, and Badiou could not get the New he wants. Badiou needs to provide a foundation for his belief that the New is possible. But this foundation, rather than determining things, needs to remain open (since a foundation that *pre*scribes does not allow for newness). The only foundation that allows for the creation of genuine novelties is the *absence* of foundation – the void. Thinking the void-like quality of the New is the task of Badiou's formidable book, *Being and Event*.

While Badiou's *Being and Event* is not the first work to think that being is in a sense void (recall Heidegger's *Being and Time*), for Badiou the void is not the same as the nothing, which, in his view, is still in thrall to the idea of the One (namely God). 'Void', by contrast, 'indicates the failure of the one, the not-one, in a more primordial sense than the not-of-the-whole' (Badiou 2007: 56).

Deducing the void is not a matter of accessing a mystical truth about the totality, it is merely the outcome of a rigorously secular reasoning. If being was ultimately something, then that something would be God. But for Badiou, an atheist, it is an axiom that God is not. Badiou (2007) thinks that this atheism is expressible in mathematical set theory, where there can be no set of all sets (one Set – or God – to contain them all). Think of a shopping list. The shopping list contains everything you want to buy, but it does not contain itself. So even if your shopping list had everything that ever has been or will be written on it, it would still not contain everything. And if you then added your first shopping list to the original list of things, this new shopping list would *still* not contain itself – and so on, to infinity. There *cannot be* a set of all sets. Being is uncontainable, which is the same as to say that it is infinite difference. And the only way we can really think infinite difference is to say that it is void-like.

This is all very abstract and difficult. But the important thing to note is that Badiou turns to set theory because it provides him with a way of saying that being is void. And he wants to say that being is void not so that he can talk about it (as Heidegger talks elliptically of the nothing) but so that he can explain the possibility of the New. In fact, the void, as void, is unpresentable in any given situation – it's what we *can't* see (Badiou 2007: 57).

But we can, occasionally, see its effects. If being is void, then it can always be something else. The Romans can say to Spartacus: you are fighting against necessity; Rome will reign forever! But this is not the case. Elders can say to young lovers from two feuding houses (I'm thinking of Romeo and Juliet): this will never work. But it can. The judgements of Rome/Capulet/Montague are based only on existing knowledge that has not – *cannot* – take account of the possibility of the New. But the New *changes* what is possible. After Spartacus, revolt is *always* a possibility, one that can never be closed down completely. Even the thousands of crosses bearing Spartacus's crucified rebels that lined the Apennine Way, and the fear of revolt they instilled, could not do this.

A compelling feature of Badiou's thought of the New is that it offers a solution to the problem of relativism, which is the view that everything is true (such that nothing is). Because Badiou's truths are built on events that didn't have to happen (Spartacus didn't have to be brave; Anthony wasn't destined to love Cleopatra), they are not necessary in the sense of predetermined. But this doesn't mean that they are only relative to their time and place. As we saw, Badiou thinks that there is something universal – in the sense of immortal – about truth. Although a truth must be taken up in accordance with its context (I cannot proclaim my love in the language of Anthony), *what* is taken up transcends time and place (love is not just for those who spoke Latin). Similarly, while a contemporary revolution will not make much headway with gladiators, the truth that slaves can throw off their masters is not confined to antiquity. Although love and revolution are human creations – creations that must be *re*created ever anew – the fact that they live on puts paid to all notions of truth as relative. A truth is a bit like the Greek hero Heracles who was immortalised by Zeus: although born to a mortal woman, on his death he was welcomed to Olympus to dwell with the gods forever. Once born, a truth can never die.

Truths are not only immortal in time but transcend place as well. Just as Paul's 'Christ is risen!' was seen by the Apostle as applying indifferently to Jews *and* Greeks, to men *and* women, a truth is true for all. For example, a revolution is only a revolution once it is addressed to everybody. If Spartacus, a Thracian, had seen his fight as only for Thracians, it would have been just another national uprising rather than the first slave revolt. As the leader of a revolt of *all* those peoples enslaved by Rome, Spartacus is a universal name honoured by anyone who would oppose empire. In a time of identity politics, Badiou insists on this point. If our struggle is only to change the circumstances of people with whom we identify then it risks reproducing the very identitarianism that we imagine ourselves to be opposing. As Badiou puts it – I'll give you your identity if you give me the possibility of change. Differences between people, while irreducible (we will always have difference), must remain provisional (we mustn't get stuck with our differences).

Badiou is a great inspiration to questioners. He reminds us that all knowledge – no matter how venerable – is only provisional. The experts can tell us how it has been, but they cannot tell us how it must be. Judged by the standards of established belief (also known as common sense), the New is nothing: it is merely dangerous in the case of revolution; deluded in the case of love; ludicrous in the case of art; and wrongheaded in the case of science. But the New sets its own standards. After the event of Einstein in physics, Newtonian physics is not wrong but irrelevant. Similarly, after impressionism, the visual arts do not have to be life-like.

In addition to their own standards, truth-events also produce their own histories. The Communards of 1871 rewrote the history of Paris as the history of workers, not of the bourgeoisie. Einstein's General Relativity, meanwhile, redescribes the absolute space and time of classical physics as relative to each other: spacetime. Truths are events that redefine the past as much as the future. As well as opening up new possibilities tomorrow, we are able to reimagine yesterday. Indeed, it is as much by doing the latter that we are capable of the former. With Spartacus, the official history of Rome as the history of a power which brought peace (the *Pax Romana*) is now pronounced as a history of violent subjugation. And this in turn rallies newcomers to the cause. New futures are enabled by alternative histories.

What does the New require of *us*? We might think that it requires constant questioning – never allowing ourselves to settle for received wisdom. Yet this is not where Badiou places his emphasis. Rather than the restlessness of constant questioning, Badiou wants us to be faithful to our truths, since they cannot be at all without our fidelity to them. The subjective declaration ('I love you'; 'To the barricades!') is essential. But talk is cheap, and declarations of love or of revolutionary courage are only as good as the deeds they inspire. For a love affair or a revolution to last, it cannot live on the glories of yesterday. We must continue to ask ourselves what it requires of us today. *This* is the questioning that Badiou calls for.

Another very important feature of Badiou's understanding of questioning is that it must start with an affirmation rather than with negation. Badiou is wary of (Socratic) negative dialectics, since to start with a 'no' is never to be able to say 'yes' to anything. Indeed, the drive to negate leads to a sort of nihilistic puritanism in which we can never start creating because there is always something in need of tearing down. This passion for destruction, for purity, is fated never to be fulfilled (Badiou 2007b: 56). If questioning is only critique, then nothing will really begin precisely because the questions never end.

In place of this negative dialectics, a questioning which can only say 'no', Badiou (2013) proposes an 'affirmative dialectics' in which the first term is 'yes'. 'A truth never appertains to Critique. It is supported only by itself' (Badiou 2003: 109). Badiou (2013: 4–5) uses the example of Paul and his relation to the Roman Empire of his time:

> In a very explicit manner, Paul explains that when you have an event that is really the creation of a new possibility in the situation, one must first create a new body [a collective] and affirm a new subjectivity before all negation and all negative consequences. The first thing is to create, to affirm the new subjectivity.

Paul does not say 'no' to Rome; he says 'yes' to the resurrected Christ: 'it is affirmation without preliminary negation' (Badiou 2003: 66). And the fact that Paul's 'yes' ultimately defeated Rome (as Nietzsche asked: who is worshipped in Rome today? Caesar or Christ?) is only a by-product, as it were, of that first 'yes'. Paul brings thought 'to the point where it no longer consists in a "critique", however radical' (Badiou 2003: 72). Rather, for Paul, 'the Christ-event is nothing but resurrection. It eradicates negativity' (Badiou 2003: 73).

Linked to this concern with yes-saying is Badiou's very Platonic conception, as set out in his *Ethics*, that the 'evil' that we seek to tear down with our critical questioning is itself nothing: 'If Evil exists, we must conceive it from the starting point of the Good. Without consideration of the Good, and thus of truths, there remains only the cruel innocence of life, which is beneath Good *and beneath Evil*' (Badiou 2001: 60). Evil has no positive content, it is only the absence of the good. But if evil is only the absence of the good, then in the same measure critique is itself 'evil'. Having no vision of the good, but only of its absence, critique participates in the very evil it denounces.

Like Weil, Badiou links our questioning not to the operation of our sovereign reason (this is the mastery required by Greek philosophy) but to the grace by which something happens to us that *forces us* to question: '"Grace" names the event [of love; of politics etc.] as condition for an active thought' (Badiou 2003: 85). For Weil, this undeserved favour is suffering; for Badiou it is the Event (of love, politics, and so on). But in each case questioning does not start with us but with the gratuitous *happening* by which we are caught up into something bigger than ourselves – saved from ourselves if you like. Against the narcissism of critique, which always questions starting from me, Badiou and Weil, after Plato, appeal to the good which is beyond us. But if Weil finds this good to be the order of the world, an order which must therefore resist our questioning, Badiou finds the good to be that truth which is constructed in the void. *This* good, as for example in the case of love, will provide me with questions, namely questions of how I remain faithful to it, questions which will persist until I draw my last breath.

But if questioning depends on an event, must we wait passively for one before we can question? 'Certainly not. Many events, even very distant ones, still require us to be faithful to them. Thought does not wait' (Badiou 2003: 111). Badiou has in mind events such as Spartacus's slave revolt, namely the 'truth of communism'. While the events linked to this truth may be mostly in our past (1848, 1871, 1917, etc.), we can still be true to them in our own time. If we have the courage of truth, that is.

With Badiou we come back to Socrates, the subject of our first chapter. For despite all his innovations, Badiou, by his own admission, is reworking the very classical theme of the true life (in Badiou's version of it: a life subject to an event of truth). But by locating the true life elsewhere than in everyday life, Badiou seems to involve himself in the ancient philosophical prejudice that finds living *as such* to be lacking in some way. Openly and unashamedly to be sure, Badiou shares the

Socratic-Platonic view that the life subject to truth is the highest life. Only the true life is worth living. Only subject to truth procedures do we escape our 'mere' animal nature, destined to be immediately forgotten, and become immortals worthy of being spoken about by future generations. 'And we know that every human being is *capable* of being this immortal [...] Beyond this there is only a biological species, a "biped without feathers", whose charms are not obvious' (Badiou 2001: 12).

18   Butler

EVER SINCE DIOGENES OF Sinope, it has been possible to question conventional ways of life by appealing to nature. What, after all, is 'natural' about an institution such as marriage or customary norms such as those that prohibit going naked in public? Yet, after Kant, can we still be so sure that 'nature' can be known in itself? Doesn't nature, like everything else, appear only in language?

Judith Butler's work goes to the heart of this problem by asking why we feel able to question gender differences but feel that differences in sex are much more certain. For example, while many people would acknowledge that there is no good reason to think that girls wear pink and boys blue, the difference between boys and girls itself seems much less questionable. For Butler (born 1956), however, the question 'How is gender constructed through the interpretation of sex?' is inadequate because it leaves the question of sex itself unposed. More radically, Butler asks: 'Through what regulatory norms is *sex itself* materialized?' (1993: xix, emphasis added).

For Butler, then, sex is no less assigned by society than is gender. Indeed, in this way, Butler questions the very basis of the distinction between sex and gender itself. If both sex *and* gender are assigned, then really there is only gender (Butler 1990: 8). Butler (1993: xiv–xv) asks: 'if gender is the social significance that sex assumes within a given culture [...] then what, if anything, remains of "sex" once it has assumed its social character as gender?' Sex, then, is merely that category that gender norms appeal to as the seemingly unquestionable basis of their differentiation between male and female. That the positing of sex as prior to gender takes place within language means that sex is only ever 'the effect of that very positing': 'something like a fiction, perhaps a fantasy, retroactively installed as a prelinguistic site to which we have no access' (Butler 1993: xv). Sex is not a natural cause of gender but its social *effect*. Butler quotes Derrida: 'There *is* no nature, only the effects of nature: denaturalization or naturalization' (1993: xi, emphasis added). Elsewhere, Marx is also invoked: 'To expose the contingent acts that create the experience of a naturalistic necessity [is] a move which has been a part of cultural critique at least since Marx' (Butler 1990: 38).

Before getting to the details of how Butler deconstructs sexual difference, it is helpful to locate her radical questioning of sex in the wider terrain of deconstruction itself. What does it mean to deconstruct something and how does deconstruction relate to questioning understood more broadly? Butler is especially close to Jacques Derrida, the philosopher who developed deconstruction as a distinctive way of questioning. But Derridean deconstruction is itself a development of Heidegger. In *Being and Time*, Heidegger used the term *Destruktion* to describe dismantling the history of metaphysics in order to arrive at a more authentic relation to being. If metaphysics leads us to 'see' only that which is immortal or timeless, then Heidegger's purpose is for mortal time to show itself once again as the forgotten basis of our seeing anything at all. In Derrida, this grandiose project becomes, more modestly, a way of readings texts in which that which is excluded from the text (in order for its identity claims to hold) is shown to be the constitutive other of the identity in question. For example, the texts of classical humanism are largely silent on the question of the animal since, at bottom, the human *is* only not-animal. This founding exclusion of the animal must itself be excluded from the text in order for the identity of the human to seem unquestionable.

In a related move, Derrida (1978) shows how Western philosophy since Plato has privileged speech over writing because, while speech is supposed to be immediate to the speaker, writing is somehow only derivative or secondary. But just as I am separated from myself in writing, so indeed I am never identical with myself at all, no more in speech than at any other time. The dream of being fully present to myself, seductive as it is, must remain only a dream.

The target of deconstruction, then, is ultimately the history of metaphysics and its fixation with presence. To portray something as fully present (such as the speaker to her speech) is to miss what in that thing is other than itself (the language that the speaker speaks predates her, for example). In *Giving an Account of Oneself*, Butler (2005: 37) puts it like this:

> If I try to give an account of myself, if I try to make myself recognizable and understandable, then I might begin with a narrative account of my life. But this narrative will be disoriented by what is not mine, or mine alone. And I will, to some degree, have to make myself substitutable in order to make myself recognizable.

Deconstruction shows that where metaphysics finds self-sameness, there is only difference. There is not first identity and then that which differs from it; rather, there is first difference and identity emerges only in relation to *it*. Think, for example, of the definition of a word. Look it up in a dictionary and all you will find is that you are referred to another word. You will never arrive at some final definition of the word, since a word's definition *is* only its difference from other words. As well as Heidegger's critique of metaphysics, this deconstructive project echoes Hegel's dialectic: that 'I' am only able to see myself through the eyes of another seeing me (Hegel 2018). In other words, difference is there in identity formation from the very beginning. This, in another register, is also the insight of psychoanalysis, which points to the formative role of infancy, when I manifestly do not belong to myself, in the appearance of adult autonomy.

But surely my body, at least, is mine alone? Butler is not so sure. Frustrated at those colleagues who responded to her ground-breaking *Gender Trouble* (1990) by invoking 'the materiality of the body' as something that 'could not be theorized away', in *Bodies that Matter* Butler (1993: xi) asks: 'why is it that what is constructed is understood as having an artificial and dispensable character?' Without bodily constructions such as gender (to which we will return), there would be no 'I' in the first place: 'bodies only appear, only endure, only live within the productive constraints of certain highly gendered regulatory schemas' (Butler 1993: xi).

The body, then, is a referent without being something to which we can point directly. My stories about myself will never 'capture the body to which they refer' (Butler 2005: 38). In fact, given how opaque the functions of bodily life are, to 'be a body is, in some sense, to be deprived of having a full recollection of one's life' (Butler 2005: 38). This is why the '"I" is the moment of failure of every narrative effort to give an account of oneself' (Butler 2005: 79). Underscoring Heidegger's notion of thrown-ness, Butler also reminds us that the narrative of our lives begins, not with us, but with all the many things that 'have already taken place to make me and my story possible in language' (Butler 2005: 39). Psychoanalysis reinforces this insight into history and language by reminding us that adult experience is always already decentred by that infantile experience to which only the unconscious has access (Butler 2005: 76). Ever in the middle of things rather than outside of them looking on, 'I am left to fictionalize and fabulate origins I cannot know' (Butler 2005: 76). The stories I tell about myself are necessarily incomplete.

This emphasis on the incompleteness of all identity enables Butler to develop an ethics based on relationship to, and responsibility for, the other person. Butler (2005: 43) acknowledges that the question 'Why be moral?' cannot be answered from within any given set of moral values without falling into circular reasoning. In place of morality, which cannot account for its own moral values, we need an ontology (an account of being) that would say why moral values are in accordance with the way things are. And if I were complete in myself, then I would not need the other. But, coming to an awareness of how contingent my own self is, I can affirm others in their incompleteness. I am forced to become both more humble and more generous because 'I will need to be forgiven for what I cannot have fully known, and I will be under a similar obligation to offer forgiveness to others, who are also constituted in partial opacity to themselves' (Butler 2005: 42). 'What I am trying to describe', Butler (2005: 78) writes, 'is the condition of the subject, but it is not *mine*: I do not own it'. Questioning, then, is central to Butler's account of ethics. Questioning the limits of what any of us can know of ourselves, we find 'reason's limit' to be a mark of our common humanity: 'my foreignness to myself is, paradoxically, the source of my ethical connection with others' (Butler 2005: 84).

An implication of being a stranger to myself is that I am inevitably susceptible to others (Butler 2005: 87). The ideal of personal autonomy requires that I know the boundaries between myself and others that I seek to defend. But in the absence of such knowledge, the other bleeds into me and I into the other. In fact, this susceptibility to others is a condition of our being responsive to them at all (Butler 2005: 87).

Following the 9/11 attacks on the United States, in *Precarious Life* (2004) Butler applied this insight to the 'war on terror'. Recognising that US global dominance tempts American citizens more than most to seek to secure their borders against threats from others, Butler tried to nudge the national conversation in another direction. Rather than viewing the terrible loss of life on 9/11 as separating America from the world, Butler suggested that grief is universal: 'for all of us have some notion of what it is to have lost somebody. Loss has made a tenuous "we" of all of us' (Butler 2004: 20).

In addition to its universal reach, loss also reveals our dependence on others. My incompleteness becomes painfully clear when, losing you, I lose myself as well: 'It is not as if an "I" exists independently over here and then simply loses a "you' over there, especially if the attachment to "you" is part of what composes who "I" am [. . .] Who "am" I without you?' (Butler 2004: 22). 'Let's face it. We're undone by each other' (Butler 2005: 23). Not only the life of nations, but bodily life itself is characterised by vulnerability and exposure to the other which prevents me from ever fully coinciding with myself. Nowhere is this clearer than when I am 'beside myself' with rage or grief (Butler 2005: 24).

But although grief can unite rather than divide us, the condition of this political possibility is that all lives are held to matter equally. Butler (2004: 34) emphasises that under contemporary conditions this is not the case:

> There are no obituaries for the war casualties that the United States inflicts, and there cannot be. If there were to be an obituary, there would have to have been a life, a life worth noting, and life worth valuing and preserving, a life that qualifies for recognition.

This question of which lives are valued anticipates the Black Lives Matter movement. It also brings us back us to Butler's earlier work on the ways in which some bodies matter more than others depending on how they are sexed and gendered.

Taking up the project of deconstruction in relation to gender, Butler has shown that sexual difference is perhaps the hardest thing of all to put into question. 'The metaphysics of gender substances' (*to be* a woman or a man) is so entrenched that showing that sex is nothing substantial and that the viability of the nouns 'man' and 'woman' are therefore questionable, is close to impossible (Butler 1990: 21). But, for

Butler, sex is a question rather than an answer: How are bodies 'materialized as "sexed" and how are we to understand the "matter" of sex?' (Butler 1990: 21).

In *Gender Trouble*, Butler recognises that sex is the basis for much feminist politics. The presupposition of struggles for greater representation is that 'women' is a natural category that pre-exists its being represented with the vote, rights, etc. Butler (1990: 2) wonders, to the contrary, whether 'women' might turn out to be something made:

> It is not enough to inquire into how women might become more fully represented in language and politics. Feminist critique ought also to understand how the category of 'women', the very subject of feminism, is produced and restrained by the very structures of power through which emancipation is thought.

This means that rather than basing its claims on the universal category of 'women', feminist practice should restrict itself to 'a critical genealogy' of the 'legitimacy practices' of specific linguistic and political constructions of this category (Butler 1990: 5). Nonetheless, although failure to acknowledge the 'specific cultural operations of gender oppression' risks reproducing the male gaze in thought, that there is worldwide gender oppression is not in doubt (Butler 1990: 13). As we shall see later, this creates the problem for Butler of whether we can reject the notion of a universal standpoint while at the same time being critical of particular patriarchal cultures, which seems to require the self-same universalism. In short, is critical genealogy a contradiction in terms? For inasmuch as critique requires some outside to what is being critiqued, doesn't the critique of (particular) social forms posit something (universal) beyond them?

As we saw earlier, when Butler (1990: 6) argues that gender 'is the cultural meanings that a sexed body assumes', this is not meant to imply that sex is more natural than gender. To the contrary, 'what is "sex" anyway?' (Butler 1990: 6). If gender has a history, then why shouldn't sex, too?

> Are the ostensibly natural facts of sex discursively produced by various scientific discourses in the service of other political and social interests? If the immutable character of sex is contested, perhaps this construct called 'sex' is as culturally constructed as gender;

indeed, perhaps it was always already gender, with the consequence that the distinction between sex and gender turns out to be no distinction at all. (Butler 1990: 7)

Gender cannot be 'the cultural interpretation of sex, if sex itself is a gendered category' (Butler 1990: 7). For transgender activists, who advocate for the right to identify with a gender other than the one that was assigned to them at birth, this argument can be used to question those, including some feminists, who want to appeal to 'man' and 'woman' as essences. As Butler puts it in the context of the feminist struggle over what it is to be a woman: 'The "one" who becomes a woman cannot be guaranteed to be female' (Butler 1990: 8).

Butler's thesis, then, is that gendering produces not only the difference between masculine and feminine, but the very distinction between men and women itself. Sex is, 'from the start, normative', forming a crucial 'part of a regulatory practice that produces the bodies it governs' (Butler 1993: xi). Far from being 'a simple fact or static condition of the body', sex is 'forcibly materialized through time' by these practices (Butler 1993: xii). As the process of this production of sex, gendering is the way in which the discourse of 'natural sex' is established as 'pre-discursive' or prior to culture' (Butler 1993: xii). Gender, then, is the construction of sex as an unconstructed thing, the artifice of a non-artificial sex. But each body, as gendered, has 'always already been interpreted by cultural meanings', which means there is no access to the body, 'male' or 'female', *as such* (Butler 1993: xii).

Like a postmodern Kant, Butler forbids us access to sex 'in itself'. Just as Kant severed critical questioning from the speculations of metaphysics, so too Butler (1990: 9) wants to have done with the 'tenets of humanism', which are always searching for something essential: 'Bodies cannot be said to have a signifiable existence prior to the mark of their gender' (Butler 1990: 8). This claim depends upon a wider commitment to the idea that access to pre-discursive reality is foreclosed to us:

> There is an 'outside' [namely the body] to what is constructed by discourse [namely the gendered body], but this is not an absolute 'outside', an ontological there-ness that exceeds or counters the boundaries of discourse; as a constitutive 'outside', it is that which can only be thought – where it can – in relation to that discourse,

at and as its most tenuous borders [...] [T]he point [of deconstruction] has never been that 'everything is discursively constructed'; that point [...] refuses the constitutive force of exclusion, erasure, violent foreclosure, abjection and its disruptive return within the very terms of discursive legitimacy. (Butler 1993: xvii)

Just because an account of 'reality' cannot be unmediated doesn't mean that the real can't come back to haunt us. Indeed, even to say 'but there are bodies with differently sexed parts' is 'formative of the very phenomenon' it insists upon (Butler 1993: xix).

Even though the body is not some essential nature prior to gendering discourses, neither is gender ever an accomplished fact. 'Gender is a complexity whose totality is permanently deferred, never fully what it is at any given juncture in time' (Butler 1990: 16). But although it is always incomplete in itself, in Western culture gender has been determined largely by heteronormative identities. Heteronormativity means recognising only those gender identities that are deemed to 'follow from' sex and which desire the other sex. In other words, those assigned female at birth should be women and desire men (and vice versa). Gender identities which fail to conform to this model can still appear, but against the backdrop of a heterosexual norm they look like 'developmental failures' or even 'logical impossibilities' (Butler 1990: 16). The bodies of those who do not materialise the norm are not considered the bodies that matter (Butler 1993: xxiv).

A significant implication of Butler's questioning of sex is that, if sex is only gender and gender is only performance, then gender identities have nothing behind them to substantialise them. The notion of gender performativity 'in no way presupposes a choosing subject' (Butler 1993: xxiii). Butler recalls Nietzsche's famous aphorism that there is no doer behind the deed. When it comes to gender, there is only playing the gender role: 'gender is always a doing, though not a doing by a subject who might be said to preexist the deed' (Butler 1990: 25). There is no *being* woman, only a *becoming* woman (Butler 1990: 38). Butler (1993: xvii) asks us to consider, for example, the role of the 'medical interpellation' by which a newborn infant is shifted from an 'it' to a 'she'. In such a naming, 'the girl is "girled"' (Butler 1993: xvii).

Yet for all that there is no substance 'woman' behind becoming-woman, the performance of gender is not a practice that could ever be completely free: 'to claim that gender is constructed is not to assert its illusoriness' (Butler 1990: 32). Indeed, the implication of there being 'no subject who decides its gender' is that 'gender is part of what decides the subject' (Butler 1993: ix). Take the gendered performance of desire, or what we call sexuality, for example. Can sexuality be delivered from the law? Following Foucault's famous refusal of the notion of a liberated sexuality, Butler (1990: 29) does not see how sexuality and power could ever be separated. Power doesn't only say 'no', it is also *productive* of pleasures (Foucault 1980). Nonetheless, although sexuality cannot be performed with complete freedom, Butler (1990: 30) is hopeful that the realisation that gender, like all identity, is 'phantasmatic' might allow 'the possibility of a repetition of the law which is not its consolidation, but its displacement'. *Playing* with the laws of gender, as in transvestism for example, we show its 'phantasmatic structure'. This is the difference between gender *as* performativity (in which we have no perspective on what we do) and the performance *of* gender (in which that perspective is won).

Although the performance of gender involves self-identification, Butler (1993: 237) is careful not to allow metaphysical identities to reassert themselves in her analysis: 'the subject as a self-identical entity is no more'. Butler (1993: 175) warns of the 'presentist conceit' which assumes that there is a choosing or willing subject without a history, one that 'makes itself in and through the magic of the name'. Identity terms must of course be used ('the temporary totalization performed by identity categories is a necessary error'), but gender performativity builds on the post-metaphysical move to decentre 'the subject as the exclusive origin or owner of what is said' (Butler 1993: 175 and 172). This is why 'it remains necessary to lay claim to "women," "queer," "gay," and "lesbian," precisely because these terms, as it were, lay their claim on us' (Butler 1993: 174). Gender performativity, then, like deconstruction in general, describes a condition 'of being implicated in that which one opposes' (Butler 1993: 184). Just as there is no deconstruction without that which it deconstructs, neither is there any queer without the straight.

Deconstructive questioning links us full circle back to Socrates's dialectic: we don't know the things we think we know. Asked to give an account of something as certain as sex, we fail to convince ourselves or others. Where we think we find an identity (or a definition in Socratic terms), actually it is only difference that we come up with (further questions about our definitions).

Given that it asks questions of each and every claim to self-evidence, it is not only fair but indeed necessary to pose a question to deconstruction in its turn. The key question here is: where does the normativity of deconstruction come from? Recall that Butler (1990: 5) describes her method in *Gender Trouble* as '*critical* genealogy' (emphasis added). Butler doesn't want only to recount the history of asymmetries of power, but to critique them from a feminist perspective. In other words, it is not enough to point to the construction of supposedly immutable forms such as male and female, the real problem is the hierarchical arrangement of men over women. Deconstruction, then, is a normative project. It wants to haunt presence with absence, to unsettle hegemonic identities with what has been excluded in order for their identity claims to hold.

But might we question why inclusion is necessary in the first place? Behind deconstruction as a mode of questioning, does there lie hidden a moral-religious view of the world in which equality is presupposed – namely, not itself put in question? In *Giving an Account of Oneself*, Butler argues that deconstructive ethics is based not in morality but in ontology: lacking self-identity, I am not fully separable from the other. But dependency on the other does not necessarily lead to inclusion of the other (as Hume said, we can't derive an 'ought' from an 'is'). For example, the Gauls were Julius Caesar's constitutive other, the other that had to be conquered in order for his identity as a glorious Roman to be secured. And he knew it. And he felt no shame in it. How then, in Western culture, did human equality become a value? Was it by way of equality in the eyes of God? And would this be the God that died, as Nietzsche argued?

These questions have the possibility of being answered, of course, but does deconstruction dare to ask them? Given how difficult it is to conceive of deconstruction within Greco-Roman ontology, where human equality was not a value, could it be that deconstruction is dependent on Biblical notions of justice? Adapting Plato: how would we recognise justice for the powerless if we hadn't already seen it before? Is deconstruction's critique of metaphysics therefore a replay of the old squabble between Athens and Jerusalem, between a Greek ethics focused on care of self (the free man) and a Biblical ethics oriented towards care for the other (the widow and the orphan)?

Another question which deconstruction leaves us with goes to the heart of the possibility of questioning itself. Everything has a history, and Butler has shown that this applies even to sex. But that everything has a history is no less true of the *questioning after* sex itself. In other words, can deconstruction have done with the subject of sex while retaining the subject that knows (or is this having its cake and eating it)? Deconstruction questions all metaphysical claims to a human essence – up to and including an essential difference between male and female – but does it want to question the knowing subject, the one who can deconstruct essences such as sex? This reticence is understandable, since, without the knowing subject, *critical* questioning would be impossible. But wouldn't the deconstruction of metaphysics finally lead to the deconstruction of any claim *to know* at all? In place of a knowing subject that takes the world as its object, the overcoming of metaphysics appears to require the abandonment of any distinction between self and world. How many questioners are ready for *this*?

Glosses

THE MOST ENDURING QUESTION asked of the Western tradition of philosophy is: why did it seek after what is timeless rather than face up to time? As mortals who live briefly and die, what use have we for knowledge of eternals? Questions about essences assume identity – that behind change there is something changeless. That behind all human lives, for example, there is 'humanity' as something essentially unchanging. In a world of time and change, this search for timeless and changeless things is bound to disappoint – to lead, ultimately, to a crisis of truth.

This misstep of asking about identity rather than difference is believed by Nietzsche to have been taken very early – by Socrates or Plato, no less. But did Socrates and Plato ask only about essences, only about what things are when considered from the standpoint of eternity? It seems to me that Socratic questioning is more fundamentally about making questioning a way of life. Anyone who has read Plato's Socratic dialogues cannot help but notice that they generally fail to arrive at an answer. At the end of the dialogue Socrates is likely to say something along the lines of, 'so we thought we knew what X was; but now we're not so sure'.

Similarly, although there is much in Plato's dialogues that asks about the eternal nature of the soul, for example, there is just as much which is concerned with *care* of the soul. Foucault (2010) demonstrated just how important the care of the self was in the world of the Greeks. He argued that even the famous injunction to 'know thyself', the one carved above the entrance to the temple of Apollo at Delphi, was only an offshoot of this deeper concern with care. This means that, for the Greeks, the question of 'Who am I?', the question of identity, was secondary to the more fundamental question of 'How should I take care of myself?'

Questioning in the Socratic tradition (and here the Cynics, Epicureans and Stoics were of one mind) generally showed greater concern with the ethics of care than it did with the question of what is always and ever the same. It was *applied* philosophy rather than metaphysical speculation. In this context, philosophical questioning had a practical aim, as we can see by recalling Epicurus's thoughts on the heavenly bodies, for example. This cosmology was aimed not at understanding the sun, moon and stars as such, but at an ethos of serenity in which the fear of the heavens (and therefore of the gods) is overcome once celestial beings are understood to be simply collections of atoms moving through the void.

Philosophers such as Epicurus and Diogenes were much more interested in the question of how we can change than in what forever remains. In this they were true to the spirit of Socrates who celebrated the fact that he and the sophist Protagoras had switched places during the course of their discussion. Protagoras had ended up arguing what Socrates started out arguing and vice versa. As Plato constructs the dialogue, it is clear that Socrates was happy that he had changed his view, whereas Protagoras, as a sophist, could not have been so cheerful. For sophists claimed to be able to sell wisdom, and changing your mind doesn't make you look very wise. The wise man should *know*. Socrates, however annoying his questions must have been, clearly didn't see himself as a know-all. He had questions, not answers.

Western philosophy has not been the same as wisdom which, in whatever culture it manifests itself (and in the ancient Greek one, too), already knows. Socratic philosophy began by posing questions, not by positing answers. And to the extent that Socratic questioning is a form of negative dialectics (proceeding not by way of affirmation of a truth claim but by the attempt to negate it), negativity has stalked Western philosophy. This infuriates Thrasymachus in Plato's *Republic*, who makes the very reasonable point that it's much easier to ask questions and then refute the answers than it is to answer them yourself.

This essential negativity of questioning is still visible in deconstruction. The dependence of deconstructive questioning on the metaphysical essences (such as sex) that it deconstructs remains vulnerable to Thrasymachus's challenge: where's your own contribution? The critique of metaphysics clearly would be nothing without the metaphysics that it opposes, which leads to the question of whether critique should love what it hates. Nietzsche (*Writings from the Late Notebooks*, note 14[31]) also struggled with this conundrum. Given the connectedness of things: 'to reject anything at all means rejecting everything. A reprehensible action means a reprehended world in general.' Indeed, the realisation of this led Nietzsche to his 'abysmal thought' of the eternal return of the same, where critique is replaced by indiscriminate affirmation of *all* that has ever come to pass, no matter how ugly. Even the small man must return if the overman is to be possible, since what would the overman be without that which he overcomes (*Z* III, 'The Convalescent')?

The epiphany of eternal recurrence changes everything for Nietzsche's Zarathustra, echoing the effect it had on Nietzsche himself in 1881, which he later compared to 'a lightning flash' (*EH*, 'Zarathustra', 1, 4). Zarathustra is initially unable to affirm this new teaching, which nauseates him: 'The now and the past on earth – alas, my friends – that is what is most unbearable to *me*' (*Z* II, 'On Redemption'). Indeed, until his vision of eternal recurrence, Zarathustra had been someone, 'who to an unprecedented degree says *no*' (*EH*, 'Zarathustra', 1, 6). Eternal recurrence, by contrast, is 'the highest possible formula of affirmation' (*EH*, 'Zarathustra', 1, 6). Finding the strength to will the return of the same, Zarathustra thereby becomes 'the eternal yes to all things' (*EH*, 'Zarathustra', 1, 6). But it nearly kills him in the process (and Loeb [2010] has even argued that Zarathustra does die at this point). How strange that Nietzsche's pitiless questioning should have been replaced (in *Zarathustra* at least) with unconditional acceptance, like Diogenes giving way to the Buddha.

And yet this strangeness is really only the working out of an inexorable logic: the questions that we pose about the world do not come from another world. They are *our* questions and could not be posed without the history that gives rise to them and us in the same movement. This means that to question our 'venerations' is also to question ourselves: '"Either abolish your venerations or – *yourselves*!" The later would be nihilism; but would not the former also be – nihilism? That is *our* question mark' (Nietzsche, *GS*, 346). The Zarathustrian yes to all things might seem like the very opposite of questioning but it is really the conclusion of questioning, the point where the essential negativity of questioning itself comes to light and becomes questionable. 'I do not want to accuse; I do not want even to accuse the accusers. Let *looking away* be my only negation! And, all in all and on the whole: some day I want only to be a Yes-sayer!' (Nietzsche, GS, 276). At this point, dizzyingly, Nietzsche's teaching coincides completely with the crucified one he above all tried to overcome. For Jesus, too, understood the messianic calling as incompatible with naysaying: 'Judge not'; 'I judge no one' (Matthew 7:1; John 8:15) As the Gospel of John (3:17) has it: 'For God sent the Son into the world not to judge the world; but that the world should be saved through him.' Questioning, with its seeming incapacity for affirmation, appears to be compatible neither with the teachings of Jesus nor with the anti-teachings of Nietzsche's Zarathustra.

Badiou's attempt (2013) at an 'affirmative dialectics' also begins with affirmation rather than negation, namely the affirmation of a truth. Yet even affirmative dialectics cannot go on without the negativity of questioning. While the first term in this dialectic might be affirmative (as we saw, Badiou gives the example of Paul's 'Christ is Risen!'), the question of what this means for the faithful (for those who believe in the resurrection, in the Pauline example), is an ongoing, potentially infinite one. And this applies to any and every one who seeks to be faithful to a truth, whether that truth is a love affair or a political revolution. Even though 'I love you' is an affirmation rather than a question, the question of what such an affirmation means *today* must always begin again.

This enduring emphasis on questions over answers brings us back to Heidegger's claim, which we started with, that the human being is the only being for which being is a question. But is this true? Apart from the question of whether there *is* such a thing as an abstract human being stripped of time and place, do most people find their very existence to be a question? Heidegger seems to retain the Socratic prejudice that the unexamined life is not worth living.

Heidegger himself changed his mind about this question. And in this sense Heidegger marks the end of Western philosophy. If the early Heidegger asked existentialist questions after authentic existence, then we find the later Heidegger 'turn' towards a poetic philosophising in which existence is rather received, gratefully, as a gift. Heidegger no longer asks the living to answer for themselves before the court of philosophy. Rather, he asks philosophy to listen, patiently, to what is; to be attentive to the miracle of 'what arrives': 'The thinking to come is no longer philosophy, because it thinks more originally than metaphysics – a name identical to philosophy. The thinking that is to come [...] is on the descent to the poverty of its provisional essence' (1998: 276). This essence, Heidegger (1998: 180) describes, is nothing other than thinking 'the advent of being' – that *there is* (something rather than nothing).

If we look closely, we can see that Western philosophy since Heidegger has largely kept to this anti-metaphysical injunction no longer to ask questions as if from the outside. After Heidegger, philosophy no longer reserves for itself a privileged God's-eye position from which to look down on existence. Even Badiou, who we saw continuing to uphold the true life as the highest form of existence, admits that philosophy has no questions of its own. Philosophy can only reflect on questions that the living subjects of truth encounter in the course of their lives together (in politics, love, art . . .). As we saw in the last chapter, this rejection of philosophy as a view from the outside has culminated in deconstruction. With deconstruction, the object of questioning is no longer the 'great outdoors' (the world 'out there') but really only philosophy itself, namely the metaphysical essences that philosophy created and which deconstruction de-creates. Philosophy eats itself.

Western philosophy is dead. But it turns out that at just the moment that philosophical questioning runs out of road, it really gets somewhere. For if Greek philosophy begins with Socrates posing the question 'Is the unexamined life worth living?', it ends by turning the question back to philosophy: from where does philosophy examine life? Socrates's question, introducing a lack into living (a living which must now endlessly justify itself), has no final answer; but the question posed to philosophy can be answered once and for all: philosophy has no privileged place from which to question the living, who are therefore not guilty as charged.

Having been what first cast the shadow of guilt, can questioning also release its captives into innocence?

References

Aquinas, T. (1959) *On Separate Substances*, trans. F. J. Lescoe, Ann Arbor: The University of Michigan Press.
Aquinas, T. (2012) *Summa Theologica*, Rochester, NY: Aquinas Institute.
Arendt, H. (1948) *The Origins of Totalitarianism*, Orlando: HBJ.
Arendt, H. (1958) *The Human Condition*, Chicago: University of Chicago Press.
Arendt, H. (1996) *Love and St Augustine*, Chicago: University of Chicago Press.
Arendt, H. (2006) *Eichmann in Jerusalem: A Report on the Banality of Evil*, London: Penguin.
Aristotle (1925) *The Nicomachean Ethics*, trans. D. Ross, Oxford: Oxford University Press.
Aristotle (1988) *Politics*, trans. S. Everson, Cambridge: Cambridge University Press.
Aristotle (1996) *Physics*, trans. R. Waterfield, Oxford: Oxford University Press.
Aristotle (2016) *De Anima*, trans. C. Shields, Oxford: Oxford University Press.
Aristotle (2019) *Metaphysics*, trans L. Judson, Oxford: Oxford University Press.
Augustine (1972) *City of God*, trans. H. Bettenson, Harmondsworth: Penguin.
Augustine (1991) *Confessions*, trans. H. Chadwick, Oxford: Oxford University Press.

Badiou, A. (2001) *Ethics: An Essay on the Understanding of Evil*, trans. P. Hallward, London: Verso.
Badiou, A. (2003) *St. Paul: The Foundation of Universalism*, trans. R. Brassier, Stanford, CA: Stanford University Press.
Badiou, A. (2007) *Being and Event*, trans. O. Feltham, London: Continuum.
Badiou, A. (2007b) *The Century*, trans. A. Toscano, Oxford: Polity.
Badiou, A. (2008) 'The Communist Hypothesis', *New Left Review* 49.
Badiou, A. (2009) *Logics of Worlds: Being and Event II*, trans. A. Toscano, London: Bloomsbury.
Badiou, A. (2012) *In Praise of Love*, trans. P. Bush, London: Profile Books.
Badiou, A. (2013) 'Affirmative Dialectics: From Logic to Anthropology', *The International Journal of Badiou Studies* 2(1).
Blumenberg, H. (1983) *The Legitimacy of the Modern Age*, trans. R. W. Wallace, Cambridge, MA: The MIT Press.
Butler, J. (1990) *Gender Trouble: Feminism and the Subversion of Identity*, New York: Routledge.
Butler, J. (1993) *Bodies That Matter: On the Discursive Limits of 'Sex'*, New York: Routledge.
Butler, J. (2004) *Precarious Life: The Powers of Mourning and Violence*, London: Verso.
Butler, J. (2005) *Giving an Account of Oneself*, New York: Fordham University Press.
Cicero (1985) *Tusculan Dispuations*, trans. A. E. Douglas, Oxford: Oxbow Books.
Deleuze, G. (2004) *Difference and Repetition*, trans. P. Patton, London: Continuum.
Derrida, J. (1974) *Of Grammatology*, trans. G. C. Spivak, Baltimore, MD: Johns Hopkins University Press.
Derrida, J. (1978) *Writing and Difference*, trans. A. Bass, London: Routledge.
Derrida, J. (1981) 'Plato's Pharmacy', in J. Derrida, *Dissemination*, trans. B. Johnson, London: The Athlone Press.
Diogenes Laertius (1925) *Lives of Eminent Philosophers* (2 volumes), trans. R. D. Hicks, Harvard, MA: Harvard University Press.
Duns Scotus, J. (1962) *Philosophical Writings*, trans. A. Wolter, Indianapolis, IN: Bobbs-Merrill.
Eckhart (1981) *The Essential Sermons, Commentaries, Treatises and Defence*, trans. E. Colledge and B. McGinn, Mahwah, NJ: Paulist Press.

Eckhart (1986) *Teacher and Preacher*, trans. B. McGinn, F. Tobin and E. Borgstadt, Mahwah, NJ: Paulist Press.
Eckhart (2009) *The Complete Mystical Works*, trans. M. O'C. Walshe, New York: The Crossroad Publishing Company.
Foucault, M. (1980) *History of Sexuality: Volume I*, trans. R. Hurley, New York: Vintage.
Foucault, M. (2010) *The Government of Self and Others*, trans. G. Burchell, Houndmills: Palgrave Macmillan.
Foucault, M. (2010b) *The Birth of Biopolitics*, trans. G. Burchell, Houndmills: Palgrave Macmillan.
Foucault, M. (2011) *The Courage of Truth: The Government of Self and Others II*, trans. G. Burchell, Houndmills: Palgrave-Macmillan.
Gillespie, M. A. (1996) *Nihilism Before Nietzsche*, Chicago: Chicago University Press.
Greenblatt, S. (2011) *The Swerve: How the World Became Modern*, New York: W. W. Norton.
Hadot, P. (1993) *Plotinus: Or the Simplicity of Vision*, trans. M. Chase, Chicago: University of Chicago Press.
Hadot, P. (2002) *What is Ancient Philosophy?*, trans. M. Chase, Cambridge, MA: Harvard University Press.
Hard, R. (2012) *Diogenes the Cynic: Sayings and Anecdotes*, trans. R. Hard, Oxford: Oxford University Press.
Hegel, G. W. F. (1991) *Elements of the Philosophy of Right*, trans. H. B. Nisbit, Cambridge: Cambridge University Press.
Hegel, G. W. F. (2018) *The Phenomenology of Spirit*, trans. T. Pinkard, Cambridge: Cambridge University Press.
Heidegger, M. (1963) 'Preface', in W. J. Richardson, *Heidegger: Through Phenomenology to Thought*, The Hague: Martinus Nijhoff Publishing.
Heidegger, M. (1978) 'The Question Concerning Technology', trans. W. Lovitt, in *Heidegger: Basic Writings*, London: Routledge.
Heidegger, M. (1978b) 'What is Metaphysics?', trans. D. Farrell Krell, in *Heidegger: Basic Writings*, London: Routledge
Heidegger, M. (1990) *Kant and the Problem of Metaphysics*, trans. R. Taft, Bloomington: Indiana University Press.
Heidegger, M. (1995) *The Fundamental Concepts of Metaphysics*, trans. W. McNeill and N. Walker, Bloomington: Indiana University Press.
Heidegger, M. (1996) *Being and Time*, trans. J. Stambaugh, Albany: SUNY.

Heidegger, M. (1998) 'Letter on Humanism', trans. F. A. Capuzzi, in *Pathmarks*, trans. W. McNeill, Cambridge: Cambridge University Press.

Heidegger, M. (1998b) 'On the Essence of Ground', trans. F.A. Capuzzi, in *Pathmarks*, trans. W. McNeill, Cambridge: Cambridge University Press.

Heidegger, M. (2000) *Introduction to Metaphysics*, trans. G. Fried and R. Polt, New Haven, CT: Yale.

Heidegger, M. (2002) *The Essence of Human Freedom: An Introduction to Philosophy*, trans. T. Sadler, London and New York: Continuum.

Heidegger, M. (2003) *Plato's Sophist*, trans. R. Rojcewicz and A. Schuwer, Bloomington: Indiana University Press.

Heidegger, M. (2004) *The Phenomenology of Religious Life*, trans. M. Fitsch and J. A. Gosetti-Ferencei, Bloomington: Indiana University Press.

Heidegger, M. (2012) *Contributions to Philosophy (of the Event)*, trans. R. Rojcewicz and D. Vallega-Neu, Bloomington: Indiana University Press.

Heidegger, M. (2015) *The History of Beyng*, trans. W. McNeill and J. Powell, Bloomington: Indiana University Press.

Horkheimer, M and Adorno, T. W. (2002) *Dialectic of Enlightenment*, trans. E. Jephcott, Stanford, CA: University of Stanford Press.

Hume, D. (1977) *An Enquiry Concerning Human Understanding*, Indianapolis: Hackett Publishing.

Jonas, H. (1958) *The Gnostic Religion*, Boston, MA: Beacon Press.

Kant, I. (1970) 'Perpetual Peace', in *Kant: Political Writings*, trans. H. B. Nisbet, Cambridge: Cambridge University Press.

Kant, I. (1977) *Prolegomena to Any Future Metaphysics*, trans. G Hatfield, Cambridge: Cambridge University Press.

Kant, I. (1991) *Groundwork of the Metaphysics of Morals*, trans. H. J. Paton, London: Routledge.

Kant, I. (1998) *Critique of Pure Reason*, trans. P. Guyer and A. W. Wood, Cambridge: Cambridge University Press.

Kierkegaard, S. (1985) *Fear and Trembling*, trans. A. Hannay, London: Penguin.

Kierkegaard, S. (1989) *The Sickness unto Death*, trans. A. Hannay, London: Penguin.

Kierkegaard, S. (2004) *Either/Or*, trans. A. Hannay, London: Penguin.

Kierkegaard, S. (2009) *Concluding Unscientific Postscript*, trans. A. Hannay, Cambridge: Cambridge University Press.
Levinas, E. (1969) *Totality and Infinity*, trans. A. Lingis, Pittsburgh, PA: Duquesne University Press.
Livy (1960) *The Early History of Rome*, trans. A. de Selincourt, Harmondsworth: Penguin.
Loeb, P. S. (2010) *The Death of Nietzsche's Zarathustra*, Cambridge: Cambridge University Press.
Lucian (1968) *Selected Satires of Lucian*, trans. L. Casson, London: Norton.
Lucretius (1968) *De Rerum Natura*, trans. R. Humphries, Bloomington: Indiana University Press.
Maimon, S. (2010) *Essay on Transcendental Philosophy*, trans. A. Welchman et al., London: Continuum.
Meillassoux, Q. (2008) *After Finitude: An Essay on the Necessity of Contingency*, trans. R. Brassier, London: Continuum.
Nietzsche, F. (1962) *Philosophy in the Tragic Age of the Greeks*, trans. M. Cowan, Washington, DC: Regnery.
Nietzsche, F. (1967) *The Will to Power*, trans. W. Kaufmann and R. J. Hollingdale, New York: Vintage Books.
Nietzsche, F. (1986) *Human, All Too Human*, trans. R. J. Hollingdale, Cambridge: Cambridge University Press.
Nietzsche, F. (1994) *On the Genealogy of Morality*, trans. C. Diethe, Cambridge: Cambridge University Press.
Nietzsche, F. (1997) *Daybreak*, trans. R. J. Hollingdale, Cambridge: Cambridge University Press.
Nietzsche, F. (2001) *The Gay Science*, trans. A. Del Caro, Cambridge: Cambridge University Press.
Nietzsche, F. (2002) *Beyond Good and Evil*, trans. J. Norman, Cambridge: Cambridge University Press.
Nietzsche, F. (2003) *Writings from the Late Notebooks*, trans. K. Sturge, Cambridge: Cambridge University Press.
Nietzsche, F. (2005) *The Anti-Christ, Ecce Homo, Twilight of the Idols*, trans. J. Norman, Cambridge: Cambridge University Press.
Nietzsche, F. (2006) *Thus Spoke Zarathustra*, Cambridge: Cambridge University Press.
Otto, W. F. (1955) *The Homeric Gods: The Spiritual Significance of Greek Religion*, trans. M. Hadas, Thetford: Thames and Hudson.

Parmenides (1984) *Fragments*, trans. D. Gallop, Toronto: Toronto University Press.
Plato (1954) *Euthyphro, The Apology, Crito, Phaedo*, trans. H. Tredennick, London: Penguin.
Plato (1956) *Protagoras and Meno*, trans. W. K. C. Guthrie, Harmondsworth: Penguin.
Plato (1966) 'II and VII Letters', in *Plato in Twelve Volumes, Vol. 7*, trans. R. G. Bury, Cambridge, MA: Harvard University Press.
Plato (1971) *Timaeus and Critias*, trans. D. Lee, London: Penguin.
Plato (1974) *Republic*, trans. D. Lee, London: Penguin.
Plato (1987) *Gorgias*, trans. D. J. Zeyl, Indianapolis, IN: Hackett Publishing.
Plato (2005) *Meno and Other Dialogues (Charmides, Laches, Lysis, Meno)*, trans. R. Waterfield, Oxford: Oxford University Press.
Plotinus (1991) *The Enneads*, trans. S. MacKenna, London: Penguin.
Schopenhauer, A. (2004) 'On the Sufferings of the World', in *Essays and Aphorisms*, trans. R. J. Hollingdale, London: Penguin.
Seneca (2007) *Dialogues and Essays*, trans. J. Davie, Oxford: Oxford University Press.
Spinoza, B. (1996) *Ethics*, trans. E. Curley, London: Penguin.
Spinoza, B. (2007) *Theological-Political Treatise*, trans. J. Israel, Cambridge: Cambridge University Press.
Stegmaier, W. (2006) 'Nietzsche's Doctrines, Nietzsche's Signs', *Journal of Nietzsche Studies* 31(21): 36–7.
Weil, S. (1952) *Gravity and Grace*, trans. E. Crawford and M. von der Ruhr, London: Routledge.
Weil, S. (1952b) *The Need for Roots*, trans. A. Wills, London: Routledge.
Weil, S. (1953) *Letter to a Priest*, trans. A. Wills, London: Routledge.
Weil, S. (1958) *Oppression and Liberty*, trans. A. Wills and J. Petrie, London: Routledge.
Weil, S. (1965) 'The Iliad, or the Poem of Force', trans. M. McCarthy, *Chicago Review* 18(2).
Weil, S. (2015) *Selected Essays 1934–1943*, trans. R. Rees, Eugene, OR: Wipf & Stock.
Xenophon (2014) *Memorabilia*, trans. A. L. Bonnette, Ithaca, NY: Cornell University Press.
Zittel, C. (2000) *Das ästhetische Kalkül von Friedrich Nietzsches* Also sprach Zarathustra, Würzburg: Königshausen und Neumann.

Index

Abraham, 126, 128, 129–31
Absolute, the, 68
Adorno, Theodor W., 19
affirmation, 20, 86, 40, 143, 145, 185, 202, 203–4
Alexander the Great, 9, 22, 26–7, 36, 54
amor fati (love of fate), 11, 145, 162, 166
Anaxagoras, 44
Anaximander, 136
anthropocentrism, 108
Aquinas, Thomas, 3, 50, 76, 84, 90
Arendt, Hannah, 3, 169–77
Aristotle, 2, 9, 21, 22, 25, 29, 35, 41–52, 57, 71, 73, 76, 84, 88, 89–90, 91, 147, 150, 160, 172
atheism, 144, 182
atomism, 9, 57
Augustine of Hippo, 3, 65, 73–82, 83, 88, 89, 90, 93, 94, 97, 104, 122, 124, 133, 174–6

Badiou, Alain, 3, 179–87, 204, 205
becoming, 1, 18, 38, 42, 78, 91, 98, 121, 196
being, the question of, 11, 39, 42, 47, 48, 50, 148–50, 154

being-in-the-world, 148
biopolitics, 173
Black Lives Matter, 193
Blumenberg, Hans, 89
body, the, 14, 42, 57, 59, 64, 66, 78, 135, 191–2, 195–6
Buddhism, 61, 162, 203
Butler, Judith, 3, 189–99

care of self, 14–15, 20, 24, 25, 46, 60, 198, 201–2
categorical imperative, the, 124, 125, 126
causality, 75, 113–14, 122
Christ, 98, 143, 147, 159–60, 181, 184–5
Christianity, 2, 5, 23, 35, 63–4, 73, 74, 77, 104, 127–8, 132, 133–4, 137, 142, 143, 144, 158–9, 166, 171, 172, 181
Cicero, 53
citizenship, 9, 23, 24–5, 28, 170–1, 173, 176
communism, 186
conscience, 77, 84
contemplation, 12, 44, 59, 84, 99, 112, 172
contingency, 76, 88–9, 139, 165

Copernican Revolution, 10, 113, 121, 153
correlationism, 10
cosmology, 7, 202
cosmopolitanism, 24–5, 29, 77, 152
cosmos, 7, 44, 48, 50, 56, 69, 78, 83, 104, 150
courage of truth, 14, 17, 23–4, 27, 162, 186
Crates, 21, 22
Cynics, 7, 8, 9, 21–9, 35, 202

Da-sein, 148–50, 152
death, 78, 82, 111, 137, 143, 161, 162–3, 165
  being towards, 151, 152, 174, 177
  fear of, 8, 18, 53–5, 57–8, 61, 63, 107, 111
  of God, 6, 139–40
deconstruction, 10, 190–1, 193, 195–6, 197–9, 202–3, 2005
Deleuze, Gilles, 92
demiurge, 6, 66, 67
Democritus, 48, 57, 60
Derrida, Jacques, 20, 39, 190
Descartes, René, 3, 90, 103, 113, 130
determinism, 55, 105, 108, 110, 11, 122, 123–4, 196
dialectics
  dialectical method, 19
  affirmative dialectics, 185, 204
  negative dialectics, 19–20, 33, 38, 185, 202
Diogenes of Sinope, 2, 7, 8, 9, 21–9, 35–6, 60, 61, 189, 202, 203
Duns Scotus, John, 3, 83–92, 93, 96–7, 105, 122

Eckhart, Meister, 3, 93–102
Eichmann, Adolf, 173–4
emanation, 64–5, 97, 159
empiricism, 114
Epicurus, 2, 8, 9, 53–61, 202
essence, 48, 51, 86–7, 104, 110, 148, 151, 155, 169, 199, 205

eternal return, 9, 143–5, 203
evil, 45, 65, 73–5, 77, 79–82, 88, 89, 93, 95, 107–8, 122, 124, 141, 160, 164, 185–6
  banality of, 173–4
existentialism, 126, 132, 151, 204

feminism, 194–5, 198
finitude, 7, 88, 121, 148, 152, 165
forms, the 7, 34–6, 49, 50, 57, 64–5, 90, 198
Foucault, Michel, 5, 7, 9, 20, 173, 197, 201
free will, 74–5, 80–2, 88, 89, 103–6, 122, 124, 164–5

gender, 189–91, 193–7
genealogy, 137, 145, 194, 198
German Idealism, 126
Gnosticism, 35, 63, 65, 66–9, 70, 73, 79, 160, 164, 166–7
Good, the, 35, 36, 38–9, 50, 65, 71, 79, 81–2, 92, 105, 133, 137, 158, 162, 164, 166, 186
Gorgias, 49
grace, 66, 67, 158, 166, 186
Greek gods, 9, 14, 25, 44, 54–7, 60, 64, 72, 76, 80, 112, 143, 165, 177, 183, 202

Hadot, Pierre, 7, 60, 70
Hegel, G.W.F., 68, 126–7, 129, 131–132, 149–50, 191
Heidegger, Martin 1, 3, 4–5, 6, 11, 18, 20, 51, 87, 119, 121, 126, 132, 147–55, 164, 169, 174, 183, 190, 205
Heraclitus, 38, 48, 91
Homer, 152, 163
Horkheimer, Max, 19
human being, 7, 11, 18, 35–6, 51–2, 87, 102, 108, 122, 142, 148–9, 152, 154–5, 160, 169, 174, 187, 204
  as rational animal, 51
human rights, 163, 170–1, 176, 182

humanism, 149, 154, 190, 195
Hume, David, 113–14, 198

identity, 5–6, 22, 37–8, 41, 71, 94–5, 100, 102, 118, 184, 190–2, 197, 198, 201–2
Iliad, the, 9, 162–5, 167
immortality, 16, 58, 71, 77–9, 82, 91–2, 161–3, 169, 171–2, 177, 180, 183–4, 187, 190
infinity, 7, 84–9, 92, 104, 121, 183
intelligibility, 34–5, 38, 67, 114, 119
intuition, 118–21

Jesus, 77, 124, 204
Jonas, Hans, 69

Kant, Immanuel, 3, 10, 104, 113–24, 125, 126–7, 150, 153, 189, 195
Kierkegaard, Søren, 3, 125–34, 151

Leibniz, G.W., 75
Levinas, Emmanuel, 117
logos, 41, 76
love, 11–12, 15, 32 44, 48, 86, 100, 110, 141, 145, 159–60, 162–3, 164–7, 174–6, 179–80, 181, 183, 184, 185, 204
Lucian, 22
Lucretius, 54, 55, 56, 58

Maimon, Salomon, 120–1
Manichaeism, 73–4
Marx, Karl, 57, 190
materialism, 48, 54, 57
matter, 48–50, 54, 64, 66–7, 78, 81–2, 104, 164
meaninglessness, 6, 89, 145
Meillassoux, Quentin, 10, 75–6, 153
metaphysics, 2, 4, 5, 6, 41, 47, 49, 76, 89, 91, 113, 114–15, 122, 137, 148, 149, 150, 154, 190–1, 193, 195, 198–9, 203, 205
modernity, 5, 9, 89, 172
moral law, 103, 122, 124, 125, 129

mysticism, 51, 71, 93–4, 100, 157, 163, 182

natural philosophy, 10, 44, 86
negative theology, 86, 163
Neoplatonism, 2, 3, 16, 35, 63–4, 75, 78, 89, 93, 95–7, 157, 158, 166
Nietzsche, Friedrich, 1, 2, 3, 6, 8–9, 20, 35, 56, 57, 61, 81, 103, 108, 132, 134, 135–45, 163, 185, 198, 201, 203–4
nihilism, 7, 10–11, 20, 89, 135, 137–8, 140, 141, 144, 203
nominalism, 89
nomos, 22–3, 26
nothingness, 82, 95, 140, 151, 159–60, 162

One, the, 11, 36, 65–6, 70–1, 79, 93, 94, 96, 97, 102
ontology, 5, 65, 77, 78, 82, 85, 88, 92, 116, 159, 160, 192, 198
Origen, 76, 158
otherworldliness, 28, 35, 36, 39, 57, 63, 64, 68, 70, 71, 103, 104, 135, 137, 139, 144, 172, 174–5
Otto, Walter F., 80
Overman, the, 140, 142–3, 203

pantheism, 104
Parmenides, 36, 37–8, 102, 136
parrhesia see courage of truth
patriarchy, 4, 194
Paul, Saint, 77, 84, 98, 147, 181–2, 184–5
Pericles, 171, 173
pessimism, 140–1
philosophy as a way of life, 8, 60
phronesis see practical wisdom
phusis, 22, 26
Plato, 2, 3, 6, 7, 13, 16, 18, 21, 25, 28, 31–9, 41, 42, 43, 44, 45, 47, 48, 49, 50, 51, 57, 65, 66, 70, 71, 73, 74, 76, 77, 81, 82, 84, 90, 101, 135, 137, 157–8, 161, 171–2, 186, 190, 198, 201, 202

Platonism, 8, 16, 28, 35, 39, 57–8, 63, 70, 77–8, 82, 84, 91–2, 100, 102, 104, 119, 136, 137, 164
Plotinus, 2, 3, 63–71, 76, 78, 92, 99, 121, 122, 147, 158, 160, 161, 166, 167
Porphyry, 64, 78, 158
potentiality, 41–2, 49–50, 51–2, 100–1, 105
practical wisdom, 44
pre-Socratics, 10, 38, 44, 136–7
predestination, 65
Prime Mover, the, 46, 76, 90
Protagoras, 17, 34, 43, 202
providence, 48, 55–6, 68, 81, 104, 106–7, 139, 166
psychoanalysis, 5, 164, 179, 191–2
pure reason, 114, 115–16, 122

rationalism, 73, 104, 114, 117
reincarnation, 78
relativism, 3, 49, 183
Renaissance, the, 57
rhetoric, 13–14, 33–4
Roman Empire, 63, 69, 142, 172, 185, 198

Sartre, Jean-Paul, 126, 132, 151
scholasticism, 84
Schopenhauer, Arthur, 140
Seneca, 135
sexuality, 5, 197
Shoah, the, 169, 171, 173
Skeptics, 91
slavery, 8, 9, 22, 23, 26, 141, 142, 164, 181, 184, 186
Socrates 1–2, 6, 9, 10, 13–20, 21, 22–3, 24, 25, 28, 31, 32, 33, 34, 37, 39, 44, 45, 57, 60, 61, 85, 114, 130, 133, 135, 171, 172, 186, 201, 202, 205
    death of, 1–2, 13, 15, 18–19, 23, 135
    trial of, 10, 13, 15, 16, 28
Sophists, 14, 17, 32, 33–4, 36–7, 43, 49, 50, 202

soul, the, 8, 14–16, 18, 33–4, 42, 44, 49–50, 51, 57, 64, 66–8, 69, 71, 79, 81, 83, 95, 97, 99, 100–1, 102, 116, 117, 142 157–8, 161, 162–3, 165, 172, 201
Spartacus, 180, 181, 183–4, 186
Spinoza, Baruch, 2, 3, 12, 56, 57, 81, 103–12, 113, 117, 121, 165, 166
spirit, 57, 66, 67, 137, 166, 167
Stoics, 7, 29, 55, 77, 83, 84, 95, 103, 104, 111, 166, 167, 202
substance, 43, 47, 48, 50, 75, 81, 85, 155, 193, 196
suffering, 57, 58, 59, 61, 68, 74, 135, 140–3, 159, 160, 161, 174, 186

technology, 4–5
Thales, 44
theodicy, 75, 80, 89, 122, 124
Thrasymachus, 32, 33, 202–3
tragic philosophy, 140–1
transcendental method, 117
transgender, 195
true world, 6, 31, 35, 63, 71, 101, 116, 136–40, 141, 144, 174

universalism, 19, 181–2, 194
univocity, 85–7, 92, 96–7

virtue, 15–17, 33, 44, 47, 60, 82, 108, 111, 123, 167

Weil, Simone, 3, 157–67, 186
will, the, 75, 80, 81–2, 89, 104, 109, 122, 123, 133, 142, 164–5
    good will, 122–4
    of God, 65, 104, 107
    to truth, 3, 10, 59
    see also free will
wisdom, 3, 8, 16–17, 18, 19, 24, 34, 44, 87, 97, 101, 107, 124, 126, 128, 135, 158, 162
    see also practical wisdom

Zarathustra, 139–40, 142–3, 203, 204

EU representative:
Easy Access System Europe
Mustamäe tee 50, 10621 Tallinn, Estonia
Gpsr.requests@easproject.com

www.ingramcontent.com/pod-product-compliance
Lightning Source LLC
Chambersburg PA
CBHW070352240426
43671CB00013BA/2475